TELLING ANXIETY: ANXIOUS NARRATION IN THE WORK OF MARGUERITE DURAS, ANNIE ERNAUX, NATHALIE SARRAUTE, AND ANNE HÉBERT

JENNIFER WILLGING

Telling Anxiety

Anxious Narration in the Work of Marguerite Duras, Annie Ernaux, Nathalie Sarraute, and Anne Hébert

UNIVERSITY OF TORONTO PRESS
Toronto Buffalo London

© University of Toronto Press Incorporated 2007
Toronto Buffalo London
Printed in Canada

ISBN 978-0-8020-9276-2

Printed on acid-free paper

Library and Archives Canada Cataloguing in Publication

Willging, Jennifer
    Telling anxiety : anxious narration in the work of Marguerite Duras,
Annie Ernaux, Nathalie Sarraute, and Anne Hébert / Jennifer Willging.

(University of Toronto romance series)
Includes bibliographical references and index.
ISBN 978-0-8020-9276-2

1. Duras, Marguerite – Criticism and interpretation.   2. Ernaux, Annie,
1940– – Criticism and interpretation.   3. Sarraute, Nathalie – Criticism and
interpretation.   4. Hébert, Anne, 1916–2000 – Criticism and interpretation.
5. Narration (Rhetoric) – History – 20th century.   6. Anxiety in literature.
I. Title.   II. Series.

PQ673.W54 2007   843.00923   C2007-900814-3

University of Toronto Press acknowledges the financial assistance to its
publishing program of the Canada Council for the Arts and the Ontario
Arts Council.

Contents

Acknowledgments

I wish to thank the College of Humanities and the Department of French and Italian at the Ohio State University for their generous support of my research. They have provided me with the leaves from teaching and the funding necessary to complete this book. I thank Diane Birckbichler and Debra Moddelmog in particular for going above and beyond their duties to help me bring this project to fruition. I am also indebted to Judith Mayne, who has been a wise and inspirational mentor to me over the past six years. Her multiple readings of the manuscript throughout its evolution have unquestionably strengthened the final product (although I take exclusive responsibility for its shortcomings). Mary Jean Green's excellent suggestions for revision, and her enthusiasm, have also been of invaluable aid to me. I thank Karlis Racevskis and Eugene Holland for their help with various sections of the manuscript, as well as for their warm collegiality. Two crucial mentors and readers of the earliest versions of the manuscript were Mireille Rosello and Gerald Mead. I am grateful to them for their expertise, kindness, and steadfast encouragement.

At the University of Toronto Press, several anonymous readers contributed to the improvement of the manuscript, and I thank them, however impersonally. Matthew Kudelka has been a talented and meticulous copy editor, leaving not a single American spelling or misused relative pronoun unaltered. Most importantly, I extend my sincere appreciation to Jill McConkey, my editor. Her guidance, praise, and constant good cheer have brightened my days throughout this process.

On a more personal note, I owe a debt of gratitude to my father, Ronald Willging, for his scrupulous and unpaid editing, and to both him and my mother, Joy Willging, for their confidence in me and for their love. I am very lucky to be their daughter. Finally, I wish to express my deepest gratitude to my husband and my own personal coach, Andrew Teitelbaum, whose 'tough love' during the writing of this rather autobiographical book on anxiety made its completion possible. I am so glad I was wrong.

Earlier versions of sections of chapters 1 and 2 have been published as '"True Down to the Last Detail": Narrative and Memory in Marguerite Duras's "Monsieur X."' in *Twentieth Century Literature* 46 (2001): 369–86; and 'Annie Ernaux's Shameful Narration' in *French Forum* 26 (2001): 83–103. I thank the editors of these journals for allowing me to reprint material from these articles.

TELLING ANXIETY: ANXIOUS NARRATION IN THE
WORK OF MARGUERITE DURAS, ANNIE ERNAUX,
NATHALIE SARRAUTE, AND ANNE HÉBERT

Introduction: Narrative Anxiety, Narrative Desire

The desire to tell a story and the anxiety that sometimes accompanies such telling are forces that can leave their trace in the narrative text. They are the forces, the energy, that convert imagination or memory into story and that turn blank pages into text. That desire is a force seems apparent; it induces human beings to take the actions necessary to obtain what they want. Psychoanalytic theory maintains that even when an individual avoids, for whatever reason, active pursuit of the object of her desire, the energy of this desire is not lost, but rather is diverted. It manifests itself elsewhere, in a sublimated form in the best of circumstances and in a physical illness in the worst.[1]

Although less obviously so, anxiety is also a force. Psychology characterizes it essentially as an emotional state – a very unpleasant and often prolonged one – in which the sufferer experiences a vague sense of immanent danger. Anxiety differs from fear in that the danger that prompts it is only *anticipated*; it is not, or not yet, real. Fear, on the other hand, is caused by a real and present danger, which activates the fight-or-flight response. Anxiety does not incite such immediate action, and therefore those who suffer from it often remain under its influence for an extended time before choosing (if ever) to act in order to alleviate it.[2] Anxiety is in a sense a process rather than an event (such as a sudden fright), and for this reason it lends itself to the process of narration. Anxiety can not only accompany narration, it can, like desire, be an impetus to it; for as psychoanalysis as well as other schools of psychology hold, articulating anxiety with language can diminish its destructive effects on the psyche.

My premise in this book is that narrating is an activity that the narrators considered here take up because they believe it will both fulfil a desire and alleviate an anxiety. Peter Brooks reminds us in *Reading for the Plot* that throughout history, narrators have wanted to tell good stories and to hold their narratees captive with them, just as narratees have wanted to hear good stories and to be held captive by them.[3] Telling and being heard fulfil the human desire to communicate, to be believed, to be taken seriously, or at least to be the centre of attention. Yet narrating can also *provoke* rather than alleviate anxiety, either when the very act of telling is itself somehow distressing, or when the narrator fears that the finished narrative will bring about an undesirable consequence. In both of these cases, anxiety is a force that hinders rather than drives forward the narration. In point of fact, Freud suggested in his later works that desire and anxiety are two sides of a single coin. Freud thought that anxiety arose from the individual's rather paradoxical fear that certain desires that possess him – specifically, those desires society has deemed illicit – will be realized.[4] Just as they often are in human life in general, then, desire and anxiety are inextricably intertwined in narration, an activity in which all human beings routinely engage in one form or another. When this narration is performed in writing, the reader can study the text for traces of the desires and anxieties that fuelled its production.

In the narratives I have chosen to examine in this book, the traces left by the desire-anxiety dyad are particularly conspicuous. These narratives are Marguerite Duras's 'Monsieur X. dit ici Pierre Rabier' (included in *La douleur*, 1985), Annie Ernaux's *La honte* (1997), Nathalie Sarraute's *Entre la vie et la mort* (1968), and Anne Hébert's *Les fous de Bassan* (1982).[5] In the last two of these texts, the narrators are fictional characters; in the first two, which are explicitly autobiographical, the narrating 'I' is intended to be read as a textual representation of the author herself. However closely a narrator might resemble her author, the two are of course never identical – the first is purely textual, the second biological and social. Still, narrators are the offspring of authors, and the fact that the narrators on whom I focus all grapple with anxiety while producing their narratives suggests at the very minimum that the topic intrigues their authors. In the two autobiographical texts ('Monsieur X.' and *La honte*), the reader is indeed encouraged to assume that each author shares her textual 'I''s anxieties and desires. In the more fictional texts, *Entre la vie et la mort* and *Les fous de Bassan*, the narrators are writers of one kind or another (Sarraute's narrator writes literary texts and Hébert's multiple narrators write sermons, personal diaries, and letters), and it is therefore not unreasonable to think that their creators have experienced some of the same anxieties and desires that they display. Yet other kinds of anxieties and desires I identify in these texts, such as those that plague the two violent and misogynist male narrators in *Les fous de Bassan*, likely belong to these fictional narrators alone. So while I do not assume that these authors are all as anxiety-ridden as their narrators, I do ascribe to them an interest in, as well as a certain experience of, the mental states at issue. Yet I am interested in the traces or signs of these states in each of these narratives regardless of whether they were left there deliberately or unconsciously, whether they are obvious or covert, and whether they are fictional or real; they are all pertinent to my object of study, which is the confluence of anxiety, desire, and narration.

However great or small their own experience of anxiety in particular might be, it is not surprising that in their texts these authors link anxiety and narration. Women, as we all know, have traditionally been discouraged or prevented from assuming authorship, and this kind of literal interdiction has surely incited many a woman's desire to write while at the same time heightening her anxiety about doing so. In their classic study *The Madwoman in the Attic* (1979), Sandra M. Gilbert and Susan Gubar maintain that the pre-twentieth-century woman writer most certainly suffered from what they call an 'anxiety of authorship,' the 'radical fear that she cannot create,' even when she found herself in the relatively rare circumstance of having the opportunity to do so.[6] Women who wanted to write found relatively few models in either fiction or real life to emulate, and they were most often told by those around them that writing was a man's occupation and that they had better just keep quiet, or risk becoming ill or mad from the unnatural effort needed to pursue a literary career. Gilbert and Gubar argue that nineteenth-century women who read literature, or who simply read the signs of their society, understood that they were supposed to be one of two things: angels or monsters, or alternatively, virgins or whores. None of these spectres looked quite at home at a writing desk. The women writers whom Gilbert and Gubar study all used, they argue, various subterfuges in order to satisfy their illicit desire to write, subterfuges whose purpose was to quell not only their fathers' and husbands' anxieties about their unseemly activity, but their own as well. In order to manage their anxieties, these writers often used such strategies as refusing or resisting publication, taking on (often masculine) pseudonyms, deprecating their own work in letters and prefaces, or reproaching themselves in those places for having the pretension to become an author. For in attempting to assume such a role, the pre-twentieth-century woman knew that she was (to borrow one of Nathalie Sarraute's superb metaphors) 'comme le petit garçon emporté par l'ardeur du jeu, revêtu de sa panoplie de général, brandissant son sabre [...] et qui, apercevant du coin de l'œil sa gouvernante apparue derriere la fenêtre, sait [...] que le moment est venu pour lui d'aller se déshabiller et prendre son bain' (like a little boy carried away by the excitement of play, dressed in his general's outfit, brandishing his sabre ... and who, out of the corner of one eye, having seen his governess through the window, knows ... that the time has come for him to go undress and take his bath).[7] While in *Entre la vie et la mort* Sarraute applies this very masculine metaphor to an anxious male writer (an indistinct *il*), her claim that the gender of any given character in her work is incidental rather than deliberate suggests that the metaphor could be applied just as well – and I would argue, better – to a woman writer.[8]

Yet, as a survey of especially post-Enlightenment literature would show, women writers have in no way held a monopoly on either the desires or the anxieties associated with their profession. Kafka, for example, was an author and a man tortured by insecurities, and the eponymous narrator of Beckett's *L'innommable* (*The Unnamable*) (1953) could rightfully be called the grandfather (and what a crotchety one!) of all angst-ridden but relentlessly driven narrators, male or female.[9] Flaubert was a wreck, as letter after letter testifies, over what he believed was his inability to turn his ideas into literature that could do them justice ('Dieu! que ma Bovary m'embête! J'en arrive à la conviction quelquefois qu'il est *impossible d'écrire*' [God, how I am fed up with my Bovary! I'm convinced at times that it is impossible to write]) (Flaubert's emphasis).[10] Simply by engaging in the act of narrating, a narrator is implying that he has something to say or write that is worth a listener or reader's time – unless, that is, he sincerely intends his texts for a Dickinsonian dresser drawer. The presumption to narrate (or worse, to write) can be and often is accompanied by anxiety, regardless of one's sex. Literary lore has it that many male authors, agonizing upon their death bed, have implored their most faithful friend or servant to destroy their manuscripts.[11] These extreme cases notwithstanding, the demonization of women authors along with all the material, social, and psychological barriers constructed to prevent women from engaging in a literary career most certainly, as Gilbert and Gubar argue, made them more susceptible to anxiety than their literary brethren.

Of course, the women writers on whom I focus in this book are the granddaughters and great-granddaughters of those discussed in *The Madwoman in the Attic*. 'If contemporary women do now attempt the pen with energy and authority,' Gilbert and Gubar write, 'they are able to do so only because their eighteenth- and nineteenth-century foremothers

struggled in isolation that felt like illness, alienation that felt like madness, obscurity that felt like paralysis to overcome the anxiety of authorship that was endemic to their literary subculture.'[12] Later twentieth-
century women writers, they claim, are 'relatively free' of the despair and
guilt that haunted earlier women who had decided, despite society's
interdiction, to pursue their indecorous literary ambitions (52). In fact,
Gilbert and Gubar argue that women writers' relative lack of female precursors could be thought of as an advantage rather than a stumbling
block: 'The son of many fathers, today's male writer feels hopelessly
belated; the daughter of too few mothers, today's female writer feels that
she is helping to create a viable tradition which is at last definitively
emerging' (50). Contemporary women writers, then, supposedly experience a creative freedom that their brothers, who suffer from the scourge
of what Harold Bloom calls the anxiety of influence, cannot.[13]

As is the case with all important books, critiques of Gilbert and
Gubar's study are now as well known as the study itself. One line of criticism takes the authors to task for making overly broad generalizations
about 'nineteenth-century' or 'twentieth-century' women writers, as if
these constituted socially and culturally monolithic groups.[14] It is true
that Gilbert and Gubar consider only white English and American writers of relatively comfortable means. Yet could it not be said that such a
critique of a groundbreaking feminist study, to borrow yet another of
Sarraute's metaphors, 'n'est-ce pas là reprocher à Christophe Colomb
de n'avoir pas construit le port de New York?' (isn't this like reproaching
Christopher Columbus for not having constructed the port of New
York?).[15] In any event, I do think it safe to say, along with Gilbert and
Gubar, that at least in Western culture today, a woman who takes up the
pen is no longer looked upon as a monster, and indeed is usually
thought to be pursuing a legitimate career – if, that is, she is thought to
be any good at it.

It can nevertheless be argued that French and French-Canadian
women have had a more difficult time assuming authorship over the past
two centuries than the Anglo-American women writers Gilbert and
Gubar discuss. The fact that women in France did not obtain suffrage
until 1944 and women in Quebec until 1940, whereas their Anglo-Cana-
dian, English, and American counterparts had gained it in 1917, 1916–
22, and 1920 respectively, confirms that at least political inequality per-
sisted longer in these places.[16] In the social sphere, French-Canadian
society before the Quiet Revolution (*la Révolution tranquille*) of the 1960s
and 1970s was deeply Catholic, conservative, and patriarchal. Women
were encouraged, or rather mandated, by their parish priests to marry

and have as many children as possible in order to counter act the progressive minoritization of their language and culture.[17] The burden of
multiple maternities (often in the double digits) and of constant and
arduous domestic duties was hardly conducive to literary production.[18]
Nor was the education available to French-Canadian women at this time;
except for a handful of classical *collèges* for women, female secondary
education in Quebec consisted for the most part of two- to four-year pro-
grams in the 'domestic sciences,' through which women learned to
become 'professional wives.'[19] Moreover, the cultural isolationism and
anti-intellectualism practised by the provincial government, especially
under the ultraconservative Maurice Duplessis in the 1930s, 1940s, and
1950s, did little to encourage the literary ambitions of either men or
women in Quebec.[20]

   In France, although many aristocratic women were involved in literary
circles in the eighteenth century, as patronesses, *salonnières,* or indeed
writers, under the Republic and the Empire, women saw their civil rights
restricted and were expected to commit themselves exclusively to the
private sphere, from which they could exercise little to no influence on
literature or the public sphere in general.[21] The relative dearth of nineteenth-century women writers included in the French literary canon
attests both to the efficacy of these restrictions and to traditional resistance to the inclusion of women in that canon. In the twentieth century,
the gender ratio of the members of the Académie Goncourt and its prize
recipients is but one indicator that barriers persist between French
women and the field of literature, or at least recognition within it. Of the
fifty-two individuals who have been members of the Académie Goncourt
over the past century, only five have been women (three of whom are
members today); and, consistent with this rate of slightly less than 10 per
cent, of the 104 Prix Goncourt laureates to date, nine have been women,
all of them since 1944.[22] Today, women writers flourish in both France
and Quebec. But in these places, women's path towards civil, sexual,
political, and professional equality (whose end the women of no nation
have yet reached) has been scattered with a certain number of historically specific obstacles perhaps more formidable than those with which
some of their Northern European and North American counterparts
have had to contend.

   Putting national differences aside, there is another reason to believe
that Gilbert and Gubar's declaration that twentieth- (and now twenty-
first-) century women writers enjoy freedom from anxiety was prema-
ture. As many feminist critics have pointed out, the notion of the 'death

of the author,' as proposed by Roland Barthes and Michel Foucault, perniciously caught on just as the women's movement was getting underway and just as increasing numbers of women were becoming authors.[23] Yet many groups within the women's movement were critiquing not only men's dominance within structures of power, but, like Barthes and Foucault, the functioning and even the very existence of certain of these structures. Nevertheless, in *Fictions of Authority: Women Writers and Narrative Voice*, Susan Sniader Lanser maintains that 'regardless of any woman writer's ambivalence toward authoritative institutions and ideologies, the act of writing a novel and seeking to publish it ... is implicitly a quest for discursive authority: a quest to be heard, respected, and believed, a hope of influence.'[24] The same is certainly true for most if not all male writers. For women, however, the desire to be an author, as I have argued, has longer been tainted by anxiety – anxiety that, moreover, has multiple and conflicting faces, for it has multiple sources: doubts about the very possibility of becoming an author in a persistently male-dominated society; fears about actually becoming one and suddenly being expected to assume the (unfamiliar) authority that is still (despite exaggerated reports of his death) generally conferred upon the author; and finally, doubts about the *legitimacy*, as well as the desirability, of claiming such authority.

As the title of this book makes clear, I have found (despite Gilbert and Gubar's optimism) that there remains plenty of anxiety in contemporary women's writing, whether it takes the form of covert narrative force, overt textual theme, or a combination of both. If there is still a preponderance of anxiety in women's writing, it is only reflective of the situation in real life, in which women, according to recent medical and psychological research, are much more likely than men (many sources say twice as likely) to suffer from anxiety. In her ambitious synthesis of recent scientific literature on anxiety, *Origins of Phobias and Anxiety Disorders: Why More Women Than Men?* (2003), Michelle G. Craske maintains that this disparity is not due, as some have proposed, to a presumed greater likelihood on the part of women to seek professional help, 'given that the prevalence data are derived from non-treatment-seeking community samples.'[25] Rather, Craske concludes that women truly are more likely to suffer from anxiety, both because of the ways men and women are socialized and because of physiological differences between them ('innate' differences, caused by evolution and/or hormones, which can in turn influence socialization) (175). Following are some of the factors Craske cites that may contribute to women's greater vulnerability to anxiety: the evolutionary and thus biological development in females of greater vigilance for and sensitivity to potential danger because of their role as caregiver (187); the tendency in females (again evolutionarily and thus biologically determined) to seek group affiliation and social support (originally in order to protect their young better), which can make them less self-sufficient and more vulnerable to anxiety in the *absence* of such support (196); and on the sociological side, greater parental acceptance of fear and timidity in girls, as opposed to parental expectations of courage and aggressiveness in boys (184–5). Another social factor proposed elsewhere is the expectation many women are still under to meet others' needs before their own.[26] In order to 'have it all,' most women (unlike their male partners in most cases) must also 'do it all' – shop for and cook the food as well as eat it; clean the house as well as relax in it; bear, feed, supervise, and transport the children as well as enjoy their company and accomplishments; and so on. One more physiological factor that has been proposed is that women's brain structure, whose development (like that of men's) is affected by sex hormones, may help explain why they are two to three times more likely than men to suffer from depression, which frequently co-occurs with anxiety[27] (but Craske warns that 'social influences may well contribute to the development of heightened negative affectivity in females').[28]

Whatever the reasons, and they are certainly multiple, it does appear to be the case that women tend to suffer from anxiety more often than men. The statistic that twice as many women as men are diagnosed with an 'anxiety disorder' might therefore appear to be a natural consequence of women's greater vulnerability to anxiety.[29] Yet how 'natural' is any progression in the diagnostic process from the identification of specific feelings a patient is experiencing (such as anxiety) to the labelling of those feelings as symptoms of a 'disorder'? As a study such as Foucault's *Folie et déraison* (*Madness and Civilization*) (1961) reveals, what constitutes a mental disorder is culturally determined.[30] Many feminists have asserted that the drug industry (like psychiatry and medicine in general) has long been guilty of 'medicalizing womanhood,' and doctors have indeed been prescribing psychotropic drugs disproportionately to women for decades.[31] In *Prozac on the Couch: Prescribing Gender in the Era of Wonder Drugs*, Jonathan Metzl studies advertisements for these kinds of drugs that have appeared in medical journals, magazines, and pamphlets over the past forty years and concludes that drug manufacturers are clearly targeting women as the primary consumers of these products.[32] From the 1950s to the 1970s, millions of American housewives were prescribed 'mother's little helpers,' tranquillizers such as Miltown and Valium, to help them cope with (or to anesthetize them to) the anxiety and depression they quite rationally felt in the face of the endless piles of dirty dishes and diapers that were their raison d'être. In the 1970s it was estimated that about 30 million American women (almost half of the adult female population at the time) were taking tranquillizers.[33] Still today, twice as many women as men are diagnosed with anxiety disorders; and moreover among all those (male and female) diagnosed, women are much more likely than men to be prescribed anti-anxiety medication.[34]

This contemporary phenomenon is in no way restricted to the United States. According to a recent *Wall Street Journal* article, the French take even more tranquillizers and anti-depressants (which are also used to combat anxiety) than Americans or Canadians: 78 pills per one thousand individuals in France per year versus 64 in the United States and 66 in Canada.[35] The French also reportedly take two to four times as many anti-depressants and anti-anxiety pills as most of their Western European neighbours.[36] Likely explanations for such a high consumption of these (as well as many other) kinds of medications in France are the lack of restrictions on how many doctors an individual can see and how many prescriptions a doctor can write, as well as the low cost (at least for consumers) of prescription drugs. Perhaps the pessimism for which the French have a certain cultural reputation plays some role in this consumption, but most experts seem to agree that the principal cause is availability. As in the United States, in France the majority of those taking anti-anxiety medication are women; the *Wall Street Journal* article in fact claims that one in every four French women has a prescription for one of these kinds of drugs.[37]

One of the negative effects of these newer anti-anxiety drugs may be that, just like the tranquillizers that preceded them (to which they are supposed to be far superior), they anesthetize women to the injustice of their still less than equal status and the constraints of the roles that continue to be 'prescribed' for them. But whatever the causes, and the legitimacy, of the disparity between women and men in the diagnosis and treatment of anxiety disorders, this disparity is a concrete reality that necessarily makes anxiety a 'women's issue.'

One way to explore this issue is by examining representations of anxiety in contemporary women's writing. Many of the anxieties revealed or presented in the narratives I study are certainly related to the anxiety of authorship that Gilbert and Gubar describe in *The Madwoman in the Attic*.

Yet many are also distinct from it, or are distinctive versions of it, as the following chapters will show. The anxieties inscribed in these four texts also distinguish themselves to a certain extent from another kind of anxiety – one which, rather than waning in the twentieth century (as has, without disappearing, that of becoming an author for women), instead reached its apogee. To this kind of anxiety I will now turn.

Representations of anxiety in Western literature, theatre, and art abound in the immediate post–Second World War period, which the modernist poet W.H. Auden went so far as to designate in his eponymous poem as the 'Age of Anxiety.'[38] For Samuel Beckett, an acutely angst-ridden author, the modern writer (indeed the modern individual) suffers from a chronic anxiety that arises especially from his inability to believe that language can be made to 'mean' in the absurd and indifferent world that human disasters on the scale of the two world wars and the Holocaust have proved ours to be. In the plays of one of Beckett's contemporaries, Eugène Ionesco, characters feel driven to speak – incessantly – yet they are maddeningly incapable of communicating anything but nonsense either to one another or to their spectators. Along with such literature, theoretical veins such as psychoanalysis, phenomenology, and Saussurian-inspired structural linguistics, with its emphasis on the arbitrary relationship between signifier and signified and the purely relational value of the former, have also eroded (often unintentionally) postwar confidence in man's presumed Cartesian ability to extract clear meaning from the world and in the efficacy of language as a tool to help him do so. Influenced by these 'hermeneutics of suspicion,' in particular notions about the limits of linguistic reference, many of the writers of what has been named the New Novel began to reject the idea of narrative mimesis. They therefore attempted to write novels that were deliberately about 'nothing' or, at most, about the futility of trying to write novels that could refer to anything outside the unreal world the novel itself created. Alain Robbe-Grillet, for example, argued in *Pour un nouveau roman* that the novel does not reveal a reality, but rather constructs and constitutes one: 'Le roman n'est pas un outil [...] Il ne sert pas à exposer, à traduire, des choses existant avant lui, en dehors de lui. Il n'exprime pas, il recherche. Et ce qu'il recherche, c'est lui-même' (The novel is not a tool ... It does not serve to expose, to translate, things that exist before it, outside of it. It does not express, it searches. And what it searches for is itself).[39]

Rather than claiming that the literary text has no referent at all, then, many such writers and theorists have suggested that the literary text creates its own imaginary or fictional referent. In *Of Words and the World: Ref-*

erential Anxiety in Contemporary French Fiction, David R. Ellison writes that
the distinction drawn in literary criticism between real and fictional referent, between real and fictional world, has been enormously fruitful,
for it 'allows the reader or critic to map the self-created topography of
the text and view it with the clear-sightedness of a theoretical perspective.'[40] Yet, Ellison argues, 'an exclusive concentration on the question of
reference *within* fiction (a study of the laws of the imaginary referent)
would limit the scope of the literary work to the aesthetic realm (the
space of forms, structures, narrative laws, and poetic figures) and would
abstract the work from the ethical domain to which it points, or seems to
point' (9; Ellison's emphasis). In his brief account of the concerns of
structuralist literary criticism in the introduction to his book *Fictional
Worlds*, Thomas Pavel maintains similarly that while 'a strongly antiex-
pressive aesthetics accompanied classical structuralist poetics, discourag-
ing reflection on those literary and artistic features that transcend purely
structural properties: style, reference, representation, global meaning,
expressiveness,' this 'moratorium on representational topics' is now
over, and questions of referentiality must be, and indeed are being,
tackled once again.[41] In *Of Words and the World*, Ellison argues through
detailed readings of several texts by writers – most of whom have been
designated as New Novelists – that despite their efforts to untether their
texts from the 'real' referent, 'the practice of writing often undermines
the theoretical constructs on which that writing seems to be based, especially those constructs that center on self-reflexivity or self-referentiality.'
That is, the referent, thought to be banished from these texts, inevitably
returns to 'haunt' them.[42] For Ellison, it is in fact those works in which
there remains a 'tension' between imaginary and real referents, between
what the author says he is doing in his text and what seems really to be
happening there in terms of reference, that are the most sophisticated
and interesting examples of postwar experimental fiction (9).

My study of anxiety in contemporary fiction in French shares some of
the same concerns as Ellison's, but also differs in several ways. Most obviously, I have focused exclusively on women writers, whereas Ellison considers women writers in only one chapter of six (chapter 4, in which he
compares the autobiographies of Alain Robbe-Grillet, Duras, and Sarraute). And while Ellison argues that in the texts he examines referential
anxiety underlies the narration, anxiety is not also a theme within most
of these narratives, as it is (to varying degrees) in the texts I read. Notwithstanding its subtitle, *Of Words and the World* is actually less about anxiety in narrative than about literary referentiality, or more specifically,

about notable and (Ellison argues) doomed refusals of such referentiality. Literary referentiality is an issue to some degree in the texts I examine as well, but it is precisely by bringing to light *all* the various anxieties present in these narratives I read (many of them not related or not directly related to the issue of referentiality) that I can best explore these authors' approaches to the relationship between text and reality, words and the world. Also, the texts I read differ from most of those chosen by Ellison in that even when the anxieties uncovered in them are linked to referentiality, they are not – or not primarily – the consequences of a *loss of faith* on the narrator's part in language's power to refer to the world. Rather, I argue that the authors concerned here have eschewed the radical linguistic scepticism of many postwar French writers and theorists and the primarily formal concerns to which they dedicated themselves. Instead, in constructing their texts these women writers begin with the premise that narrative and story, words and the world, can and must maintain a practical connection in literature, and that language can be made to point, however imperfectly, to social, historical, and psychological realities. Let it be clear, however, that these writers have no naive conceptions of linguistic representation; they are profoundly wary of language and its inherent artificiality and indeterminacy. If they attempt to represent in their work a certain reality, they do so self-consciously and without employing outmoded 'realist' narrative techniques.[43] But any anxieties they or their narrators experience while writing or narrating stem less from radical doubts about language's capacity to gesture towards the world than, first, from doubts about their own ability to make language do so, and second, from an apprehension of the *responsibility* that writing about the world entails. The anxieties concerning language and its referential function that surface in these texts are thus intimately related, but not identical, to the multiple anxieties of authorship described above. If there is a general anxiety that subsumes all the particular anxieties inscribed in these authors' texts, it is a double-edged anxiety produced first by the recognition of the *difficulty* of attempting to speak about or reveal some kind of reality in language, and second, by the recognition of the very *possibility* of such revelation. That is, the narrators of these texts (and often the authors behind them, I maintain) fear at the same time both success and failure in their endeavour to say something about themselves and the world.

Very roughly sketched, the particular reality whose exploration in narrative is each of these writers' goal is the following: for both Duras and Ernaux, it is the (nearly) ineffable ways in which human memory functions and the degrees to which memory is reliable and communicable; for Sarraute, it is the 'true' nature of human interaction, which lies hidden beneath social and linguistic conventions; and for Hébert, and also for Duras and Ernaux, it is the violence of social and political marginalization, that is, both the violence that engenders this marginalization and that which is in turn engendered by it. Although the narrative styles of the texts studied here are all innovative, and some 'difficult' (this is especially true of Sarraute's and Hébert's texts), these texts are all 'realist' in the very specific sense that their narrators all try to get to the bottom of a particular social, psychological, political, and/or historical phenomenon.

From at least the early nineteenth to the mid-twentieth centuries, one of the goals of many French writers was to diminish in their texts the perceived temporal and epistemological distance between 'story' (in Genette's sense, the 'signified or narrative contents')[44] and narration, as well as that between narration and reception. Flaubert attempted to reduce this distance through the use of *discours indirect libre* (free indirect discourse), which gave the reader the impression that she had direct access to characters' minds without the mediation of a narrator. Proust went one step further by abandoning altogether the patently artificial device of the omniscient narrator in favour of a homodiegetic narrator, to whose mind the reader thus had 'direct' and presumably reliable access.[45] Some writers then attempted to lessen even more the reader's perception of temporal distance in particular by having, as in sections of Sartre's *La nausée* (*Nausea*) (1938), a homodiegetic narrator narrate in the present tense, as if he were living and recounting his experiences simultaneously.[46] The purpose of narrative techniques such as these was to give the reader the impression that living and telling, life and language, were not so very separate. Structuralist and then poststructuralist theorists of the latter half of the twentieth century, however, insisted that the difference between these two did and would always exist, no matter how good an illusion of their coincidence a narrator might create. This demystification of the notion of *presence* in literature, and in language in general, has been essential to the effective critique of oppressive discourses, and the women writers I study have embraced as well as contributed to such a demystification. They have not, however, lost faith in the use of the literary text as a tool (a role which at least the early Robbe-Grillet denied it) that can, however crudely and imperfectly, help them gain and convey a better understanding of what they see as *realities*, realities that merit reflection and, if 'hidden,' revelation.[47]

In loosely defining these diverse writers as practitioners of a kind of 'realism' rather than of, for example, the *nouveau roman* (which has been associated with a hyperpreoccupation with form) or *l'écriture féminine* (feminine writing) (associated with an ahistorical essentialism), I want to underscore the connection maintained in at least the texts I study here between words and the world, between the narrative and the cultural, historical, and social context in which it is constructed and to which it gestures.[48] If I study only female writers, I do so in part to emphasize the very breadth of the kinds of issues they address in their texts, issues concerning the inner as well as the outer worlds (psyche and society) that we all, both men and women, inhabit. Duras, Ernaux, and Hébert could all be characterized as feminist writers (although their feminisms differ), but they are not exclusively that. Of the four principal narratives I analyse in the following chapters, only one – Hébert's *Les fous de Bassan* – deals explicitly with feminist, or even specifically women's, issues.[49] Taking the case of Duras, for instance, Jane Bradley Winston argues that from the publication of *Moderato cantabile* (1958) to that of *L'amant* (*The Lover*) (1984) and beyond, the media and many critics constructed 'Marguerite Duras' as a writer preoccupied principally if not uniquely with 'feminine' themes such as desire and jealousy.[50] Winston maintains that they did so in order to obfuscate the more manifestly political, and especially anti-colonial, content of her texts. A certain amount of this kind of journalistic and critical manipulation might be detected in regards to Ernaux's and Hébert's images as well, for both are strongly 'political' writers. And while women's oppression is a central issue in much of Ernaux's work, I would argue that class oppression is an even more significant one.[51] As for Sarraute, she unequivocally refused the label not only of 'feminist' writer but of 'woman' writer as well, and she resisted that of 'New Novelist,' which she felt also threatened to limit the significance of her literary project. As Sarraute insists in both her fiction and her theoretical writings, ready-made labels, of any kind, always imperil the 'life,' the vitality, of the reality to which they are applied.[52]

I should doubtless explain my use of such a loaded term as 'reality.' To borrow yet again the words of Nathalie Sarraute, in this case spoken when she was asked what *she* meant when she used the term (as she so often did), I will begin with the caveat, 'Je ne suis pas philosophe.'[53] I use the word 'reality' because the authors of the texts I analyse here do (especially Ernaux and Sarraute, but also Duras and Hébert), and I do not lend it any specialized or obscure meaning. In my usage, 'reality' means simply, 'the quality or state of being real,' wherein 'real' means 'having objective independent existence,'[54] although neither I nor my authors purport to have 'objective' understandings of the realities about which we write. These authors do believe, however, that what they investigate in their texts has an existence that precedes and therefore is not (or at least not wholly) dependent on the text (the language) that reveals them. I use the word 'reveal' here, because what the authors of these texts are trying to do, more or less explicitly (Sarraute more, Hébert less, for example), is to 'show' the reader something he had not already, or had only imperfectly, perceived (which is exactly what Robbe-Grillet, in the quote reproduced earlier, claimed a novel should *not* do). Once again, these authors are well aware that language is not a mirror that can reflect reality without leaving traces of itself upon that reflection. Ernaux and Sarraute in particular treat explicitly and extensively in their texts the question of language's role in our comprehension and communication of a reality. To what extent, they ask, does language distort or falsify that which it is meant to represent? How well can non-linguistic perceptions, sensations, or memories be 'translated' into language? Or is language always already implicated in the processes of perceiving, feeling, and remembering? Although these authors' answers to such questions are sometimes ambivalent, the fact that they pose them suggests that for them, there exists something that is not language but that can be indicated by language, even if only with a great deal of difficulty and imprecision.

Because 'Monsieur X.' and *La honte* are explicitly autobiographical texts – texts whose narrators claim to represent the authors of the text and to describe real rather than fictional events, experiences, and feelings – their narrators often use the terms 'vrai' and 'vérité' ('true' and 'truth') along with, or instead of 'réel' and 'réalité' ('real' and 'reality'). One way of looking at the difference is to consider that the first set stresses the quality of faithfulness or accuracy, whereas the second emphasizes that of existence. A lie actually told is 'real,' for example, but the information it proffers is not 'true.' The meanings of 'reality' and 'truth' nevertheless frequently intersect; both words have multiple definitions, and the first ('reality') is evoked in one of the definitions of the second ('truth'), which reads, 'the body of *real* things, events, and facts: ACTUALITY,' or, in other words, 'the state of being the case: FACT' (my emphasis).[55] Duras's use of the terms 'vrai' and 'vérité' includes, as I will show, the notion of sincerity, but both she and Ernaux most often employ them as synonyms for 'réel' and 'réalité.' Remaining aware of each concept's specificity, I will at times problematize the seeming interchangeability of the two concepts in these authors' texts.

The conclusions I draw about the presence of anxiety in contemporary women's writing in French will necessarily be limited, as my intention is to offer, along with general reflections on the topic, thorough and original readings of a small number of texts I consider to be particularly 'anxiety-laden.' Another caveat I will make is that it is not my objective to identify in these texts anxieties that belong exclusively to women. Rather, it is to point out some of the innovative ways in which anxiety is textualized in contemporary women's writing in French and also to reflect on what these textualizations might tell us about contemporary notions of anxiety in both France and Quebec. Although the four writers I study differ widely in their writing styles and interests, I find at least one broadly conceived commonality among them (aside from that they are all women and that they all wrote in French in the twentieth century). What they share is the experience, to a greater degree than most people of their respective generations and milieux, of what I will call *displacement.* The displacements these writers underwent were geographical, cultural, or social or a combination of any of these three. I elaborate on the nature of the particular displacements each writer experienced in the following, brief biographical sketches.

Marguerite Duras was born in 1914 of French schoolteachers who had settled in colonial Indochina to earn the fortune that colonialist propaganda had promised them.[56] She grew up speaking both French and Vietnamese and playing in rice fields with native children, a fraternization of which most white colonials disapproved. Her father died when she was seven, and her widowed mother's plan to build a prosperous plantation was thwarted by a corrupt colonial administration. Duras escaped her family's poverty and her mother's madness to attend university in France when she was seventeen, and she never returned to her 'homeland.' During the latter part of the Second World War, she and her then-husband, Robert Antelme, joined a resistance group headed by François Mitterrand. Duras spent the last year of the war in desperate search of news of Antelme, who had been arrested in the summer of 1944 (the story is recounted in the first two texts of *La douleur.* I examine the second of these in chapter 2). She published her first novel in 1943 (*Les impudents*), but did not gain much recognition until the late 1950s and 1960s, with texts such as *Moderato cantabile* (1958), the scenario for Alain Resnais's film *Hiroshima mon amour* (1959), and the India cycle (1964–73).[57] Her writing would be neither popular (that is, of best-seller status) nor truly lucrative until 1984, when she won the Prix Goncourt, along with an entire hour on Bernard Pivot's populo-intellectual television show *Apostrophes*, for *L'amant*. From Kampot to Saint-Germain-des-Prés, from barefoot colonial girl to turtle necked French *intello*, from obscure and esoteric writer ('Marguerite Durasoir'[58]) to wildly popular and wealthy 'romance' novelist, Duras experienced to a rather profound degree, then, all three kinds of displacements – geographical, cultural, and social – noted above.

Annie Ernaux was born of French parents in Normandy in 1940 just after the German advance into that province.[59] Her mother had been a factory worker and her father a farmhand before buying, on credit, a tiny café and grocery shop in a working-class section of a small Norman town. They vowed throughout their daughter's childhood never to lose their footing on the social ladder they had managed to climb ever so slightly, and their fierce social struggle informs Ernaux's entire œuvre, just as Duras's mother's drawn-out battle with corrupt colonial authorities does her daughter's. Yet it is Ernaux's own, more radical and consequently more painful social ascendancy – from shopkeeper's daughter, to university student, to *professeur agrégé*, to prize-winning and wealthy author – that is the focus of many of her texts.[60] While the displacement that Ernaux underwent was solely one of social class, her literary work, like the theoretical work of her contemporary Pierre Bourdieu, reveals that intracultural class differences can be as profound and as irreconcilable – and as susceptible to calculated 'naturalization' – as intercultural ones. Ernaux herself underscores this point by calling herself 'une "immigrée à l'intérieur" de la société française' (an 'immigrant within' French society).[61]

Nathalie Sarraute was born in Russia at the dawn of the last century to educated members of the upper-middle class. Her parents were liberal activists who had a number of run-ins with the czarist government.[62] Unlike Duras and Ernaux, Sarraute grew up in an economically and culturally privileged environment. Her mother – herself a writer of novels and stories – and her father – a chemist and entrepreneur – were divorced when she was two years old, and she spent much of her childhood travelling back and forth between France, where each of her parents lived for a time and where her father eventually settled, and Russia, to which her mother returned for good when Sarraute was eight. From that point on, Paris was Sarraute's permanent home; there she earned a law degree, married a Frenchman, and had three daughters. Because she was Jewish, during the Second World War she left Paris with two of her daughters to live in a village under an assumed name. She went so far as to divorce her husband, whose mother was Jewish, in order to protect him from anti-Semitic laws (the couple remarried in 1956). Like Duras, then, Sarraute underwent several displacements during her life, displacements between two countries, two cultures, and two languages (but not, like Duras or Ernaux, between two social classes).[63] She also, interestingly, experienced three quite different identities: Natacha Tcherniak (her Russian maiden name), Nathalie Sarraute (her French married name, as well as her authorial name), and Nicole Sauvage (her war-time, Aryan pseudonym).

Anne Hébert was born in 1916 into a wealthy and prominent family near Quebec City.[64] Her father was a respected poet and literary critic as well as a civil servant, and her cousin, Hector de Saint-Denys Garneau, was one of the century's most celebrated *québécois* poets, along with Hébert herself. Hébert began publishing in the late 1930s, before gaining attention in 1950 with *Le torrent* (*The Torrent*), a collection of short stories.[65] She published the volume at her own expense, because editors found the subject matter of the title story – the physical and emotional abuse of a young boy by his puritanical mother and his own consequent misanthropy (and especially misogyny) – too shocking for Catholic French Canadians, and most certainly too critical of the repressive and reactionary atmosphere of pre-'revolutionary' Quebec. Alienated from her native society, which was itself alienated from and dominated by anglophone Canada, in 1954 Hébert was awarded a grant that allowed her to spend a year in Paris. One year turned into three, and in 1965 she settled permanently in Paris, a city that offered her, as it did so many other North American expatriates, the personal and creative liberty she could never have found at home. Because of this cultural and geographical displacement, Hébert witnessed the cultural revolution that her fellow *Québécois* carried out during the 1960s and 1970s, and to which her iconoclastic writing contributed, principally as an outsider.

Because of the various kinds of displacements they have in common, along with their status as women and francophones, the four authors I have selected can also be said to share, to varying degrees, the status of 'other.' Almost all human beings experience alienation in one form or another during their lives. Yet because the displacements these authors underwent were multiple, significant, and in most cases permanent, their sensitivity to and understanding of 'otherness' was doubtless more acute than is typical. Consequently, anxieties about otherness emerge (again, to varying degrees) in their work. Many of the narrators and characters in their texts suffer from a deep sense of alienation, be it self-imposed, or imposed by others, or both. Such anxiety is not unrelated to the anxiety of authorship. If these authors believe, as I argue they do, that language can be used to describe, organize, and interpret the outside world, however imperfectly, their common experience òf being the other to a majority has made them aware (often painfully so) that language, because of its power, is a potentially dangerous tool. In their writing, they therefore use it carefully, and at times, as I will further argue, anxiously.[66]

I have divided this book into two parts, each of which describes the particular anxiety-provoking subject matter with which the narrators of the texts I read grapple. Part I, 'Narrating the Self, Narrating the Other,' focuses on two openly autobiographical texts. Chapter 1, '"Truth" in Memory and Narrative: Marguerite Duras's "Monsieur X. dit ici Pierre Rabier",' examines the second narrative in Duras's *La douleur,* a collection of short texts about resistance and collaboration during the Second World War. It is, Duras claims, a 'true' account ('une histoire vraie jusque dans le détail' [a true story, right down to the details]) of her attempts to learn what happened to her husband in the months following his arrest for resistance activities.[67] Chapter 1 explores how remembering – often a disorderly, fragmented, and unreliable process – impels but also confounds narration – an inherently ordering, completing, and meaning-imposing force. I call attention to the heterogeneity of the text's narrative style and argue that it is an effect of the first-person narrator's need to draw from two very different kinds of memory in order to tell her account. In constructing the story of 'Monsieur X.,' the narrator must constantly negotiate between a desire to tell the 'truth' about her experience, with all the pain and guilt that attend such telling, and an accompanying, anxious desire to bury the memories that inform this truth. In the end, the truth told by the text is less a truth about what happened to Marguerite Duras during the summer of 1944 (although Duras certainly attempts to get at such a truth) than a truth about how the act of remembering both invites and hinders the act of narrating.

Chapter 2, 'Shame in Memory and Narrative: Annie Ernaux's *La honte,*' is another exploration of how memory and narrative intertwine. In *La honte,* the autodiegetic narrator (an incarnation of Ernaux herself) describes a violent scene that took place between her parents when she was eleven years old. Although by 1997 Ernaux had already published several accounts of her childhood and adolescence, in them she had made no explicit reference to this scene, which the narrator of *La honte* nevertheless names as the most shameful experience of her life. While Ernaux's multiple and seemingly compulsive returns to her adolescence in works previous to *La honte* reveal an implacable desire to expose this shameful scene, the scene's very absence from these works points to an anxiety so powerful that it overrode for more than twenty years the drive towards revelation. By finally narrating this traumatic memory, the narrator of *La honte* hopes to weave it into the larger text of memories that make up her life story. When she rereads the narrative she has at last produced, however, she is struck by the feeling that it is somehow false. She thus experiences a double, as well as paradoxical, anxiety: on the one hand an anxiety about exposing her shame, and on the other about not being able to communicate this shame truthfully or accurately. In this way Ernaux questions – as does Duras in 'Monsieur X.' – the fidelity, first, of memories to the lived experience they supposedly record, and second, of narrative to wordless memories. Her persistent, even obsessional efforts to represent her experiences accurately, not only in *La honte* but also in many of her other narratives, attest to the very seriousness with which she undertakes literary representation and authoring.

Part II, 'Narrating Life, Narrating Death,' encompasses chapters 3 ('The Anxiety of Influence and the Urge to Originate: Nathalie Sarraute's *Entre la vie et la mort*') and 4 ('The Sound of the Semiotic: Anne Hébert's *Les fous de Bassan*'). The two principal texts that I analyse in these chapters differ from those in the preceding chapters in at least one significant way: their narrators are male.[68] Chapter 3 reveals the desires and anxieties of a fictional writer, a shadowy, composite figure referred to simply as *il*, a pronoun that Sarraute claims she is using simply to avoid marking the gender of a figure she intends to be universal – *un écrivain* (a writer) (in this chapter I nevertheless problematize Sarraute's use of gender in *Entre la vie et la mort*). In her highly abstract as well as comical fashion, Sarraute presents the typical experiences of a writer as he tries to produce a text not in a vacuum but in the society of others whose spoken and unspoken (or 'tropismic,' in Sarraute's vocabulary) communications with him constantly distract him from what he senses to be his crucial objective. This objective is similar to that of both Duras's and Ernaux's narrators in that it is a search for a way to represent in narrative a reality that lies outside of language, without falsifying (or 'killing,' as Sarraute would say) that reality. The writer also harbours the more mundane desire to attain literary greatness through absolute originality; yet at the same time he struggles against this ambition, feeling that it interferes with his first and less egotistical goal. As Sarraute's essays and interviews suggest, she herself was in no way immune to either the 'noble' or the 'petty' anxieties suffered by her fictional writer. Yet in *Entre la vie et la mort*, as I will argue, these anxieties cannot be thus differentiated, because the anxious desire to produce an original text (unlike those of one's predecessors) is indispensable to the writer interested in producing a 'living' text (one that is faithful to the reality it is meant to reveal).

Chapter 4 examines the narrative anxieties and desires of two of the multiple homodiegetic narrators of Hébert's *Les fous de Bassan* (1982), a novel about the brutal murder of two adolescent girls in rural Quebec in the 1930s. In their narratives, these two male characters demonstrate a pathological sensitivity to sound in general, and to the sound of certain human voices and vocal emissions in particular. I read their narratives in part through the lens of Kristeva's theory of the semiotic. The semiotic is the material side of all language (aspects of it such as rhythm, tone, pitch, gestures, etc.); through it, bodily drives that are normally repressed under the symbolic order are 'furtively' discharged. I argue that what makes certain voices so unpleasant to these male narrators (who are both products and propagators of a fiercely patriarchal and misogynist society) is the striking palpability in them of the semiotic, which challenges the disciplined, rational, and eminently masculine order of the symbolic. These men's narratives are similar to those of the female narrators in 'Monsieur X.' and *La honte* in that they are narratives of memory (although of a fictional memory). Yet they distinguish themselves from these latter in at least one very important way: whereas Duras's and Ernaux's narrators recount the violence they have endured, Hébert's narrators tell of the violence they have committed. The anxieties that affect their narration are nevertheless similar in that, though these men struggle to keep their stories of violence hidden (one of them in order to save his own skin), the drive to narrate overrides in them the desire for secrecy. Telling their unseemly stories, however, offers them none of the relief or redemption that it does, at least in some small part, their more innocent counterparts.

In summary, the objectives I hope to achieve through the textual analyses that follow are multiple. A first goal is to mine the content and the narrative structure of each text in order to determine what kinds of anxieties and desires (whether they belong to the narrator, or the author, or both) have left their mark on it. A second is to uncover ways in which these forces appear to have affected the narration of the narrative, and how, in turn, the (anxious) narration produced might affect the reader's reception of that narrative. A third and broader goal is to glean from these texts, by comparing the anxieties and desires inscribed in each of them with those in the others, some insight into the role that anxiety played (as theme, impetus, hindrance, or something else) in the literary production of women writing in French in the second half of the twentieth century. Some additional and related questions I will address in this book include these: Just how free from the anxiety of authorship in particular do these granddaughters of Gilbert and Gubar's madwomen appear to feel? If indeed these authors seem to be not just interested in but also personally affected by anxiety, how have they harnessed the energy of that anxiety in order to convey better their vision of reality to their readers? And finally, how do the literary representations and/or manifestations of anxiety in these four texts relate to the hyperpreoccupation with anxiety displayed in postwar Western society as a whole?

PART ONE:
NARRATING THE SELF, NARRATING THE OTHER

1 'Truth' in Memory and Narrative: Marguerite Duras's 'Monsieur X. dit ici Pierre Rabier'

La douleur ('pain' or 'grief') distinguishes itself from most of what Marguerite Duras published between the late 1950s and early 1980s in that the first several texts it contains are narrated overall in a less abstract and more classically realist mode than these earlier texts.[1] That is, while these short narratives still contain plenty of narrative 'particularities' as I will call them (for lack of a more precise term that would still encompass the variety of narrative techniques I will point out below), they are peopled by identifiable characters who live in a recognizable and coherent world and who behave in more or less logical ways.

Although not typically 'Durassian' in this sense, then, these narratives do resemble two texts that Duras published just prior to *La douleur* – *L'été 80* (*Summer 1980*) (1980) and the Prix Goncourt–winning *L'amant* (*The Lover*) (1984) – in that they are *explicitly* autobiographical.[2] That is, in prefaces to these texts and in interviews, the author has concluded with the reader what Philippe Lejeune calls an 'autobiographical pact.' This is to say that Duras has confirmed *l'identité*, the sameness, of the author, narrator, and protagonist of each of these texts.[3] So although several of Duras's earlier, less 'experimental' novels, such as *Les impudents* (*The Impudents*) (1943) and *Un barrage contre le Pacifique* (*The Sea Wall*) (1950), contain many autobiographical elements, they are fictions in that their protagonists have different names from their author, and Duras has never claimed their strict identity with her.[4] Lejeune's notion of 'identity' in this context does not necessarily entail what he terms 'ressemblance'; that is, for Lejeune, a text's status as autobiography depends not on factual accuracy but rather on the author's stated intention to present the reader with a truthful representation of his or her life, notwithstanding any omissions, exaggerations, dubious analyses, or lapses of memory readers may discover in the text. Autobiographical texts, like biographies, histories, and scientific texts, Lejeune maintains,

> prétendent apporter une information sur une 'réalité' extérieure au texte, et donc se soumettre à une preuve de *vérification.* Leur but n'est pas la simple vraisemblance, mais la ressemblance au vrai. Non 'l'effet de réel', mais l'image du réel. Tous les textes référentiels comportent donc ce que j'appellerai un '*pacte référentiel*', implicite ou explicite, dans lequel sont inclus une définition du champ du réel visé et un énoncé des modalités et du degré de ressemblance auxquels le texte prétend.

> claim to provide information about a 'reality' exterior to the text, and so to submit to a test of *verification.* Their aim is not simple verisimilitude, but resemblance to the truth. Not 'the effect of the real,' but the image of the real. All referential texts thus entail what I will call a '*referential pact,*' implicit or explicit, in which are included a definition of the field of the real that is involved and a statement of the modes and the degree of resemblance to which the text lays claim.[5] (Lejeune's emphases)

Yet unlike in the other kinds of referential texts Lejeune mentions, in autobiography, 'le pacte référentiel peut être mal tenu sans que la valeur référentielle du texte disparaisse' (the referential pact can be badly kept, without the referential value of the text disappearing).[6] Intention, or at least stated intention, thus takes precedence over result in the case of autobiography.[7] The texts published in the early 1980s in which Duras concludes this 'pacte autobiographique' can be said to signal, then, a certain 'return to the referent' that critics at the time noted not just within Duras's œuvre but within French letters in general.[8]

Criticism of *La douleur* tends to focus on the first of the six texts in the volume (the *journal* [diary] entitled 'La douleur'), in which Duras writes of the last month of her agonizing wait for the return of her husband, Robert Antelme, from a German prison camp (April to May 1945). Antelme had been arrested for participating in the Resistance in June 1944, and Duras's year-long ignorance of Antelme's fate created ideal conditions for the development of an excruciating, almost debilitating anxiety. This anxiety, along with a range of other physically painful emotions that Duras subsumes under the term *douleur,* is an object of the narrator's examination in this first narrative. The narrative on which I will concentrate in this chapter is the second in the book, 'Monsieur X. dit ici Pierre Rabier' (Monsieur X, Here Called Pierre Rabier).[9] It tells the earlier but equally anxiety-laden story of Duras's frequent encounters during the last few months of the Occupation (June through August 1944) with one of the French Gestapo agents who had arrested Antelme. It also tells of the relationship, of sorts, that Duras maintained with him in order, she says, to obtain information about her husband's whereabouts. In her preface to this second story, Duras writes that frequenting a man who had the power to make another man disappear and who could choose to exercise that power on *her* at any moment was 'terrible ... terrifiant à vivre, au point de pouvoir en mourir d'horreur' (terrifying to live through, enough to make you die of horror) (90; 71–2). Wondering whether and when Rabier would arrest her, and wondering what would happen to her husband, placed her then in a doubly profound state of anxiety the likes of which she says she had never before experienced.

The leader of the Resistance group in which Duras and Antelme participated in 1944 was François Mitterrand, later president of the French Republic (1981–95). In *Une jeunesse française: François Mitterrand, 1934–1947* (1994), an examination of Mitterrand's right-wing youth and wartime whereabouts, Pierre Péan devotes a chapter to this group's activities.[10] In the early 1990s, Péan interviewed many of its surviving members, including Mitterrand himself, and in his book he offers an alternative version – indeed, several alternative versions – of many of the events Duras describes in 'Monsieur X.' That there are differences in the story told is not in itself surprising. Yet the bold claim Duras makes as part of her 'pacte autobiographique' in the preface to 'Monsieur X.' – that in this text, 'Il s'agit d'une histoire vraie jusque dans le détail' (This is a true story, right down to the details) (90; 71) – does tempt one to take interest in conflicting accounts. Some of the discrepancies between Duras's and Péan's narratives can be attributed simply to divergent subjective interpretations of events by the various people involved, but others are more difficult to explain. Certain details in *Une jeunesse française* that contradict or at least differ from those in *La douleur* are presumably verifiable facts (they are derived from court transcripts or corroborated by several witnesses, for example) and thus seem to belie Duras's prefatory assertion. If we assume that Péan's more 'historical' account is more accurate at least to some extent than Duras's more literary version, to what can we attribute the 'errors' in a text the author calls true to the very last detail? Did Duras deliberately fictionalize elements of the story, as she did Rabier's name, for reasons of prudence or respect (thereby making at least one significant if above-board exception to her statement)? 'C'est par égard pour la femme et l'enfant de cet homme nommé ici Rabier,' she writes in the preface to the story, 'que je ne l'ai pas publiée avant, et que ici encore je prends la précaution de ne pas le nommer de son vrai nom' (It's out of consideration for the wife and child of the man here referred to as Rabier that I haven't published it before, and that even now I take the precaution of not using his real name) (90; 71). Or did she change some details of the story in order to render her text more dramatic, as Leslie Hill suggests she did in the first text in the volume, 'La douleur,' and as Gabriel Jacobs argues she did in all six texts?[11] Is Duras's statement concerning the story's truth value therefore just an example of artistic hyperbole? Or are the discrepancies due not to deliberate alteration of the facts but rather to faulty memory (for Duras said that she wrote much of 'Monsieur X.' ten years after the war's end)?[12]

While attempting to determine a definitive truth about the historical events recounted in 'Monsieur X.' would be a misguided endeavour, taking note of the variances among different versions of the story is nevertheless worthwhile. It is so because such an examination throws light on the ways in which remembering and narrating – two activities Duras and Péan's interviewees undertake – intersect. In the first part of this chapter, I will consider 'Monsieur X.' by itself, paying particular attention to elements of its narration, such as voice, mood, tense, and chronology. In doing so I will examine the relationship in it between what Gérard Genette calls 'story' (*récit* – the 'signified or narrative contents') and 'narrative' (*histoire* – the 'signifier, statement, discourse or narrative text itself').[13] Of course, in reading Duras's text alone, the only knowledge about its story we have is what we can infer from its narrative. But because of certain peculiarities in the narrative that I will examine below, there appears to the reader to be some distance between the inferred story (the story that the reader could mentally reconstruct in a more straightforward manner based on clues given in the text) and the somewhat idiosyncratic narrative.[14] Because of this distance, the reader might be more aware than when reading a more conventional narrative that the narrator, like all narrators, made certain choices in the construction of her narrative. In my reading of 'Monsieur X.,' I will examine these narrative choices – or rather 'particularities,' because 'choices' implies that the narrator is fully aware of them all. I will also speculate on the reasons for or at least the causes of these particularities and point out their effects on the reception of the text.

In the second part of the chapter, I will read 'Monsieur X.' alongside Péan's chapter, as well as in the light of two interviews Duras gave shortly after the publication of *La douleur*. These texts provide alternative versions of events, as well as information that is 'missing from' or at least not provided by Duras's narrative. What I will be comparing for the most part, then, is not a narrative to its story, but rather a narrative to other narratives. I do not make any assumptions about the truth value of the narratives told by Péan's interviewees as compared to the one told by Duras. Especially remarkable in the narratives of these interviewees is the vehemence with which many of them express their disagreement with Duras's version of the facts, fifty years after the events in question. Considering the gravity of the subject matter in these narratives – loyalty, treachery, desire, love, deportation, execution – it is only natural that the desires and anxieties that both fuel and hamper their narration are particularly acute. What I search out are the traces that these desires and anxieties have left in the multiple narratives I examine.

In the third and final section of this chapter, I will briefly discuss four other texts by Duras that shed more, and at times very different, light on the relationships among desire, anxiety, and narration in her work. First I will look at three earlier, fictional texts that also have homodiegetic narrators who narrate the story of another person. These texts are 'Madame Dodin,' a short story included in *Des journées entières dans les arbres* (*Whole Days in the Trees*) (1954), *Le ravissement de Lol V. Stein* (*The Ravishing of Lol V. Stein*) (1964), and *Le vice-consul* (*The Vice-Consul*) (1965).[15] Unlike the narrator of 'Monsieur X.,' the narrators of these texts do not also narrate their *own* story; rather, they focus almost exclusively on that of another who, for different reasons in each case, fascinates them and presents to them a kind of enigma to be solved (as does Monsieur X., in many ways, to his narrator). I will then consider a newspaper article Duras wrote the year *La douleur* was published in which she herself, following several of her narrators in *La douleur*, attempts to tell the 'truth' about another person, this time a real one. My objective in these four analyses will be to ascertain whether (and if so, how) the desires and anxieties that accompany the act of narration differ when the principal subject of the narrative is not the narrating self, but another, and when the principal source of the story recounted is not memory but historiography, hearsay, imagination, or something else.

Narrating 'Monsieur X. dit ici Pierre Rabier'

The narrator of 'Monsieur X.' provides a great number of concrete details, such as exact dates and times and the names of real people and places, all of which have the effect of anchoring the story in a historical time and space. In this forty-five-page narrative, she refers, for example, to no fewer than thirty different topographical points within the city of Paris (streets, squares, Metro stations, gardens, and cafés). And by situating the opening of the story on a date and in a place that are both highly significant and recognizable to most readers – 'C'est le 6 juin 1944 au matin dans la grande salle d'attente de la prison de Fresnes' (It's the morning of 6 June 1944 in the main waiting room of the prison at Fresnes) (91; 73) – the narrator embeds the story not just within a personal history but within a collective one as well. At the same time, most of the story is narrated in the present tense, which tends to lend it an atmosphere of immediacy and open-endedness. The reader has, or at least is meant to have, the impression that the narrator is still living out her terrible yet true ordeal as a spy of sorts for the Resistance, and that she is living it alongside her.[16] These two aspects of the narration – the present tense and the inclusion of factual details – work together to create a realistic text that seems to be situated somewhere between literature and history. Much of the story is recounted in a series of episodes, each several paragraphs or pages long and most of which describe a particular meeting between the narrator and the Gestapo agent she calls Rabier. The narrator meets Rabier at Gestapo headquarters on the rue des Saussaies in Paris while trying to have a package delivered to her imprisoned husband. In most of these episodes, which take place in a historical moment when imprisonment, deportation, and execution were all too real dangers, the present-tense narration creates not only immediacy but suspense. While the reader knows very well that Marguerite Duras, the implied 'I' of the narrative, lived to tell this tale of the Occupation many years later, this narrative style asks the reader to bracket this extra-diegetic knowledge and to 'believe' in the presentness and indeterminacy of each of these episodes.

In one of the first episodes of the narrative, for example, the narrator serves (as did many women in the Resistance) as liaison agent for her group: she must bring into contact two other *résistants* who do not know each other.[17] The passage begins with the kind of precise and factual detail that creates the text's realism: 'Le premier lundi de juillet à onze heures trente du matin, je dois mettre en contact Duponceau [...] et Godard [...] Nous devons nous rencontrer à l'angle du boulevard Saint-German et de la Chambre des Députés du côté opposé à la Chambre' (At eleven-thirty in the morning on the first Monday in July I'm to establish contact between Duponceau ... and Godard ... We're to meet at the corner of the boulevard Saint-Germain opposite the Chamber of Deputies) (95; 76). The episode, worth quoting more fully, continues thus:

> J'arrive à l'heure. Je trouve Duponceau [...] Cinq minutes ne se sont pas passées quand je m'entends héler à quelques mètres de moi: Pierre Rabier. Il m'appelle en claquant des doigts. Sa figure est sévère. Je nous crois perdus. Je dis à Duponceau: 'C'est la Gestapo, on est faits.' Je vais vers Rabier sans hésiter. Il ne me dit pas bonjour.
> 'Vous me reconnaissez?
> —Oui.
> —Où m'avez-vous vu?
> —Rue des Saussaies.'
> Ou la présence de Rabier est un pur hasard, ou il vient nous arrêter. Dans ce cas la '11 légère' de la polizei attend derrière l'immeuble, et c'est déjà trop tard [...] Je serre les mâchoires pour m'empêcher de claquer des dents.

> I arrive on time. Duponceau is there ... Before five minutes have passed I hear someone calling me from a few yards away: Pierre Rabier. He snaps his fingers as he calls me, his expression is severe. I think, we're done for. I say to Duponceau, 'It's the Gestapo – we've had it.' I go over to Rabier without showing any hesitation. He doesn't say good morning.
> 'Do you recognize me?'
> 'Yes.'
> 'Where did you see me before?'
> 'In the rue des Saussaies.'
> Either he's here by pure chance or he's come to arrest us. In the latter case the police car is waiting around the corner and it's already too late. ... I clench my jaws to keep my teeth from chattering. (95–6; 76–7)

Here, the present tense creates the sense that the character-I (the 'I' living out the events of the story) and the narrator-I (the 'I' who is later telling or writing down her past experiences) are one, and that the events are being narrated as they are unfolding.[18] In addition, with her 'Ou [...] ou' (Either ... or), the 'I' claims ignorance as to what Rabier's presence there means, further collapsing any distance between herself as character and narrator. These lines create suspense by inviting the reader to forget what he knows of the narrator's fate (alluded to in the story's preface) and to wonder if she really is 'done for.'

The narration continues for a time to generate the same sense of immediacy and suspense: '[Rabier] est gai, cordial, il me donne des nouvelles de ma belle-sœur qu'il a vue et à laquelle il a remis le colis dont s'est chargé Hermann [a Nazi official],' and so on. ([Rabier] is cheerful, cordial, gives me news of my sister-in-law, whom he's seen and to whom he's given the parcel Hermann took charge of) (96; 77). Methodically built up over the first five pages of the narrative, this suspense is then suddenly tempered by the intervention of a narrative voice that clearly belongs to a narrator-I situated in a *different* present, a present posterior to that in which the events of the story are occurring: 'Je ne me souviens d'aucun autre de ses propos' (I don't remember anything else he said) (96; 77). This intervention reminds the reader that the character-I has lived through this harrowing episode to become the narrator-I who can later recall the experience (even if her memory of it is only partial) as part of her past. The present-tense telling of the episode as it unfolds immediately resumes after this intervention – 'Nous sommes, Rabier et moi, à cinq mètres devant et cinq mètres derrière encadrés par mes deux camarades. Cette situation d'un comique répertorié et éprouvé, ne fait rire personne' (We, Rabier and I, are sandwiched between two of my colleagues, one five yards in front and the other five yards behind. This classic comic situation doesn't make anyone laugh) (96; 77). But this telling is once again interrupted by a voice from a 'future' present tense: 'Je me demande *encore aujourd'hui* comment Rabier ne s'aperçoit pas de mon trouble' (*Even today* I still wonder how it is that Rabier didn't notice my agitation) (96; 77 – emphasis mine). Again, the narrator retains the present tense for the second verb in this sentence, even though this present is anterior to that of the first verb. Despite her anachronistic intervention, it would seem that the narrator wants to conserve for the reader the continuity and immediacy of her story.

What is clearly the voice of the narrator-I rather than the character-I emerges in this episode several more times, yet most of these subsequent narratorial interjections are made in the *past* instead of the present tense. More so than those in the present tense, these past-tense interjections break the rhythm of the present-tense narrative and function as reminders to the reader that the events recounted are part of a finished and determined past. 'À travers ma peur,' the narrator continues in the same episode, 'à mesure que le temps passe, un espoir se fait jour, celui d'avoir affaire à un fou. Le comportement de Rabier *par la suite a fait que je n'ai jamais été* tout à fait démentie de ce sentiment' (As time goes by a hope starts to glimmer through my fear: perhaps I'm dealing with a madman. *Because of Rabier's subsequent behavior,* I've never quite abandoned this impression) (96–7; 78 – emphasis mine). The 'I' who experiences fear ('*ma* peur' [*my* fear]) and who has only a faint suspicion that she is dealing with a madman is distinct from the 'I' in the second sentence, who is able to tell the reader that Rabier's subsequent behaviour indeed confirmed the first 'I''s suspicion. While the first 'I,' the character-I, feels but a glimmer of hope at this moment, and while this hope will be confirmed only much later in the *story*, it is nevertheless confirmed here, prematurely as it were, in the *narrative*. Each time the posterior narrator-I intervenes in this episode, she further diminishes suspense by 'giving away' more of its outcome before the episode itself comes to a close. In the last paragraph of the episode, rather than simply interrupting, this narrator-I actually takes over the narration. Rabier's presence on the street that day, she explains in the past tense,

> était bien un hasard. Il s'était arrêté parce qu'il avait reconnu la jeune Française qui avait porté le colis à la rue des Saussaies. *Je l'ai appris ensuite,* Rabier était fasciné par les intellectuels français, les artistes, les auteurs de livres. Il était entré dans la Gestapo faute d'avoir pu acquérir une librairie de livres d'art (*sic*).

> really was an accident. He had stopped because he recognized the French girl who'd brought the parcel to the rue des Saussaies. *I found this out afterward.* Rabier was fascinated by French intellectuals, artists, authors. He'd gone into the Gestapo because he hadn't been able to buy an art bookshop (*sic*). (97–8; 79 – emphasis mine)

Rabier told the narrator he knew she was an author because he had seen (and taken) copies of her two novels that had been lying on a table in the apartment in which he had arrested her husband (94; 75). The 'sic' at the end of this passage, the narrator's own, is rather curious. One possible explanation is that the narrator is quoting Rabier verbatim, from a confession he must have made to her 'par la suite' (afterward). The reader therefore surmises that the narrator will somehow come to know and to maintain a relationship – a relatively intimate one if he confides in her thus – with this man who had arrested her husband.

This is not all the narrator-I gives away only one-third of the way through 'Monsieur X.,' a narrative that had begun like a suspense story. This past-tense, retrospective voice goes so far as to inform the reader that Rabier was arrested and tried immediately after the Liberation: 'J'ai appris pendant son procès que l'identité de Rabier était fausse, qu'il avait pris ce nom à un cousin mort dans les environs de Nice. Qu'il était

Allemand [sic]' (I learned during his trial that Rabier used a false identity, that he'd taken the name from a cousin who'd died somewhere near Nice. That he was German) (108; 88). This prolepsis, covering an event – Rabier's trial – that the narrator will revisit several more times in her narrative, not only gives away the ending of the story – villain gets his desserts – but also unveils this villain's 'real' identity.[19] Such a revelation is of course typically reserved for the *end* of a suspense narrative. Prolepses such as this one occur frequently throughout 'Monsieur X.' and disrupt the logical chronology of many of the episodes. Instead of moving from the temporal beginning through the middle to the end of the story being narrated in each episode, the reader often encounters the temporal order beginning, ending, middle; or even ending, beginning, middle. For example, one-quarter of the way through the text (102–3; 83), the interjecting narrator-I brings up a scene that she identifies as the character-I's last meeting with Rabier. This scene then reappears thirty pages later in its 'correct' place at the end of the narrative.

What is the effect of these multiple prolepses? For the reader, the effect of most of them is to expose as lies many of Rabier's statements to the character-I. Their presence suggests that the narrator-I wishes to disabuse the reader as quickly as possible of misinformation that a faithful, present-tense transcription of the 'naive' (that is, without hindsight) character-I's perceptions and thoughts would give.[20] For example, in an episode that occurs near the beginning of the relationship between the *résistante* and the Gestapo agent, the narrator reports the following: '[Rabier] prétend qu'il lui [Antelme] a évité un jugement et que mon mari est maintenant assimilé aux réfractaires du S.T.O. Moi aussi je le tiens: si j'apprends que mon mari est parti en Allemagne, je n'ai plus besoin de le voir, et il le sait. *L'histoire du S.T.O. est fausse, je l'apprendrai plus tard*' ([Rabier] claims that he saved [Antelme] from being put on trial and that he's now being treated like the people who resist the S.T.O. But I have him in my power, too. If I find out that my husband's been sent to Germany I won't need to see him anymore, and he knows this. *The story about the STO is false, as I will learn later*) (99; 80 – emphasis mine).[21] Because of the future tense of this last verb, its subject, the last 'je,' must still refer to the character-I. Only the narrator-I, however, is privy to the information reported in this sentence. In this way, the voice of this posterior narrator-I intervenes in these present-tense episodes, in any one of three tenses: the present (for example, 'Je me demande encore aujourd'hui' [Even today I still wonder] [96], 'Je me souviens' [I remember] [96, 108, 126, 128]); the past ('je l'ai appris ensuite'

[I learned later] [98], 'J'ai appris' [I learned] [108]); or the future ('je l'apprendrai' [I will learn] [99], 'J'apprendrai plus tard' [I will learn later] [121]). The effect of all these interventions is to distance the reader, if only momentarily and even imperceptibly, from the immediate action of the story.

In a later episode, another kind of temporal disorder invades the text. This episode is similar to the one discussed in depth above in that in it, the narrator recounts in the present tense another meeting (this time planned) between the narrator and Rabier, a meeting in which once again the narrator's anxiety is high. Short, matter-of-fact sentences again deliver the kind of concrete detail that renders the episode vivid and realistic. In this episode, there are no prolepses that prematurely give away the outcome. In the midst of recounting the episode, however, the narrator suddenly and inexplicably switches from the present to the past tense. The reproduction of a rather lengthy passage is needed to show this shift in context:

> Cette fois-ci c'est rue de Sèvres, nous venons de Duroc, nous passons just-ement devant la rue Dupin, où mon mari et ma belle-sœur ont été arrêtés. C'est cinq heures de l'après-midi. C'est déjà le mois de juillet. Rabier s'arrête. Il tient sa bicyclette de la main droite, il pose sa main gauche sur mon épaule, le visage tourné vers la rue Dupin, il dit: 'Regardez. Aujourd'hui il y a exactement quatre semaines jour pour jour que nous nous connaissons.'
>
> Je ne réponds pas. Je pense: 'C'est fini.'
>
> 'Un jour, continue Rabier – il prend le temps d'un large sourire – , un jour j'ai été chargé d'arrêter un déserteur allemand. Il m'a fallu d'abord lier connaissance avec lui et ensuite il m'a fallu le suivre où qu'il aille. Pendant quinze jours, jour après jour, je l'ai vu, de longues heures chaque jour. Nous étions devenus des amis. C'était un homme remarquable. Au bout de quatre semaines je l'ai mené vers une porte cochère où deux de mes collègues nous attendaient pour l'arrêter. Il a été fusillé quarante-huit heures après.'
>
> Rabier *a ajouté*: 'Il y avait ce jour-là également quatre semaines que nous nous connaissions.'
>
> La main de Rabier *était* toujours sur mon épaule. L'été de la Libération *est devenue* [sic] de glace.

This time it's in the rue de Sèvres. We come from the direction of the Duroc metro, go past the rue Dupin, where my husband and sister-in-law were arrested. It's five o'clock in the afternoon. It's July already. Rabier stops. He's holding his bicycle in his right hand, his left is on my shoulder, his face is turned toward the rue Dupin. 'Look,' he says. 'Today it's exactly four weeks to the day since we met.'

I don't answer. I think, 'It's all over.'

'One day,' Rabier goes on, with a broad smile, 'one day I had to arrest a German deserter. First I had to get to know him, and then I had to follow him wherever he went. For two weeks I saw him every day, for hours and hours every day. We became friends. He was a remarkable man. After four weeks I led him to a doorway where two of my colleagues were waiting to arrest him. He was shot forty-eight hours later.'

He added, 'That day, too, we'd known each other for four weeks.'

His hand *was* still on my shoulder. The summer of the Liberation *turned* to ice. (105–6; 86–7 – emphases mine)

While, as I have noted, the narrator employs the past tense outside of quoted dialogue before this passage, her use of it here is distinct. Whereas the 'I' in a remark such as 'Je l'ai appris ensuite' refers to the narrator-I, the 'I' implied in the next to the last sentence of the passage above ('La main de Rabier était toujours sur *mon* épaule') refers to the character-I. It is on the character-I's and not the narrator-I's shoulder that Rabier's hand is (was) resting, as it was (is) in the first paragraph narrated in the present tense ('il pose sa main gauche sur mon épaule'). There is no interjection from a posterior narrator-I here and no addition of information gathered at a later date; the narration simply shifts without warning to the past tense. The narrator appears to adopt the tense that Rabier uses to recount *his* narrative when she resumes her own, as if his narrative mode were somehow contagious, as if his control over the character-I's fate had extended even to the narrator-I's narration. Whatever its cause, I want to suggest that the effect of this tense change is similar to that of the interjections discussed above: it is to distance, temporally as well as emotionally, the reader from a highly suspenseful and anxiety-provoking scene. Furthermore, this tense change distances not only the reader from the scene, but the *narrator* as well, for with this past tense, the narrator-I dissociates herself from the character-I and thus escapes, in a sense, the mental torture to which Rabier submits this latter.

Yet as quickly as the past tense appears, the present returns: 'Je vois les grands immeubles du carrefour de Sèvres tanguer dans le ciel et les trottoirs se creuser, noircir. Je n'entends plus clairement' (I see the tall buildings at the Sèvres crossing swaying in the sky and the sidewalks going hollow and black. I can no longer hear clearly) (106; 87). These highly charged lines bring the reader back (or rather forward?) to the moment of the story's unfolding, a distinctly oppressive summer of 'liberation.' The reader is encouraged to feel that he is with the character-I on this Parisian street corner in 1944 and to share the vertigo her terror induces. The tense shifting continues, however, with the return of the past tense nine lines later: '—Pourquoi me raconter ça?' the narrator asks Rabier. '—Parce que je vais vous demander de me suivre', dit Rabier. / Je *découvrais* que je *m'y attendais* depuis toujours' (—'Why are you telling me this?' / —'Because I'm going to ask you to come with me,' says Rabier. / I *realized* I *had always been expecting* it) (106; 87 emphases mine). The narrator then alternates several more times between these two tenses, past and present, over the final page of the episode:

> Rabier parle de nouveau : 'Mais à vous je vous demanderai de me suivre dans un restaurant où vous n'êtes jamais allée. J'aurai l'extrême plaisir de vous inviter.'
>
> Il s'est remis à marcher. Entre la première phrase et la deuxième phrase, il s'est passé le temps de faire une certaine distance, un peu moins d'une minute et demie, le temps d'arriver au square Boucicaut. Il s'arrête de nouveau et cette fois il me regarde.

> Rabier speaks again: 'But I shall ask *you* to come with me to a restaurant where you've never been before. It will give me great pleasure to ask you to be my guest.'
>
> He has started to walk on. Before the first and second sentences there's been time to go a certain distance, a bit less than a minute and a half, long enough to get to the square Boucicaut. He stops again, and this time he looks at me. (107; 87)

Just as do the interjections described above, these alternations of tense disrupt the flow of the narrative. They also appear for the most part at moments of high anxiety for the character-I, when the suspense felt by the reader, consequently, is particularly acute. In this episode the narrator does not intervene and prematurely give away the meaning of Rabier's narrative (that it was just a rather sick joke to scare his 'captive') but instead lets the reader (slowly) discover this meaning alongside the character-I. Yet at key moments, the narrator dispels some of the anxiety produced by her narrative by taking refuge, as it were, in a distancing past tense. She nevertheless appears unable to sustain for long her use of this comforting tense; the present continually reappears, as if the narrative itself demanded its return. This tense alternation reflects in part, as I will argue below, the dynamic interaction of the forces of memory and narration (or remembering and narrating) in the production of the text. But first I will point out a few more particularities in the narrative structure of 'Monsieur X.'

Interspersed between what I have named the episodes, which are narrated predominantly in the present tense, are passages of a different nature.[22] They are also narrated in the present tense, but this time in an *iterative* present. That is, instead of recounting in detail individual incidents more or less from their beginning to their end, as she does in the episodes, the narrator describes *recurring* events in each of these passages.[23] The following is exemplary of these iterative passages: 'Je vois Rabier *chaque jour.* Il m'invite *quelquefois* à déjeuner, *toujours* dans des restaurants marché noir. *La plupart du temps* nous allons dans des cafés. Il me raconte ses arrestations [...] Je m'arrange pour *chaque fois* lui rappeler l'existence de mon mari' (I see Rabier *every day. Sometimes* he invites me to lunch, *always* in black market restaurants. *Usually* we go to cafés. He tells me about the arrests he's made ... I make sure *every time* to remind him about my husband) (98; 79 – emphases mine). The 'je' in this passage refers to the character-I, yet the narrator-I's presence is felt behind that of the former. This is because only she can know, after a necessary passage of time, that the kinds of events described here happen (or rather have happened) more than once. The several iterative adverbs highlighted stress the repetitive nature of the activities described. Iterative narrative, of course, is a common feature of many narratives. It helps speed along the telling of a story, which can never be told in its 'entirety.' Yet in 'Monsieur X.,' interspersed as they are between the episodes, these iterative passages, like the interjections described above, tend also and more importantly to distance both the narrator and the reader from the emotional force field of the high-anxiety episodes. These passages are necessarily devoid of detail, because the distinctiveness of each of several, similar events must be effaced for the narrator to be able to encompass them in one iterative narration (for example, 'La plupart du temps nous allons dans des cafés'). What were in real life singular and presumably terrifying meetings between a sadistic Gestapo agent and his prey thus become in the narrative only imprecise and seemingly innocuous abstractions. The narrator's use of the iterative present makes it clear that these excruciating meetings were multiple and that they therefore prolonged and periodically refuelled her agonizing anxiety that summer; at the same time, though, it obscures the particularities of these meetings in the narrative and therefore dilutes their emotional force for both the narrator and the reader.

I have identified, then, three distinct types of narration in 'Monsieur X.': one that presents a number of distinct episodes in an orderly present tense and that gives the illusion of simultaneity between the events recounted in each episode and their present-tense narration; a second that intervenes within these episodes in the present, past, or future tense and that often adds retrospective, correcting information; and a third that uses the iterative present to evoke in an abstract and distanced way recurring events in the story and which therefore cannot be seen as simultaneous to these events. These last two types of narration, or narrating instances, are similar to each other in that the voice narrating them speaks from a time and place beyond the character-I's immediate present.[24] Even when narrating in the present tense, this voice describes events not as they are perceived by the character-I but rather as they appear to a narrator now distanced from them, a narrator who has since had time to reflect on their meaning. Although I have discussed the effects produced by each of these types of narration, I have not yet speculated on their causes. One could say simply that their 'cause' is the will of Marguerite Duras; that is, perhaps Duras chose to write 'Monsieur X.' as she did precisely in order to produce tension and suspense, with intermittent attenuation of that suspense. Perhaps each and every tense shift and change in the narrating instance was deliberate and its effect calculated. Yet this explanation is not consistent with Duras's own account of the way she wrote. When asked in a 1990 interview to describe her writing style (to explain what 'du Duras' was), Duras replied, 'C'est laisser le mot venir quand il vient, l'attraper comme il vient, à sa place de départ, ou ailleurs, quand il passe. Et vite, vite écrire, qu'on n'oublie pas comment c'est arrivé vers soi. J'ai appelé ça "littérature d'urgence"' (It's letting each word come when it comes, catching it as it comes, at its point of origin, or elsewhere, when it passes by. And it's writing quickly, quickly, so that you don't forget how it came upon you. I call this 'literature of urgency').[25] And in *Écrire* (1993), Duras writes that what she dislikes about most books is that 'ils ne sont pas libres. On le voit à travers l'écriture: ils sont fabriqués, ils sont organisés, réglmentés, conformes on dirait. Une fonction de révision que l'écrivain a très souvent envers luimême' (they are not free. One can see it in the writing: they are fabricated, organized, regulated; one could say they conform. This is the result of revision, which the writer often feels he must impose upon himself).[26] Resisting the temptation to edit, she says, is not easy – 'C'est peut-être ça, le plus difficile, de se laisser faire. Laisser souffler le vent du livre' (This is perhaps the hardest part, letting go. Letting the book take its own shape) – but it is nevertheless her goal, if we take her at her word.[27]

However speculative it may be, I want to propose an explanation for the 'causes' of the narrative particularities of 'Monsieur X.' that is consistent with Duras's stated credo of writing. The force behind many of these shifts in narrative voice can perhaps be found in the interaction – the 'collision,' one might say – between the two processes necessary for the production of an autobiographical text: remembering and narrating. Whereas it seems likely that it is especially her imagination that Duras attempts to 'let go' ('laisser faire') when creating her more fictional texts, in the production of her more autobiographical texts, it is likely her memory that she primarily strives to unleash.[28] The two principal narrative voices in 'Monsieur X.' – that of the present-tense episodes and that of both the interjections and the interative passages, which I suggested create similar effects – might be thought of, then, as expressions of two different kinds of memory. The memory that informs this second voice seems to be an informed, mature, and panoramic memory, a memory that can organize and calmly recount originally troubling and confused impressions. In *Holocaust Testimonies: The Ruins of Memory,* Lawrence Langer discusses the distinction Charlotte Delbo makes in her memoirs precisely between two kinds of memory.[29] Delbo calls the kind of memory I have just described 'mémoire externe' (external memory) or 'mémoire intellectuelle' (intellectual memory).[30] This is a memory that, over time, reworks raw impressions, subduing their emotional force and organizing them into coherent patterns of meaning that can then be communicated by their bearer and understood by others. In other words, this kind of memory *narratizes* its raw material: it selects, orders, and edits individual memories, and it does so according to culturally recognizable narrative codes.

Like the interjections and the iterative passages, the episodes in 'Monsieur X.' are presumably also the products – at least in great part – of memory. I would suggest, however, that they are the products of a different type of memory, one that Delbo calls 'mémoire profonde' (deep memory) or 'mémoire des sens' (sense memory) (13–14). As Roberta Culbertson eloquently puts it, Delbo's 'mémoire des sens' is 'the persistence of the past in its own perpetual present.'[31] It is more passive than active, more like a container that stores impressions than a machine, like 'mémoire intellectuelle,' that reworks them. According to Delbo, sense memory is more faithful to lived experience than is intellectual memory, for it retains past impressions not in words but in sensations, not in the intellect but in the body.[32] When recalled, memories stored in sense memory revive in a sense the present in which they were formed, or at least they revive the sensations and emotions the subject experienced during that present.[33] Yet since this 'present' is different from the one in which the rememberer now dwells, its resurgence can provoke feelings of alienation, isolation, and indeed terror if the 'material' of the memory is a traumatic experience.

If the bearer of such sense memories wishes to communicate them to others, she must 'convert' them into language. What the reader of 'Monsieur X.' is privy to, then, are not sense memories per se, but approximate linguistic, as well as narratized, transcriptions of them. 'The demands of narrative,' Culbertson maintains, 'operate in fact as cultural silencers to this sort of memory, descending immediately upon an experience to shape notions of legitimate memory, and silencing the sort of proto-memory [sense memory] described.'[34] Sense memory, then, cannot be conveyed to others without first being distorted by language and narratization. Many writers and theorists of especially the postwar period have contended that even perception is not free from language; they maintain that language acts as a grid which separates the individual from the world and through which she (the individual) instantaneously categorizes and labels her perceptions.[35] If language is always already implicated in perception, then it must be implicated in memory, the storehouse of past perceptions. Culbertson, however, discusses Delbo's notions of memory specifically in the context of trauma, and she distinguishes traumatic memory from normal memory precisely in that the former defies language.[36] Duras's prefatory description of the period during which she frequented Rabier (reproduced on the first page of this chapter) indeed suggests that it was for her a traumatic experience.[37]

Whatever the precise nature of traumatic memories (I will examine such memories in more depth in chapter 2), the memories communicated in 'Monsieur X.' have all, as we know, been narratized. Yet as I have argued, these memories (*souvenirs*) have been narratized in different ways at different moments of the narration, depending, I am now suggesting, on what kind of memory (*mémoire*) is 'taking over' at any given moment. Langer writes that 'in [Delbo's] own narrative and even more in oral testimonies,' the two kinds of memory Delbo defines – intellectual and sense – 'interact and intersect continually, and the challenge to us as audience is to recognize and interpret those moments.'[38] The narrative structure of 'Monsieur X.' suggests that this same kind of interaction between two types of memory has occurred in its narration. The first voice I have identified, which strives to describe events as they are immediately experienced by the character-I, is the voice of sense memory. This voice very often does invoke the sensorial, as amply demonstrated in the following passage, some of which I have already quoted:

> Dans la peur le sang se retire de la tête, le mécanisme de la vision se trouble. Je vois les grands immeubles du carrefour de Sèvres tanguer dans le ciel et les trottoirs se creuser, noircir. Je n'entends plus clairement. La surdité est relative. Le bruit de la rue devient feutré, il ressemble à la rumeur uniforme de la mer. Mais j'entends bien la voix de Rabier.

> In my fear the blood ebbs from my head, the mechanism of vision wavers. I see the tall buildings at the Sèvres crossing swaying in the sky and the sidewalks going hollow and black. I can no longer hear clearly. The deafness is relative. The street noises are muffled, like the regular murmur of the sea. But I hear Rabier's voice distinctly. (106–7; 87)

Here the character-I *feels* the blood draining from her head, *sees* the streets and the buildings around her reel, *hears* the sinister voice of Rabier, although the noise from the street is strangely muffled. These are memories of sensations that have been stored in the body and that are physically re-experienced in the present in which they are recalled. 'De ce souvenir de l'agent de la Gestapo que j'ai fréquenté pendant trois mois,' Duras said in a 1986 interview about the story of 'Monsieur X.,' 'la peur est tellement intense que même le souvenir ne la change pas. C'était trop peut-être. C'était une peur mortelle, je mourais de peur, je maigrissais de peur' (As for this memory of the Gestapo agent I frequented for three months, the fear it evokes is so intense that even the fact that it's just a memory hasn't lessened it. It was perhaps too much. It was a mortal fear; I was dying of fear, I was wasting away from fear).[39] The *souvenir* of which she speaks, the memory of the terrible fear unaltered even after forty years, is sense memory. In recalling and putting into text these memories, the author herself claims to re-experience in the flesh the excruciating anxiety – the terrible uncertainty over both her and her husband's fate – of those few months.

It is precisely at such emotionally charged moments that the second voice tends to break into the narrative. The passage from 'Monsieur X.'

reproduced just above, describing a moment of utter terror for the character-I, is then interrupted by a voice of a different quality: 'Je découvrais que je m'y attendais depuis toujours. On m'avait raconté que dès la confirmation de l'épouvante, survient le soulagement, la paix. C'est vrai. Là sur le trottoir, je me suis trouvée déjà arrêtée, inaccessible désormais au facteur même de la peur: Rabier lui-même, lui échappant' (I realized I'd always been expecting it. I'd been told that as soon as terror is confirmed, relief follows, peace. It's true. There on the sidewalk I was already arrested, inaccessible to, escaping from, the very creator of fear: Rabier himself) (107; 87). This change in voice is signalled not only by a sudden shift to the past tense but also by a new tone of reflection and assessment. The previous voice, on the other hand, had simply described – sensations, principally – without commentary. The second and third sentences in this passage ('On m'avait raconté [...] C'est vrai' [I had been told [...] It's true]) have the effect, moreover, of universalizing the character-I's experience; others ('on') have felt such a fear and have reacted to it in the same way as she. The terrifying feeling of isolation expressed by the first voice – the character-I is separated from what is going on around her as if by a cloud ('Je n'entend plus clairement' [I can no longer hear clearly]) – is thus assuaged by the second voice's invocation of an 'on' who has experienced the same sensation.[40] In multiple ways, then, this second voice dissipates the atmosphere of terror that the first has created. When the telling of sense memories becomes too painful, the narrator must take refuge in intellectual memory, a narratizing memory that cleanses sense memories of their affect.

This kind of 'cleansing' inevitably alters, and therefore falsifies in some way, these sense memories. At the same time, however, as noted, the voice of intellectual memory often *corrects* information given to the character-I (and thus to the reader) that later proves to be false. The interventions of the voice of intellectual memory in this way work to render the scenes described in fact *more* truthful from the perspective of the narrator-I, but less truthful from that of the character-I. The voice of sense memory is faithful to the character-I's true feelings at any given moment, but often does not, indeed cannot, speak about that moment's overall truth. In any case, it is perhaps only with the continual interjections of the second voice, its constant alternation with the first, that 'Monsieur X.' manages to be told at all; for it seems that a purely present-tense, spy novel–like telling of the story would have been too painful for the narrator to sustain. Indeed, the placement of 'Monsieur X.' in *La douleur* also works to dampen the pain of the memories it contains. It appears second in the book, directly after the diary 'La douleur,' in which the narrator describes her wait for Robert L. (Antelme) and his eventual return, in a state near death, in May 1945. The question that haunts the character-I in 'Monsieur X.' in July 1944 – will Robert L. return home safely? – is therefore already answered for the reader by the time he begins this text. The diary thus acts as a prolonged external prolepsis, which technically eliminates from the outset any suspense that might arise from the narration of 'Monsieur X.' In fact, the events in all three of the autobiographical texts that follow the diary – 'Monsieur X.,' 'Albert des Capitales' (Albert of the Capitals), and 'Ter le milicien' (Ter of the Militia) – chronologically *precede* those described in the diary. It is as if only by placing the narrative of the return and recovery of Robert L. *first* could the narrator allow the events of the agonizing year preceding this miracle to be narrated.

In 'Spectres of Remorse: Duras's War-Time Autobiography,' Gabriel Jacobs argues that the order of the six texts in *La douleur* creates a 'kind of decrescendo' from the most factual and non-literary (the diary) to the most fictional and literary ('Aurélia Paris'). This decrescendo, Jacobs proposes, represents 'the expiation of a long-felt guilt. By the end of *La douleur*, the confession is complete; literature has replaced repugnant memories of the real self during the period of the Occupation and the Liberation.'[41] For Jacobs, the narration of the diary provokes the most guilt in the narrator, because in it she informs Robert L. of her intention to divorce him, despite his ordeal in the camps and the anguish she experienced while waiting for him. In making his argument, however, Jacobs implies that the narrator tells her husband of her decision only *after* his return from the concentration camps: 'when Robert L. is convalescing, she casually announces to him ... that their marriage is over' (52). In fact, the narrator of the diary makes it clear that she had already announced her desire for a divorce well before her husband's arrest: 'Je lui ai dit qu'il nous fallait divorcer [...] *que je n'avais pas changé d'avis depuis deux ans*' (I told him we had to get a divorce ... *that I hadn't changed my mind over the previous two years*) (emphasis mine).[42] While I agree that the diary was likely the most 'difficult' text for Duras to write, I would suggest that the primary emotion that this narration resuscitated was not guilt but rather anxiety – the agonizing anxiety of ignorance, of not knowing what had or would become of Robert L. Because the narration of events in the diary is presented (whether authentically or not) as simultaneous to their occurrence, their outcome is unknown (at least to the reader) until the end of the narrative. It is therefore the most suspenseful of the four autobiographical texts and, because of this, perhaps the most painful to narrate. The author thus places it first in the volume in order to be done with it and to move on to (relatively) less troubling material.

Yet because it covers not only a segment of the narrator's anguished wait for Robert L. but also a segment of her longer wait for the expulsion from France of the Nazis (and of their petty henchmen, men like Rabier), 'Monsieur X.' could have been the most painful of the texts to narrate. 'Les Allemands,' the narrator of that text insists, 'faisaient peur comme les Huns, les loups, les criminels, mais surtout les psychotiques du crime' (The Germans were frightening in the same way as the Huns, in the same way as wolves, criminals, and above all, psychotic criminals) (108; 88). But the terrible anxiety that its narration arouses is abated not only by the narration of Robert L.'s return *before* the narration of his arrest, but also and perhaps more importantly by the periodic retrospective interventions of the voice of intellectual memory, which is 'a form of reassurance,' writes Langer, 'designed to sedate the surge of deep [sense] memory, that constantly threatens to erupt' in the narration of a traumatic experience.[43] In 'Monsieur X.,' however, sense memory does more than erupt – it often dominates the narration, in particular in the present-tense episodes. This predominance of the voice of sense memory perhaps explains in part *La douleur*'s lack of what Langer calls a 'coherent moral vision,' which, he says, only intellectual memory can impose on the narration of otherwise inchoate and amoral sense memories.[44] The ambiguity of the 'moral vision' of 'Monsieur X.' is concretely confirmed in its final pages.[45] Here the narrator states that she testified three times at Rabier's trial: the first two times for the prosecution and the third for the defence. This third time, she told the judge that Rabier had saved the lives of several Jews whom he apparently did not have the heart to arrest. 'Le procureur général a hurlé, il m'a dit: "Il faudrait savoir ce que vous voulez" [...] J'ai répondu que je voulais dire la vérité' (The judge yelled at me, 'Make up your mind!' ... I answered that I wanted to tell the truth).[46] The truth about Monsieur X., like the narrator's dual testimony, is not unequivocal, and in the end the narrator is neither overjoyed nor guilt-ridden about the guilty verdict. Rather, she feels a mixture of fear and pity, hatred and solicitude, towards the pathetic yet highly dangerous man: 'Il est seul dans le box des accusés [...] Il nous [the narrator and 'D.'][47] regarde avec amitié ... Il dira de nous: "Ils ont été des ennemis loyaux"' (He is alone in the dock ... The looks he gives us are friendly ... Rabier will say of us, 'They've been loyal enemies') (119; 98). Thus the narrator imagines that Rabier himself was not immune to the profound ambivalence ('des ennemis loyaux') that pervades the story. This ambivalence is very clearly reflected in the double-voiced narration of the text; these two voices alternate expressing fear then calm, deference then mockery, and in the end, they take their turns damning and exonerating the man designated as 'Monsieur X.'

This alternation of voices reveals conflicting desires on the part of the narrator: one of these desires is to allow sense memory to take over and to tell the story as it was lived at the moment, the other is to rely on intellectual memory to tell it as a part of objective history, from a distance, with retrospective, anxiety-dispelling insight. In the second part of this chapter, I will discuss how these opposing narrative desires manifest themselves still further in the text when it is read alongside other narratives – in particular, Péan's biography of Mitterrand and an interview of Duras and Mitterrand together – that (re)produce, in part and with variances, the story of 'Monsieur X.'

The 'Truth' about Monsieur X.: 'Literature' versus 'History'

Like 'Monsieur X.,' the chapter in Pierre Péan's *Une jeunesse française: François Mitterrand, 1934–47* of interest here ('Marguerite, Edgar, François et les autres' [Marguerite, Edgar, François, and the Others]) focuses on the months leading up to the liberation of Paris in August 1944. While Péan's narrative of Mitterrand's life from 1934 to 1947 generally unfolds in chronological order, the chapter immediately *preceding* 'Marguerite' is entitled 'Libération,' an event which it indeed covers. At the beginning of 'Marguerite,' Péan explains that the 'bref retour en arrière' (brief turn backwards) that he will make in this chapter 'est ici indispensable pour évoquer ce temps de l'épuration' (is indispensable here in order to evoke this time of the Purge) (449). In this way, interestingly, he introduces the same anachrony into his text as Duras does in *La douleur* when she places the diary (April 1945 to summer 1946) before 'Monsieur X.' (June to August 1944). In the chapter in Péan's book entitled 'Libération' (and which, again, anachronistically precedes 'Marguerite'), we learn that Duras, Antelme, Dionys Mascolo (Duras's lover and Antelme's friend), and Edgar Morin (a well-known French intellectual today) all belonged to a Resistance group headed by Mitterrand called the Mouvement de Résistance des Prisonniers de Guerre et des Déportés (Resistance Movement of Prisoners of War and Deportees). 'Marguerite' then opens with the arrests of several members of the group, including Antelme, in the spring and early summer of 1944. These arrests, carried out on different days and in different places, provoked the suspicion among some members that there were informants among them. After the Liberation, the group interrogated, along with other alleged collaborators, those members who were suspected of being moles (Duras writes of such interrogations in the third and fourth texts of *La douleur,* 'Albert des Capitales' and 'Ter le milicien'). In 'Marguerite,' Péan writes at length of Duras's relationship with Rabier, whose real name was Charles Delval.[48] He does so because Mitterrand's group apparently attempted to execute the *gestapiste* before the Liberation. They failed, but on his arrest by the French police after the Liberation, they did interrogate Delval in order to discover the identities of the alleged informants.

When he begins his narrative of Duras's encounters with Delval, Péan writes in a footnote, 'L'histoire des relations entre le gestapiste français et Marguerite est tirée de l'instruction du procès du gestapiste après la Libération' (The story of the relationship between the French Gestapo agent and Marguerite is derived from court records from the former's trial).[49] Throughout the chapter, however, he quotes and paraphrases several passages from 'Monsieur X.,' which he then cites as *La douleur* rather than specifically as 'Monsieur X.,' in a separate footnote. In this footnote, he mistakenly refers to the preface to the first narrative in the volume, 'La douleur,' as the preface to the entire text: 'En avant-propos de ce livre [...] M. Duras précise qu'elle a "retrouvé ce *Journal* dans deux cahiers [...] Je sais ... que c'est moi qui l'ai écrit" [...] Dans ce "Journal," le personnage identifiable à Delval s'appelle Rabier' (In the preface to this book ... Duras notes that she 'found this *Journal* in two notebooks ... I know ... that it's I who wrote it' ... In this 'Diary,' the character that can be identified as Delval is called Rabier) (454).[50] Now, there is no mention of Rabier in 'La douleur'; he appears only in 'Monsieur X.' Perhaps by conflating 'Monsieur X.' (whose title he never mentions) with the diary (the *journal* to which Duras refers in her preface to it and which she claims to have written near the time of the events), Péan wanted to strengthen the historicity and reliability of the former text. Indeed, he often seems to place it on the same footing as his other, presumably more 'historical' sources (court transcripts and interviews). He paraphrases or weaves passages from it into his own narrative, unobtrusively naming the source in footnotes, just as he does his other sources.

On the other hand, in the first footnote in which he cites Duras's text (reproduced above), Péan puts the word 'journal' in quotation marks, as if its status as such were questionable. On the following page, Péan also warns the reader about the possible fictionality of Duras's narrative, describing her account of Rabier/Delval's interest in Mitterrand, for example, as 'une version plus littéraire que celle qu'entendirent jadis les murs du Palais de Justice' (a more literary version than that once heard within the walls of the Paris courthouse) (455).[51] As noted, Péan also derives much of the information he offers in this chapter from interviews, specifically interviews he conducted in 1993 and 1994 with surviving members of Mitterrand's resistance group – including Mitterrand, but not, significantly, Duras, who was alive at the time, although ailing. In response to an e-mail I sent him asking why he had not also interviewed Duras, Péan wrote (rather ironically, it seemed to me, considering my analysis of 'Monsieur X.'): '*ma mémoire n'est pas très lumineuse* mais il me semble que Duras n'était déjà plus en état de répondre à mes questions' (*my memory is fuzzy*, but it seems to me that she was no longer in any shape to answer my questions) (emphasis mine). Yet Péan then goes on to offer another reason for not interviewing the author of La douleur, as if in case the first reason he cites were to appear insufficient: 'Je ne crois pas que j'ai beaucoup perdu car je ne pense pas qu'elle aurait volontiers parlé d'un sujet aussi délicat, déjà trituré par son imagination romanesque' (I doubt I missed out on much, because I don't think she would have willingly spoken about such a delicate subject that had already been filtered through her romantic imagination).[52] Péan claims here to believe that Duras would have been too discreet to talk about a personal matter she had already exposed at length in a best-selling book, even if in a 'romanticized' way. But perhaps he meant to say that he doubted she would tell him anything *more than* or *different from* what she had already written in the book; that is, presumably, he doubted she would tell him the 'truth' about the events described. Indeed, much of the chapter in Péan's book about these events is dedicated, as I will show, to investigating the veracity of Duras's statements in 'Monsieur X.,' especially those concerning the two suspected informants. Péan therefore appears to alternate between relying on and questioning the authenticity of Duras's version of the story and between treating the text as a historical document and reading it as fiction. He approaches this intriguing text, in other words, in a manner not unlike that in which many of the literary critics who have written about it, including myself, do. This is not surprising, as Péan's and others' ambivalence towards 'Monsieur X.' only reflects the ambivalence or duality that, as I have argued, is present in the text's own narrative voice.

Despite his footnoting, it is nevertheless difficult at times to know exactly from which of his sources Péan has drawn a particular bit of information. Péan's necessary effort to weave different strands from different sources together in order to create a coherent and readable narrative himself inevitably works to obscure distinctions in the origins of these strands. Péan's narrative thus becomes a version of the story in its own right, differing from the other versions while at the same time being entirely derived from them. The proliferation of narratives about or touching on many of the events recounted in 'La douleur' and 'Monsieur X.' is indeed remarkable: besides Péan's narrative and its sources (the oral narratives of those who gave testimony at the trial and of those whom Péan interviewed), there are Antelme's *L'espèce humaine* (*The Human Race*) (1947), Mascolo's *Autour d'un effort de mémoire* (*Concerning an Effort of Memory*) (1987), several interviews of Duras in which she speaks of that period (three of which I cite in this chapter), and finally, numerous biographies of the people involved.[53] This proliferation is supremely Durassian. Like the multiple stories of Lol V. Stein, Anne-Marie Stretter, and the Chinese lover, the stories of Monsieur X. and of the Duras of 1944–5 have no definitive version. And Duras is only one of many who have rewritten and continue to rewrite these latter stories. About the only participant whose full version of the story we do not have (though we do have his testimony) is Monsieur X. himself.

Some of the discrepancies between Duras's narrative and Péan's (part of which, as noted, he derived from the former) seem minor and can probably be attributed to differences in the perspectives of the people involved and/or to the varying reliability of their memories. For example, in 'Monsieur X.,' Duras insists upon the fact that when Rabier hailed her on the street, she was speaking with only one of the agents she was to put into contact (Duponceau), and that the other (Godard) thankfully did not mistake Rabier for Duponceau and approach her while she was speaking to the *gestapiste*. 'Godard arrive et, je ne sais pas par quel miracle, ne m'aborde pas' (Godard arrives and, miraculously, doesn't approach me).[54] Yet in Péan's version of this scene, which is based, he says, on testimony Duras herself gave at Delval's trial after the Liberation, all three *résistants* were speaking together when Delval called out to Duras: 'Tous trois bavardent,' Péan writes, 'quand elle est hélée par l'homme de la rue des Saussaies' (All three of them are chatting when she is hailed by the man from the rue des Saussaies).[55] If Péan's version is correct, did Duras's memory fail her when writing 'Monsieur X.'? Or rather did she disregard her pledge of truthfulness and deliberately change the scene for dramatic reasons? If, on the other hand, the version told in *La douleur* is correct, did Duras's memory fail her on the witness stand but return to her while writing 'Monsieur X.'? Or did she 'lie' in court but not in her text? Or is it Péan who is mistaken?

The possibilities are many, and I will not belabour the point concerning such a minor detail. A more significant discrepancy is the following: whereas court documents reveal, according to Péan, that it was one of Delval's neighbours who denounced him as a collaborator and had him arrested during the Purge (465), Duras makes no mention of this and seems rather to take full responsibility for his arrest and eventual execution: 'moi,' she rather dramatically writes on the final page of 'Monsieur X.,' 'moi par qui il mourra' (I because of whom he was to die).[56] It was indeed because of her knowledge of him and his activities that her resistance group had tried to execute him, but they had failed. Did Duras write this line because she believed it to be true? Or did she include it precisely for its dramatic effect? That is, did she write it in order to make of herself (depending on each reader's sensibilities) either the heroine of this tale of Resistance or a self-appointed dispenser of the dubious justice of the Purge, like the character in 'Albert des Capitales' (whom Duras identifies as herself in the preface to this narrative and 'Ter le milicien')?[57] If we take seriously Duras's statements in interviews and in *Écrire* regarding her desire to write in as instinctive a manner as possible, then the first hypothesis would seem more likely than the second. About the autobiographical texts in *La douleur*, Gabriel Jacobs asks pointedly, 'Do the four texts reveal an uncommonly honest Duras, or a vainglorious Duras congratulating herself on her honesty, or an honest but supremely self-conscious Duras whose self-indulgence is part of her honesty?'[58] To these I might add a fourth question, which is similar but not identical to Jacobs's last: If Duras is indeed being honest here (if she is telling the truth *as she sees it*), to what extent does this honesty produce texts that are factually accurate? Relevant to this question, to which I will return, is the interplay between remembering and narrating that I am examining here.

In a 1986 interview of Mitterrand and Duras together, the two friends and former *résistants* discuss many of the events represented in *La douleur*, which had just been published the previous year. At the time of the interview, Duras was seventy-one, Mitterrand sixty-nine. An attentive reader of the interview might be struck by what appear to be lapses in Duras's short-term – *very* short-term – memory. For example, near the beginning of the interview, Mitterrand relates a brief anecdote about his

experience as a soldier on the front before the Occupation: 'Je me souviens d'un moment, devant Verdun – le Verdun de 1940, pas celui de
1916, mais enfin c'était quand même un Verdun qui n'était pas très
fréquentable, une nouvelle fois – l'attaque allemande s'est produite' (I
remember a moment, near Verdun – the Verdun of 1940, not of 1916,
but at any rate it was a Verdun that once again wasn't very hospitable –
the German attack took place).[59] Even though he pronounces the word
'Verdun' three times at the beginning of this story (the entire text of
which fills only a little over half a newspaper column), when he finishes,
Duras immediately asks, 'C'était où?' (Where was this?) (32). Her question could be attributed simply to a momentary lack of attention, but
there is more. Later in the interview, Mitterrand brings up Duras's latest
book: 'Dans la *Douleur,* j'ai retrouvé la trace de tous ces événements
vécus, qui sont un tissu de rencontres assez extraordinaires' (In *La
douleur,* I rediscovered the thread of all those events we lived through,
which weaves together a number of quite extraordinary encounters)
(33). He goes on to tell in detail the story – narrated in 'La douleur' – of
how he stumbled upon the gravely ill Robert Antelme at Dachau and
arranged for him to be secretly taken out of the quarantine camp and
driven home to Paris (an action that most certainly saved his life). What
is surprising here is that even after Mitterrand mentions Duras's book a
second time – telling the author, ironically enough, that he thinks her
memory of Delval's trial is faulty ('Vous ne le racontez pas précisément
dans le livre [...] Ça ne recoupait pas exactement mes souvenirs' [You
don't tell it quite right in the book ... Your version doesn't exactly fit my
memories of it] [35]) – Duras asks him, 'Vous l'avez lu, mon livre?'
(Have you read my book?) (38)! Mitterrand responds by reminding her
that she sent him a copy herself (38). Duras later asks Mitterrand, 'Au
fait, où a-t-il été arrêté, Robert?' (By the way, where was Robert arrested?)
(39). Mitterrand tells her that it was 5 rue Dupin, which, firstly, he had
already mentioned earlier in the interview ('Et j'étais, moi, dans la poste
en-dessous du 5 rue Dupin, au-dessous de l'appartement, au moment
même où [Robert] a été arrêté' [And I was myself in the post office
below 5 rue Dupin, below the apartment, at the very moment Robert was
arrested] [34]), and which, secondly, Duras *herself* mentions, once earlier
in the interview itself (32) and four times in 'Monsieur X.'[60] One might
be tempted to wonder whether Duras herself had read the book.

Of course, decades of alcoholism, added to the simple passage of time,
can wreak havoc on fragile human memory.[61] In this interview, Duras is
indeed aware of her memory lapses, for she describes herself as someone

'qui oublie tout' (who forgets everything), and she uses the same verb ('oublier' [to forget]) four more times in reference to herself. But my point is not to claim that Duras got it all wrong in *La douleur*. In another interview about the book, she says that she wrote the first text, the diary she calls 'La douleur,' immediately after the war and much of 'Monsieur X.' within ten years after it, when her memory was likely more intact.[62] Her description in this interview of the genesis of 'Monsieur X.' has interesting implications with regard to my analysis of the text's double-voiced narration: 'J'avais essayé plusieurs fois de l'écrire dix ans après la guerre. J'y avais renoncé. Rien ne survenait jamais. Beaucoup d'épisodes étaient écrits, presque tous. Ce qui n'était pas écrit, c'était le quotidien. La durée n'était pas là. Un temps morne' (I had tried several times to write it ten years after the war. I had given up. Nothing ever came of it. A lot of episodes were written, almost all of them. What wasn't written was [a description of] day-to-day life. The feeling of endlessness, of bleakness, wasn't there).[63] What Duras calls 'episodes' likely correspond in large part to the segments of the text I have also named 'episodes': the mostly present-tense, detailed narrations of specific meetings with Rabier. These are the sections of the narrative, Duras says, that she wrote closest to the time of the war. In the text itself, the narrator even speaks of writing about Rabier while the relationship was still running its course: 'Je note chaque soir ce qui s'est passé avec Rabier, ce que j'ai appris de faux ou de vrai sur les convois des déportés vers l'Allemagne [...] Je prends ces notes à l'intention de Robert L. pour quand il rentrera' (Every evening I write down what happened each time I saw Rabier, what I learned, true or false, about the trainloads of deportees being sent to Germany ... I take these notes for Robert L. when he returns home).[64] It is in these episodes that the first narrative voice – the voice of deep or sense memory – is the strongest. Duras also says in the above quote that it was 'le quotidien' that was missing from this original text. 'Le quotidien,' the ensemble of repeated rather than singular daily activities and events, is normally narrated in the iterative mode. The iterative passages I have identified in 'Monsieur X.' therefore probably constitute much of the 'quotidien' that was lacking and that Duras filled in for the book's publication in 1985. If this is the case, the detail-poor and emotionally neutral iterative passages came from the pen of a writer much further removed from the incidents described than the writer of the episodes. During this later writing period, it seems likely that intellectual memory would have taken over as the main source of the information added to 'Monsieur X.' Gabriel Jacobs also comments on the account of the writing of *La douleur* that Duras gives in this interview as well as in the preface to 'Monsieur X.,' where she says that she hadn't published the text earlier in part because 'ça ne s'agrandissait jamais, ça n'allait jamais vers le large de la littérature' (it never became anything greater, never took off into literature) – that is, it wasn't literary, or perhaps romanticized, enough to be interesting.[65] Jacobs writes that the 'quotidien' that Duras said she added later was then 'presumably created by literary means.'[66] Jacobs is implying by this that the material Duras wrote later must have been more fictional than the rest. I would add that if what Duras wrote later is indeed more fictional, it is so, at least in part, because it is a product of a different kind of memory. It is a product of intellectual memory, which, as Delbo contends, *necessarily* fictionalizes the material it holds.

Returning to a comparison of Péan's and Duras's texts, the former is interesting not only for the ways in which it differs from the latter but also for the additional information, to whatever degree factual, it provides. Indeed, after consulting Péan's text, the reader might begin to feel that there are important omissions in Duras's story. Certainly, every narrator must pick and choose among the myriad possible elements of a story, whether that story be fact, fiction, or something in between. The 'whole' story can never be told, and therefore even narratives that are 'vrai[s] jusque dans le détail' are always only partial accounts of what happened. Yet by discovering through other sources more about what was going on in Duras's circle during the period in question, it is possible to learn something about the narrative choices Duras made in constructing 'Monsieur X.'

For example, in 'Monsieur X.,' the narrator states that Rabier told her that there was a traitor in their movement, someone who under threat of torture had told the Gestapo about the meeting to be held at 5 rue Dupin, where Antelme and others were subsequently arrested: 'Rabier me donne le nom. Je le donne à D. [Dionys Mascolo]. D. le donne au mouvement' (Rabier gives me the name. I give it to D. D. gives it to the movement).[67] The group makes plans to execute the mole, but the Liberation comes too quickly: 'On abandonnera le projet à l'unanimité' (We unanimously decided to abandon the plan) (104; 85). In his interview with Péan, however, one of Duras's fellow *résistants*, Philippe Dechartre, declares flatly in reference to 'Monsieur X.' that 'tout ce que raconte Marguerite Duras est faux' (everything Marguerite Duras says is false).[68] It is not clear whether Dechartre means to restrict his statement to Duras's contention that there were traitors or to condemn her entire account of the affair (he, as well as Péan's other interviewees, all appear

to have read *La douleur*). In either case, he is making an interesting assertion about an author who claims that her story is 'vraie jusque dans le
détail.' According to Péan, another *résistant* in Duras's group, Georges
Beauchamp,

> partage la conviction de Dechartre à propos de Marguerite. Lui aussi est
> convaincu que toute cette histoire [of the traitors] lui est imputable. Il
> trouve 'inconvenant' le récit qu'elle a fait de cette période ['Monsieur X.']:
> 'Elle n'a pas reçu d'ordre de Mitterrand pour aller vers Delval. C'est elle-
> même qui a décidé de 'vamper' le gestapiste qui avait fait arrêter son mari
> [...] C'est Marguerite qui nous a parlé de Savy et Bourgeois [the *noms de
> guerre* of the two men Duras denounced as traitors].

> shares Dechartre's conviction about Marguerite. He also is convinced that
> she is the source of the entire story (of the traitors). He finds the narrative
> she constructed of that period ('Monsieur X.') 'unseemly.' 'Mitterrand
> never ordered her to see Delval. She herself decided to "vamp" the Gestapo
> agent who had arrested her husband [...] It's Marguerite who spoke to us
> about Savy and Bourgeois (the *noms de guerre* of the two men Duras accused
> of being traitors). (461)

Beauchamp therefore disputes not only Duras's accusation of treachery but also the legitimacy of her relationship with Delval. Edgar Morin
also makes it clear to Péan that he frowned upon the connection, calling
it a 'fréquentation dangereuse et équivoque' (dangerous and equivocal
relationship) (458). Mitterrand himself, however, contradicts these
men's assertions. He affirms in the joint interview with Duras that she *did*
ask him whether she should see Delval, and that he decided she should:
'Ça a été une délibération absolument mûrie, on vous a fait un devoir de
continuer à le voir' (That was a thoroughly deliberated decision, we
ordered you to continue seeing him).[69] Yet regardless of whether Mitterrand did in fact order or at least condone Duras's meetings with Delval,
it is clear that the three men cited above (Dechartre, Beauchamp, and
Morin) liked neither the relationship nor the information Duras
claimed to glean from it. Nor, it would appear from their remarks, did
they much like her.

The attitude of these men could be attributed at least in part to simple
misogyny. Female *résistants* were generally supposed to play only support-
ing roles (like that of liaison agent, precisely), while men were to be the
real actors in the effort. Perhaps Duras's adoption of the role of spy

among the Gestapo conflicted with these men's conception of women's function in 'their' organization, and threatened their view of their own usefulness or performance within that organization. Beauchamp's choice of the term 'vamper' to describe Duras's actions and Morin's qualification of her relationship with Delval as 'équivoque' imply, moreover, that they assumed there was a (sordid) sexual element to the encounters. While in 'Monsieur X.' the narrator in fact affirms that Rabier wanted more from her than just a dinner date ('la dernière fois que j'ai vu Rabier il m'a demandé d'aller prendre un verre avec lui "dans un studio d'un ami absent de Paris"' [the last time I saw Rabier, he asked me to have a drink with him 'in the studio of a friend of his who was out of town']), she also makes it clear that she did not oblige him ('J'ai dit: "Une autre fois." Je me suis sauvée' [I said, 'Another time.' Then I escaped]).[70]

However, yet another (male) member of the group reported to Péan that, in reference to one of her meetings with Delval, Duras once told him, 'J'ai failli franchir le Rubicon' (I almost crossed the Rubicon).[71] What Duras was implying by this, according to Péan's source, is that she almost slept with Rabier. If this is indeed true, for what reasons would she have 'almost' succumbed to Delval's advances? Two possible explanations are (1) that fear for both her and her husband's lives made it difficult for her to rebuff him, and (2) that she thought that sleeping with him might induce him to give her more information about Antelme. A third possibility, one that some of her fellow *résistants* seem to have entertained, is that she felt an odd sexual attraction to this collaborator who had arrested her husband and possibly sent him to his death. There is no evidence of this in the narrative itself; what the narrator of 'Monsieur X.' appears to feel towards Rabier is a mixture of horror and pity, not lust. On the other hand, in the preface to 'Albert des Capitales' and 'Ter le milicien,' Duras does write that the protagonist of these stories, Thérèse, a *résistante* 'qui a envie de faire l'amour avec Ter le milicien' (who feels like making love with Ter the militiaman), 'c'est moi' (that's me).[72] Such a 'confession' seems likely to have compounded doubts about Duras's motivations in maintaining contact with Delval. If, as Jacobs argues, the texts in *La douleur* are placed in the order less to more literary (or more to less autobiographical), then perhaps, just perhaps, Thérèse's desire for Ter is a displaced, more literary version of Duras's desire for Delval, a desire so illicit (a woman's desire for her husband's would-be executioner) that even Marguerite Duras felt a need to transpose it.

If such a desire were purposefully omitted from 'Monsieur X.,' it would not be the only one, nor, as it turns out, the most bizarre. The only female actor in the Rabier/Delval drama whom Péan interviewed was Paulette Delval, the *gestapiste*'s wife. The narrator of 'Monsieur X.' mentions her once, giving her no other name than 'sa femme' (his wife) and describing her (as did another witness at the trial, she says) as 'insignifiante et belle' (insignificant and beautiful) (134; 111). Yet Duras knew quite a bit more about Paulette than her narrator implies. According to Péan, she interrogated her while this latter was temporarily imprisoned by Mitterrand's group shortly after the Liberation, and she also witnessed her testimony at Delval's trial.[73] Through Péan's chapter, we also learn that this 'insignificant' woman must have figured rather significantly in Duras's life, more so, we can imagine, than the writer would have liked. During the months preceding Delval's trial in December 1944, Paulette Delval became the lover of Dionys Mascolo, the man with whom Duras was living at the time and for whom she would leave Antelme after the war. Interestingly enough, it was when he was called upon to interrogate her alongside Duras that Mascolo first laid eyes on the beautiful Paulette. Péan does not say if the details about this (second) rather aberrant relationship came directly from the participants' mouths, but in their interviews with him both Mascolo and Paulette do confirm that it happened. In reminiscing about Paulette, Mascolo tells Péan: 'Elle était passionnée' (She was passionate) (470). Yet Paulette asserts that if she was passionate, she was so only about her husband: 'J'ai fait l'amour avec [Mascolo] pour sauver mon mari' (I slept with [Mascolo] in order to save my husband), she flatly tells Péan. Indeed, according to Péan, she defends her husband to this day (470). It is possible that Mascolo cast himself in the same role in relation to Paulette as Delval had in relation to Duras: as the man who held a husband's fate in his hands and who used, or tried to use, this power to seduce that man's wife. Neither man possessed such power in reality. We know that Delval had no control over or even knowledge of Antelme's whereabouts, and despite Paulette's liaison with Mascolo, Delval was executed at Fresnes at the beginning of 1945. According to Péan, who does not specify his source for this information, 'Les relations entre Dionys et Marguerite sont entre-temps devenues très difficiles. Mascolo revoit régulièrement Paulette. Pendant quelques années, il restera tiraillé entre les deux femmes. La bataille est d'une rare violence. Paulette a un enfant en juin 1946. Marguerite, l'année suivante' (Meanwhile, the relationship between Dionys and Marguerite became very troubled. Mascolo saw Paulette regularly. For several years, he would remain torn between the two women. The battle was an exceptionally violent one. Paulette had a child in June 1946, Marguerite, the following year) (473).

It would appear that what we have here is not just a triangle of desire – a very Durassian and somewhat prosaic figure – but a *quadrangle* of desire: Paulette desires Delval who desires Duras who desires Mascolo who desires Paulette. And if we believe certain participants, the arrow of desire could be reversed – Paulette desires Mascolo who desires Duras who desires Delval who desires Paulette – and still hold true, either simultaneously or at different moments in the story. It is uncertain whether Duras herself could have conceived of a novel containing as complicated and surprising a web of desire. Fact sometimes is indeed stranger than fiction, even when the author of that fiction is Marguerite Duras.[74]

Duras and Mascolo's relationship, like Duras and Antelme's, was apparently an open one – the three of them lived together in Duras's apartment on the rue Saint-Benoît both before and after Antelme's deportation.[75] This is not to say, however, that Antelme was not pained by Duras's feelings for Mascolo – according to Frédérique Lebelley, one of Duras's biographers, he was.[76] It is hard to imagine that Mascolo's liaison with Paulette Delval did not trouble Duras, and the narrator's curt dismissal of Paulette in 'Monsieur X.' could be indicative of ill feelings. During her interview with Péan, Paulette, for her part, 'profère sur Marguerite Duras des propos qui ne peuvent être reproduits ici' (uttered some remarks about Marguerite Duras that cannot be reproduced here).[77] Paulette appears to believe that it was Duras who single-handedly sealed her husband's fate. She therefore gives Duras as much credit for his death as the writer takes ('moi par qui il mourra' [I because of whom he would die]). Interestingly, while Paulette Delval is mute (or gagged, as it were) in Duras's text, it is she who has the last word in Péan's chapter. Or rather, she *almost* has the last word, for her word was apparently too salacious to be reproduced. When Péan asked Paulette about the hypothesis that Charles Delval was actually a German, which Duras puts forth in 'Monsieur X.'[78] and repeats in the Duras–Mitterrand interview,[79]

elle a opposé un démenti formel à cette rumeur. Elle m'a affirmé avoir bien connu toute la famille de Charles Delval: 'C'est encore une histoire romanesque, née probablement rue Saint-Benoît, à un moment délicat dans les relations entre Marguerite et Dionys'. Et elle a de nouveau conclu par quelques formules peu amènes sur l'auteur de *L'Amant...*

she vehemently denied that rumor. She affirmed to me that she had known Charles Delval's entire family very well. 'It's just another fiction, conceived most likely in the apartment on the rue Saint-Benoît at a delicate moment in the relationship between Marguerite and Dionys.' And once again she concluded with a few choice words about the author of *The Lover* ... (Péan's ellipses)[80]

It would thus seem from Péan's text that few are those who take Duras at her word when she declares that her story is true down to the last detail. Along with many of his interviewees, Péan himself does not appear to put much stock in this claim. Literary critics of *La douleur* also agree that Duras's assertions of truth are not to be taken literally. For Jacobs, for example, 'Monsieur X.' 'is no more a completely faithful record of events than "La douleur,"' a text whose accuracy he disputes at length in his article.[81] That neither of these texts is historically accurate in all details seems certain. Just how many of these inaccuracies are the work of a deliberately dishonest Duras – as opposed to a forgetful Duras, or a Duras carried away by her own invention – is and will forever be unclear. Yet once again, if we listen to Duras not only in the text's preface but also in *Écrire*, we might believe in a generally honest (if sometimes mistaken) Duras. Or, at least, half of us might: 'Je n'ai jamais menti dans un livre,' she writes in that essay. 'Ni même dans ma vie. Sauf aux hommes. Jamais' (I have never lied in a book. Nor even in my life. Except to men. Never).[82] The juxtaposition of 'jamais' (never) and 'sauf' (except) attests to either poor logic or a coy rejection of logic. The second is certainly consistent with Duras's project as a writer. One thing the reader of 'Monsieur X.' knows for certain, at least, is that the character-I (a textual representation of a past Duras) lies. These lies do not contradict Duras's statement in *Écrire*, however, because they are told to a man: the character-I lies consistently to Rabier, telling him, among other falsehoods, that she is not involved in the Resistance and that she does not know François Morland (Mitterrand). But of course lying to save one's skin is hardly indicative of a more general dishonesty. Moreover, the question of honesty in 'Monsieur X.' concerns not the character-I, but rather the narrator-I, for it is upon her that the reader is entreated to rely.

One possible answer to the question of honesty – an answer to which the first part of this chapter points – is that the narrator of 'Monsieur X.' is honest to the extent that intellectual memory allows her to be. To draw exclusively from sense memory – 'the persistence of the past in its own perpetual present'[83] – in order to narrate the story of a painful or terrifying experience proves impossible for the narrator. At certain moments in the narration, intellectual memory must come to the rescue, so to speak, of the narrator in pain. To use a literary metaphor, intellectual memory edits sense memory – or indeed censors it – and in doing so inevitably falsifies it, to however great or small a degree. The narration of 'Monsieur X.' is thus double-voiced. But perhaps it is precisely in the text's display of this duality, in the alternations of voices, that 'Monsieur X.' is most truthful. Of the account of her Auschwitz experiences that she gives in *La mémoire et les jours*, Charlotte Delbo writes, 'tout en sachant très bien que c'est véridique, je ne sais plus si c'est vrai' (even while knowing very well that it's truthful, I no longer know if it's true).[84] One definition of 'véridique' (truthful) is 'vrai' (true), but another is 'sincère,' and it is likely this latter meaning that Delbo intends here. 'Une histoire *véridique* jusque dans le détail' might have been a more apt description of 'Monsieur X.,' whose narrator, at least, is sincere in her efforts to get at the truth – or at least a certain truth – about her experiences. Jeanine Parisier Plottel argues effectively that 'the texts of *La douleur* are meant to instruct us in how things really were in France when the war ended. While the historian may aspire to this achievement, in fact Marguerite Duras's narrative aims at apprehending the complexities of her experience in order to convey what really happened in 1944 and 1945. It seems to me that the discourse here both undermines and makes use of literary devices for the purpose of creating a discourse more truthful than literature and more historical than history.'[85]

Plottel, like most critics, stresses the constructedness of the texts in *La douleur* and Duras's use of literary devices in order to create the *illusion* of truth. Like me, however, Plottel maintains that Duras did in fact manage, at least in many instances, to get at the truth not only of her personal experiences but also of the atmosphere of the historical period. I have nevertheless argued that the narration of 'Monsieur X.' is less calculated than most critics assume. I have argued that in the telling of the story, this narration, if not entirely created by, then at least deeply affected by a sort of competition for primacy between intellectual and sense memory. Certainly, Duras was an accomplished writer who knew how to achieve the effects she desired through narrative devices. Yet because I place some faith in her comments on the manner in which she strove to write, it seems to me entirely possible that certain characteristics of the narration, such as the sudden changes in verb tense, were not calculated. While Duras likely became aware of these tense shifts when rereading her text, they nevertheless could well have been produced by the spontaneous and inscrutable workings of memory. If so, they reflect the true psychological state in which the writing of the text placed its writer.

In the middle of her narration of 'Monsieur X.,' the narrator, using the more distanced voice of intellectual memory, says, 'Je n'ai jamais trouvé comment le dire, comment raconter à ceux qui n'ont pas vécu cette époque-là, la sorte de peur que c'était' (I've never figured out how to express it, how to tell those who didn't live through it what sort of fear it was).[86] For reasons I have outlined above, the reader cannot be sure when Duras wrote this particular line. It is also unclear whether she means here that she felt this way – incapable of truthfully and accurately expressing what she experienced in 1944 – only *before* having produced 'Monsieur X,' or whether she continued to feel this way despite her attempt to do so in this text. Multiple and conflicting desires, along with their concomitant anxieties, doubtless informed Duras's composition of this text: the desire to tell the story in as uncensored and uncalculated a manner as possible in order to free herself from the grip of traumatic and as yet unnarrated memory (an 'expiation' less of guilt than of stifled terror and pain); the desire to tell the story in a way that would show her wartime self and activities only in the most seemly light possible (unlike in the more fictionalized 'Albert des Capitales' and 'Ter le milicien,' in which Duras seems to revel in the portrayal of herself as ethically suspect); and finally, the desire not to tell the story at all, but to let the painful memories at its source remain buried forever (for it did take four decades for the story to be told). If it is not always true, the narrative is truth*ful* in the way it reveals the multiple selves, memories, voices, desires, and anxieties at work in its creation.

Narrating the Self, Narrating the Other

The vehemence with which many of Péan's interviewees dispute Duras's account of events testifies to the seriousness with which the written word in particular tends to be taken, especially when that word comes from the pen of a world-renowned author, and also when it claims to tell the truth, not only about the author herself, but about others as well (such as, in the case of *La douleur*, Charles and Paulette Delval, 'Savy' and 'Bourgeois,' Edgar Morin, François Mitterrand, and so on). It was clearly both recognized by and bothersome to many of those involved in the events recounted that Duras's version of the story would be the principal, if not the only, version known to the general public. A certain understanding on Duras's part of the impact her narrative might have on others can be evinced (if, that is, she is being sincere) when she writes in her preface to 'Monsieur X.' that, in consideration of Rabier's wife and

child, she had not published the story earlier and that she uses pseudonyms in it. Yet in that preface she also displays a certain amount of
naivety, or else insouciance, when she predicts (erroneously, as we have
seen) that, since 'quarante ans ont recouvert les faits, on est vieux déjà,
même si on les apprend ils ne blesseront plus comme ils auraient fait
avant quand on était jeune' (the facts lie buried under forty years, everyone is old, and even if they learn about those facts for the first time, they
won't be wounded by them as they would have been before, when we
were young).[87]

   Still, the gravity and consequences of the written word, especially
when it is used to tell the story of *another*, is underscored in several of
Duras's earlier texts, which it will be useful to discuss briefly here. In
'Madame Dodin,' a little-known and masterfully comical story, Duras
plants the seed of a narrative technique that will become a highly significant feature of some of her most important texts: that of using one character within the narrative to tell the story of and for another.[88] In
'Madame Dodin,' a nameless and nearly sexless tenant of number 5, rue
Sainte-Eulalie (a conspicuous deformation of 5, rue Saint-Benoît, an
apartment in the Saint-Germain-des-Prés quarter of Paris where Duras
lived for more than fifty years) attempts to perform a character analysis
of her wily and quarrelsome concierge, whom she obviously both fears
and admires.[89] But despite her desire to do so, this homodiegetic narrator never seems to bring herself to write down her reflections about her
concierge; rather, she only speaks about doing so in the *conditional* tense:
'Qu'il *faudrait* pouvoir raconter ces choses si bien qu'on *oserait* sans rou-
gir les donner à lire à Mme Dodin elle-même' (If only I *could narrate*
these things so well that I *would dare* give them to Mme Dodin herself to
read without blushing) (147; 102 – emphases mine).[90] 'Peut-être,' she
ponders, 'faudrait-il que l'un d'entre nous écrive aux autres une lettre
en faveur de Mme Dodin. J'ai quelquefois pensé que je pourrais être ce
locataire' (Perhaps one of us should write a letter to the others on Mme
Dodin's behalf. I have sometimes thought that I might be just the tenant
to do so) (126; 89). Yet when she goes on to describe such a hypothetical
letter, she forever forecloses the possibility of actually writing one with
the use of the *past* conditional: 'faute de destinataire, voici, ici, les deux
sortes de lettres que j'*aurais aimé faire*' (for lack of an addressee, I'll set
down here the two types of letter I *would have liked to write*) (126; 90 –
emphasis mine). She wants to compel her fellow bourgeois tenants to
have some sympathy and consideration for their concierge, but knows
she would only succeed in this were she able to dignify Mme Dodin's

story by writing it down, and not in a mere letter, but in a *book*: 'on ne peut leur parler de leur concierge que noir sur blanc, dans un livre, autrement, ils deviennent de fer' (one can't speak to them about their concierge except in black and white, in a book; otherwise they turn to stone) (128; 90). Making literature out of someone or something, the narrator therefore implies, lends it a credibility and importance it would not otherwise command.

Yet a multitude of anxieties prevent 'Madame Dodin''s narrator from becoming the author she would like to be. For one thing, as the first quote above indicates, she fears being a poor writer, being nothing but one of the nameless 'crivains' (sic) (writers) who, according to a contemptuous Mme Dodin, already overpopulate the neighbourhood (142; 99).[91] In addition to desiring her own success as a writer (and conversely fearing her failure at this effort), the narrator also desires, as mentioned, to make her fellow tenants understand and appreciate their concierge. But in a discussion of Mme Dodin's continual complaints about having to dispose of her tenants' trash, the narrator's comment that 'il en est de nos poubelles comme, je le répète, de nos idées. Comment connaître leur vrai destin une fois que nous les avons lâchées dans le monde?' (I repeat: as our garbage cans go, so go our ideas. How can we know their true destiny once we have launched them into the world?) (130; 92) expresses her understanding that once a text is made available to others, it is forever liberated from its author, her intentions, and her control. This analogy fittingly calls to mind one of Jacques Lacan's *jeu de mots*, 'la poubellication,' by which he wryly suggests that the publication of a text is always in some sense a profanation or trashing of it.[92] The narrator of 'Madame Dodin' suspects that any attempt to effect a change in the tenants' attitude even through literary means would be doomed, for even if they were moved to feel sympathy for a textual concierge, they would still be unwilling to transfer that sympathy to a flesh-and-blood one.[93]

Yet even greater than her anxiety over the possibility of writing an ineffectual text is her anxiety over the possibility of writing an *effective* one, for deep down, the narrator of 'Madame Dodin' knows that her concierge wants neither the homage nor the good will of her tenants: 'elle ne veut pas qu'on lui veuille trop de bien parce que cela lui confirme le mieux que rien ne pourra atténuer la véritable négation que, concierge, elle subit du locataire' (she doesn't want us to care too much about her, because that confirms all the more for her the fact that nothing could attenuate the true neglect to which, as a concierge, she is subjected by the tenant) (126; 89). Mme Dodin needs the tenants to fulfil their role as tyrants if she is to triumph in the complementary, and much more sympathetic, role of martyr. A text about Mme Dodin would in fact benefit only its writer, and not its subject. The voice and will expressed in it would not be Mme Dodin's, the narrator fears, but rather her own. In the end, therefore, this would-be author lets her narrative anxieties prevail over her narrative desires, and 'Madame Dodin' turns out to be a text about not writing a text.

Two of Duras's later and much better known texts, *Le ravissement de Lol V. Stein* and *Le vice-consul,* also have homodiegetic, as well as voyeuristic, narrators whose objective – indeed, obsession – is to tell the story of another human being.[94] The act of narrating (and in *Le vice-consul,* that of writing) becomes an even more manifest theme in these texts, as do the issues raised by it, such as the authority and the reliability of narrators. Two significant differences between these two texts and 'Madame Dodin' are, first, that their narrators are male, and second, that each of these men narrates the story of a woman who, unlike the sturdy and strong-willed Mme Dodin, appears not to resist the appropriation of her story by another.[95] A third and perhaps more important difference is that, instead of causing them to doubt the legitimacy of their narration, as it does the narrator of 'Madame Dodin,' the awareness of their own subjectivity and epistemological limitations make these male narrators pursue with all the more vigour their projects of (re)constructing another's story through narrative.

These two narrators in fact openly state from the beginning of their narratives that they are imagining much of the story they are telling about their subjects. *Le ravissement*'s narrator, Jacques Hold, peppers his account of the life of Lol V. Stein – a woman abandoned by her fiancé for another woman and reportedly driven mad by it – with caveats such as 'j'invente' (I am inventing) and 'je crois' (I think).[96] In *Le vice-consul,* Peter Morgan admits that in constructing the story of another presumed madwoman, a beggar who hovers around the embassy where he works in colonial Calcutta, '[il] voudrait [...] substituer à la mémoire abolie de la mendiante le bric-à-brac de la sienne' ([he] would like ... to fill the beggar-woman's obliterated memory with the bric-a-brac of his own).[97] Both men would thus appear to be voluntarily abdicating the authority traditionally conferred upon narrators by declaring their ignorance of their subjects. In admitting to a fundamental lack of *savoir* (knowledge), they are abandoning all pretension to the *pouvoir* (power) that is its corollary. They could also be considered New Novelists of sorts, in that they appear to be eschewing any attempt to reflect an exterior reality in their narratives and to be privileging rather the fictional 'realities' that are the very texts they have created. Susan Suleiman sees Jacques Hold in this way, arguing that he 'makes no claim to understand Lol V. Stein and abandons any attempt to create a discourse of mastery over her.'[98]

Martha Noel Evans, on the other hand, argues that the narrative 'honesty' of both Jacques Hold and Peter Morgan is in truth nothing but a facade:

> By 'honestly' emphasizing the very subjectivity of his writing, the male narrator does not in fact deconstruct the reliability of his narrative, but merely recasts it on another, less obvious but also less vulnerable level of credibility and authority ... The truth function of [Jacques Hold's] narrative is thus diverted from its base in objectively grounded language onto a more unstable but finally less assailable terrain: the trustworthiness of the narrator ... His appeals to his own fallibility are a lure, a con, which encourages the reader to trust him even if what he says is not wholly reliable.[99]

Evans suggests that in spite of Hold's disclaimers, or perhaps because of them, the reader in a sense 'forgives' his ignorance and 'forgets' that what she is reading is 'made up' (a forgetfulness that is simply expected of the reader of traditional fiction). I agree with Evans, as well as with a number of other critics, who maintain that *Le ravissement de Lol V. Stein* is *not* the story of Lol V. Stein, but rather the story of the *narration* of Lol's story, or more specifically, the story of Jacques Hold's narration/creation/fantasy of Lol.[100] Peter Morgan, for his part, chooses a subject whose real life-story would be not just difficult but probably impossible to reconstruct: the beggar-woman speaks a language no one understands, and she is believed to be too mad to be able to recount or even to remember her own history. Neither she nor anyone else, therefore, could ever contest Morgan's version of that history. Armed with stories that are more complete and likely more compelling than the 'real' ones – which the women in any case cannot or do not tell themselves – these narrators are able to 'colonize' the memories of their two subjects with impunity.[101] Less scrupulous than the anxious narrator of 'Madame Dodin' Jacques Hold and Peter Morgan shirk the responsibilities of truthful representation and instead give free reign to their desires and imaginations. They relieve themselves of narrative anxiety by theatrically relinquishing any claims to truth, yet they manage to maintain mastery over their narratives by choosing subjects who will never challenge their authority, and on whose behalf no one else will either.

Peter Morgan is not the only character in *Le vice-consul* to feel driven to become an author. This desire seems contagious in Duras's fictional Calcutta, like the leprosy that encircles and so terrifies the white colonials. The French ambassador, for example, 'a essayé d'écrire des romans, autrefois,' but, 'sur le conseil de sa femme,' Anne-Marie Stretter, 'il a abandonné' (once tried his hand at writing a novel, but had given up on the advice of his wife).[102] The director of the European circle, expressing himself in the same conditional as 'Madame Dodin''s narrator, laments, 'eh bien, je regrette de ne pas savoir écrire... quel roman cela ferait, ce que j'ai vu... ce que j'ai entendu...' (It's too bad I don't know how to write... what a novel that would make, the things I've seen, the things I've heard!) (Duras's ellipses).[103] Yet were he to possess such writing skills, it is doubtful he could remain sober and awake long enough to put pen to paper. These two men are only would-be authors; but unlike the narrator of 'Madame Dodin,' they are held back not by any scruples concerning the integrity of their subject matter, but rather by their own incompetence or indolence.

What kind of author was Marguerite Duras? For one thing, she was one of the most prolific writers of the twentieth century, having produced upwards of eighty narratives, plays, and films. If she suffered from the kinds of narrative anxiety 'Madame Dodin''s narrator experiences, they certainly did not prevent her from writing. She was, nevertheless, intimately familiar with the plight of those, like the beggar-woman, whose voices have literally or figuratively been taken away from them. Her mother's numerous and increasingly strident complaints to the colonial administration in French Indochina that it had sold her infertile land fell upon deaf ears. Her cries for justice were as nonsensical to these administrators as the beggar-woman's singing is to the fictional administrators of *Le vice-consul*. Despite Duras's radical displacement from the rice paddies of Cochin China to the cafés of Saint-Germain-des-Prés, her memories of childhood did not suffer the same fate as those of the beggar-woman during her circuitous journey from Cambodia to Calcutta. Duras wrote of her mother's unrelenting anxiety over her land, her money, her place in colonial society, and her children's fate for more than fifty years. Her mother's story, transposed multiple times in several different genres, represents all the unwritten stories of those who have been made victims of the greed, pride, prejudice, or cruelty of men (and women) in power.[104]

At the same time, the mother's story is also the story of how victims of violence, oppression, or indifference often become themselves perpetrators of the same (as the textual mother's tyranny over her children and her racism attest). Ironically and unfortunately, an event in Duras's own life in the year *La douleur* was published (1985) illustrates this. As Frédérique Lebelley relates in her biography of Duras, over the course of that year, French newspapers followed the investigation of the disappearance of a four-year-old boy whose body was found in the Vologne River nine months after he was last seen.[105] An autopsy revealed that he had been murdered, and suspicions were raised about the mother, Christine Villemin. In July of that year, shortly after Villemin was arrested but before she was tried, Duras – who had an insatiable appetite for accounts of *les crimes passionnels* – published a dramatic three-page article in *Libération* about the case, of which she was no more an authority than her readers. In this article, 'Sublime, forcément sublime Christine V.' (Sublime, Necessarily Sublime Christine V.), Duras simultaneously condemned and exculpated the suspect, writing, in short, that the pain of a mother who is driven to kill her own child can be neither fathomed nor judged by anyone, certainly not by any court.[106] It can be understood by no one, that is, except for Duras herself, apparently. 'L'enfant a dû être tué à l'intérieur de la maison' (The child must have been killed inside the house), she wrote, thus implicating the family and – the rest of the article made clear – the mother specifically. She based this and other assertions on 'intuition': 'C'est ce que je vois. C'est au-delà de la raison' (This is what I see. It's beyond reason).[107] The 'evidence' Duras had gathered by reading newspaper reports, visiting the village in which the crime took place, and studying photos of Christine Villemin 'me porterait à croire que l'enfant n'aurait pas été le plus important dans la vie de Christine V.,' she wrote. 'Il arrive que les femmes n'aiment pas leurs enfants, ni leur maison, qu'elles ne soient pas les femmes d'intérieur qu'on attendait qu'elles soient' (would lead me to believe that the child must not have been the most important thing in Christine V.'s life ... It sometimes happens that women don't love their children, or their house, and that they are not the kind of housewife they are expected to be) (4). Under the linguistic cover of multiple conditional and hypothetical constructions, such as 'elle a dû' (she must have), 'il ne devait pas' (he must not have), 'il se pourrait que' (it's possible that), 'il me semble que' (it seems to me that), and 'dit-on' (they say), which in effect did little to mitigate the article's implications, Duras constructed an elaborate story about the profound unhappiness from which Christine V. supposedly suffered because of an unsuitability for the role of housewife and the severity of an imperious husband: 'il se pourrait que Christine V. ait vécu avec un homme difficile à supporter ... Je vois la dureté de cet homme s'exercer sans trêve aucune, être de principe, éducative, etc.' (it's possible that Christine V. lived with a man who was difficult to bear ... I see that man ruling with an iron fist, without fail, out of principle, for her own good, etc.) (4). Duras wrote that this pain 'could have' led Christine V. to kill her child so as to escape definitively the imprisonment of her home and marriage: 'cette femme des collines nues, dit-on, aurait trouvé comment défaire en une fois, en une minute, la totalité du bâtiment de sa vie. On le dit. Ce n'est pas sûr [...] Dans ce cas, la mort de l'enfant aurait été le seul moyen qui lui serait resté, parce qu'il aurait été le plus sûr' (that woman from the bare hills, they say, would have found in an instant a way to undo her entire life. That's what they say. It's not certain ... In that case, the death of the child would have been the last way out for her, because it would have been the surest) (5–6). Because Villemin was herself a victim (of a society that had imposed upon her a feminine role that robbed her of her liberty), she could not also be a criminal, Duras reasoned: 'si Christine V. est consciente de l'injustice qui lui a été faite durant la traversée du long tunnel qu'a été sa vie, elle est complètement étrangère à cette culpabilité que l'on réclame d'elle ... Qu'elle ait été, elle, victime de traitements injustes, oui, mais coupable, non, elle ne l'a pas été' (If Christine V. is conscious of the injustice she endured during the long tunnel that was her life, that sense of guilt they demand of her is completely foreign to her ... That she was herself a victim of unjust treatment, yes, but guilty, no, that she was not) (6). This strange article echoed Duras's equivocal testimony at Charles Delval's trial, by which she first damned and then defended the accused. In the trial of Christine Villemin, however, Duras's performance as a 'witness' (whom no one had summoned) later caused her to have to play the role of defendant: decidedly less compliant than either Anne-Marie Stetter or the beggarwoman, Christine Villemin successfully sued both Duras and *Libération* for libel. Duras was forced to pay damages, and in February 1993, Villemin was acquitted due to a lack of evidence.[108]

According to Lebelley, Duras never recanted her capricious and very public presumption of Villemin's guilt, nor did she apologize for this gross abuse of her power as a public figure (especially in the wake of *L'amant*'s acclaim), so certain was she of the 'vérité' of her version of events. 'Au contraire,' Lebelley writes, 'chaque fois qu[e Duras] se relit, elle succombe au même éblouissement: "Je crois que plus jamais je ne pourrai écrire aucun article aussi beau. Il est somptueux de vérité ... J'ai complètement sauvé Christine Villemin"' (On the contrary, every time [Duras] rereads her own article, she is equally dazzled: 'I don't think I'll ever be able to write another article as beautiful as that one. It is laden with truth ... I completely saved Christine Villemin') (Lebelley's ellipses).[109] Dominque Denes writes in her recent book on the impetuous author that, 'Duras refuse à "assagir l'émotion", se déclarant même incapable de le faire. Elle privilégie l'expression brute, souvent brutale, irrationnelle, souvent déraisonnable, jaillie tout droit de l'émotion. Son art poétique se fonde sur la force native de l'émotion et la forme première de l'écrit' (Duras refuses to 'tame emotion,' going so far as to declare herself incapable of doing so. She favours raw, often brutal, irrational, often unreasonable expression, rising straight up from emotion. Her poetic art is based on the innate force of emotion and the first draft of the text).[110] It is precisely this kind of writing that makes so many of Duras's literary texts, among them *La douleur*, so very engaging and seem so very truthful to the reader. When this kind of 'brutal' writing is transferred into the realm of journalism, however, its very effectiveness (that it can persuade the reader of its truth value) makes it a highly dangerous tool, one that Duras wielded with appalling carelessness in her article on the Villemin affair.

In this article, Duras treats 'Christine V.' as a character in one of her literary texts (like Emily L.,[111] Robert L., or Monsieur X.), replacing her surname with an initial as if this would suffice to fictionalize the textual Christine and thus 'protect' the real one. But the Durassian character whom the Christine V. constructed in the article most resembles is Claire Lannes, the protagonist of Duras's play *Les viaducs de la Seine-et-Oise* (*The Viaducts of the Seine-et-Oise*) (1959) and of her novel *L'amante anglaise* (*The English Lover*) (1967), whose plots are based on another *fait divers*. Claire Lannes kills her cousin and chops her body into pieces, then throws these parts from a viaduct onto trains travelling to the four (or rather six) corners of France.[112] Although Claire is without question guilty of the crime, the narrative of *L'amante anglaise* suggests that since both the crime and the criminal defy comprehension, so they defy judgment. Claire Lannes further resembles Christine V., as well as many of the female characters I have been discussing here, in that someone (in Claire's case, a professional writer) wants to co-opt her story. This writer arranges a number of interviews with Claire in prison, and while she docilely cooperates by answering most of his questions to the best of her ability, she nevertheless resists the total confiscation of her story by remaining silent on at least one, 'capital' point: she refuses to tell him what she has done with the victim's head.

While Duras's intransigent defiance of authority and disregard for conventional morality often made her an ally of victims of reactionary and unjust institutions, her 'defence' of Christine Villemin as an 'innocent' murderer was as misguided an attempt at writerly engagement as perhaps ever was. In her article, Duras does precisely what several of the male narrators in her literary texts are implicitly censured for doing – appropriating another's voice and telling 'her' story in her place. Like Jacques Hold in *Le ravissement*, Duras does 'confess' her ignorance in her article – 'j'écris sans savoir' (I write without knowing), 'C'est ce que je crois' (This is what I believe), and so on[113] – but this disarming 'honesty' only serves – as Evans argues it does for Hold – to reinforce readers' confidence in her and her story.[114] The Duras who wrote this inflammatory article certainly does not appear to suffer from an anxiety of authorship; on the contrary, she tells Lebelley that the author is not only allowed but *obligated* to write (and to publish, apparently) the narrative that takes form within her: 'La littérature m'a emportée. Une raison inhumaine. Emportée par l'article, la miason, la chose ... C'est la passion. Si c'était à refaire, je le referais' (I was carried away by literature. An inhuman force. Carried away by the article, the house, the thing ... It's passion. If I had the choice of doing it all over again, I would) (Lebelley's ellipses).[115] Perhaps Duras's ego, never humble to begin with but likely inflated by the enormous success of *L'amant*, got the better of her. In her defence (to adopt the equivocal spirit of both 'Monsieur X.' and the Villemin article), she also seems to have sincerely believed that her 'testimony' would serve to exonerate Christine V.; indeed, the outcome of the case did not belie this assumption. Yet according to Lebelley, the real effect of the article was not to vindicate Villemin, but to discredit Duras.[116] The great writer did not heed her humble narrator's warning (in 'Madame Dodin') that a written text is like a fish tail or a pair of old shoes ('Comment connaître leur vrai destin une fois que nous les avons lâchées dans le monde?' [How can we know their true destiny once we have launched them into the world?]).[117] In the end, Duras paid a very literal price for such insouciance.

In contrast to the recklessly oblivious author of the Villemin article, 'Monsieur X.'s narrator (like that of 'Madame Dodin') is patently anxious about her writing project. Hers is not principally an anxiety about claiming authority, however. Instead, it is an anxiety about attempting to convey the emotion of a past experience – the emotion of acute anxiety, as it happens – truthfully and forcefully in narrative. The narrator of Annie Ernaux's *La honte* (*Shame*) (the text examined in chapter 2) shares this anxiety. She is preoccupied with creating a truthful representation of herself, her family, and her social milieu during a particularly difficult period of her childhood. She seeks to discover and to communicate what she calls her 'réalité d'alors' (reality at that time).[118] Like 'Monsieur X.''s narrator, *La honte*'s narrator desires to convey accurately not only certain events, but also, and more importantly, certain psychophysical states – certain emotions and their effects on her body. Whereas the two related emotions that predominate in 'Monsieur X.' are anxiety (in the face of potential danger) and terror (in the face of what appears to be certain danger), that which overshadows all other sentiments in Ernaux's text, as its title makes clear, is shame. But both narrators are burdened with memories of a traumatic experience (though vastly different), memories of which they wish to unburden themselves by narrating them. *La honte* contains none of the drama of 'Monsieur X.'; the traumatic experience, or the 'scene,' as the narrator calls it, is narrated in the past tense and in a neutral, measured language that Ernaux adopted in 1984's *La place* and has used ever since. Ernaux's narrator exudes much less confidence than Duras's about the truth value of her text. The primary source of her anxiety is neither the trauma itself nor its memory, but rather her doubts – first, about the possibility of finding a narrative style that will convey her past self's reality accurately (a worry that 'Madame Dodin''s narrator shares in her abortive attempt to narrate *another's* reality), and second, about the adequacy of language as a means of representing fundamentally non-linguistic phenomena (a worry that, as I will suggest in chapter 3, the 'writer' in Sarraute's text shares). While the reality finally presented in *La honte* is less equivocal than that put forward in 'Monsieur X.,' as well as less subject to dispute because of its more profoundly personal nature, its narrator is often as sceptical of its truth as Duras's critics are of that of *La douleur.* Yet like the doubts of these critics, the scepticism of Ernaux's narrator is a textually productive one, as her creator's multiple returns to her past in other texts demonstrate. These also will be examined in the following analysis of *La honte*'s anxious narration.

2 Shame in Memory and Narrative: Annie Ernaux's *La honte*

In Annie Ernaux's autobiographical *La honte* (*Shame*) (1997), the autodiegetic narrator describes a painful childhood experience to which there is no explicit reference in any of the several accounts of her youth the author had previously published.[1] In that unembellished style she calls 'l'écriture plate' (flat writing),[2] Ernaux writes: 'Mon père a voulu tuer ma mère un dimanche de juin, au début de l'après-midi' (My father tried to kill my mother one Sunday in June, in the early afternoon).[3] It quickly becomes evident that the memory of this 'scene' (as the author refers to it), which Ernaux struggles to recount in the first part of *La honte* and to understand throughout the rest of it, remains after forty-five years a powerful force in the writer's life. Why did she make no mention in her previous autobiographical texts of what *La honte* makes clear was an experience of primal significance for her? What can explain what becomes to the reader of *La honte* such a glaring omission in these texts?[4] As the title of the book suggests, the most obvious, if incomplete, answer is that she was ashamed of what happened that day in June 1952.

While Ernaux is certainly not a writer who shies away from personal revelation, in *La honte* she does claim, as Duras does about the story of Monsieur X., to have had much difficulty writing about the episode exposed in that text.[5] In *La honte* and elsewhere, she also, once again like Duras in reference to 'Monsieur X.,' staunchly defends the truth value of her narrative (this is a subject to which I will return later in the chapter). Unwittingly echoing the author of *La douleur* (although speaking with more caution), Ernaux states in an interview published in 2003 (*L'écriture comme un couteau [Writing Like a Knife]*) that in all her texts since 1984's *La place* (*A Man's Place*), 'toute fictionnalisation des événements est écartée et [...] sauf erreur de mémoire, ceux-ci sont *véridiques dans tous leurs détails*' (I have avoided any fictionalization of events and ... except for lapses in memory, these events are *truthful in every detail*) (emphasis mine).[6] Interestingly, in this same interview Ernaux firmly rejects the interviewer's suggestion that there are similarities between her writing and Duras's, asserting that, along with Duras's poeticism, it is 'l'absence d'historicité et de réalisme social' (the absence of historicity and social realism) in this latter's work that separates their œuvres) (94). Immediately following this statement, however, Ernaux notes that she did enjoy reading *La douleur*, among a few other of Duras's texts. This is perhaps not surprising given that, as demonstrated in chapter 1, *La douleur* squarely belies the charge that Duras's work lacks historicity and social realism. *La douleur* has yet more in common with Ernaux's œuvre in general and with *La honte* in particular in that this latter is an autobiographical text whose narrator experiences anxiety while attempting to portray as realistically and truthfully as possible past emotions, one of which is anxiety itself (as in 'La douleur' and 'Monsieur X.'), and another (as in 'Albert des Capitales'), shame.[7]

Yet was the scene in *La honte* really that much more difficult to narrate than, for example, the abortion explicitly recounted in *Les armoires vides* (*Cleaned Out*) (1974) and *L'événement* (*The Event*) (2000), or the obsessive, even debilitating passion for a married man revealed in *Passion simple* (*Simple Passion*) (1991) and *Se perdre* (*To Lose Oneself*) (2001)?[8] If so, why? What anxieties kept Ernaux from writing about this scene for more than twenty years (the time between the publication of her first text and *La honte*)? In this chapter I will read the revelatory text that is *La honte* alongside several of Ernaux's earlier works, as well as alongside interviews with the author, in order to comprehend why this critical scene was not included in those texts that cover precisely the time period in which it occurred. Interestingly, when (re)read *after La honte*, these texts appear to foreshadow it; a rereading of them here will therefore contribute to a better understanding of *La honte* and the scene contained within it. In turn, *La honte* acts as a missing piece of the puzzle that these other texts had incompletely formed, and it therefore elucidates their meanings and seems to fill in the image of the author's childhood and adolescence that they had sketched.

Related to the question of why the scene was not narrated earlier in Ernaux's œuvre are the questions of why, and perhaps more significant to this study of the narration of anxiety, how it *was* finally narrated in *La honte*. What desires finally drove Ernaux towards its exposure? What specific narrative strategies does she use to recount this previously unnarratable scene? What does she hope to accomplish by creating this narrative, and, in the end, to what extent does she feel she has achieved these goals? Efforts to answer these questions will lead in the first part of this chapter to a discussion of traumatic experience (touched upon in chapter 1), the clinical definition of which the scene Ernaux describes in *La honte* appears to fit. This discussion of the personal and psychological aspects of the scene will then open up to a consideration of its sociological dimensions – that is, to the ways in which social forces are implicated in both its occurrence and its significance for the narrator. This transposition of the scene from the personal to the social sphere is already performed by the text itself, by the necessary translation of private, wordless memories into the inherently social codes of language and narrative. The performance of this difficult transposition/translation will be, as I will show, a source of much anxiety for the narrator. Yet it is also the means by which she hopes to liberate herself of anxiety, as well as of a related but still more debilitating emotion for her, that which she names in the text's title.

The 'Scene'

The narrative of the actual scene, which took place on a Sunday afternoon after an ordinary family dinner, fills only three pages of the 133-page text:

> Ma mère était de mauvaise humeur. La dispute qu'elle avait entreprise avec mon père, sitôt assise, n'a pas cessé durant tout le repas. La vaisselle débarrassée, la toile cirée essuyée, elle a continué d'adresser des reproches à mon père, en tournant dans la cuisine, minuscule – coincée entre le café, l'épicerie et l'escalier menant à l'étage – , comme à chaque fois qu'elle était contrariée. Mon père était resté assis à table, sans répondre, la tête tournée vers la fenêtre. D'un seul coup, il s'est mis à trembler convulsivement et à souffler. Il s'est levé et je l'ai vu empoigner ma mère, la traîner dans le café en criant avec une voix rauque, inconnue. Je me suis sauvée à l'étage et je me suis jetée sur mon lit, la tête dans un coussin. Puis j'ai entendu ma mère hurler: 'Ma fille!' Sa voix venait de la cave, à côté du café. Je me suis précipitée au bas de l'escalier, j'appelais 'Au secours!' de toutes mes forces. Dans la cave mal éclairée, mon père agrippait ma mère par les épaules, ou le cou. Dans son autre main, il tenait la serpe à couper le bois qu'il avait arrachée du billot où elle était ordinairement plantée. Je ne me souviens plus ici que de sanglots et de cris. Ensuite, nous nous trouvons de nouveau tous les trois dans la cuisine.

My mother was in a bad mood. The argument she started with my father as soon as she sat down lasted throughout the meal. After the table was cleared and the oilcloth wiped clean, she continued to fire criticism at my father, turning round and round in the tiny kitchen – squeezed in between the café, the store, and the steps leading upstairs – as she always did when she was upset. My father was still seated at the table, saying nothing, his head turned toward the window. All of a sudden he began to tremble convulsively and to wheeze. He stood up, and I saw him grab hold of my mother and drag her through the café, shouting in a hoarse, unfamiliar voice. I rushed upstairs and threw myself on to the bed, my face buried in a cushion. Then I heard my mother scream: 'My daughter!' Her voice came from the cellar adjoining the café. I rushed downstairs, shouting 'Help!' as loud as I could. In the poorly-lit cellar, my father had grabbed my mother by the shoulders, or maybe the neck. In his other hand, he was holding the scythe for cutting firewood which he had wrenched away from the block where it belonged. At this point all I can remember are sobs and screams.[9]

'J'écris cette scène pour la première fois,' Ernaux's narrator states. 'Jusqu'à aujourd'hui, il me semblait impossible de le faire, même dans un journal intime. Comme une action interdite devant entraîner un châtiment. Peut-être celui de ne plus pouvoir écrire quoi que ce soit ensuite' (I am writing about this scene for the first time. Until now, I have found it impossible to do so, even in a diary. I considered writing about it to be a forbidden act that would call for punishment. Not being able to write anything else afterward, for instance) (16; 15). Although the scene appears nowhere else in Ernaux's œuvre, the narrator of *La place*, a narrative about the author's father and her estrangement from him due to her social ascent into the bourgeoisie, does mention her parents' frequent shouting matches: 'Sous l'insulte, sortant de son calme habituel : "CARNE! J'aurais mieux fait de te laisser où tu étais." Échange hebdomadaire: "Zéro! – Cinglée! / Triste individu! – Vieille garce!" / Etc. Sans aucune importance' (Shedding his customary reserve, he responds to the insult: 'You SLUT! I should have left you back where I found you!' Every week they would exchange insults: 'A nobody, that's what you are!' / 'You're crazy!' / 'You're pathetic!' / 'You stupid old bitch!' / And so on. It didn't mean anything).[10] These kinds of exchanges were exclusively verbal and without consequence – except, *La place*'s narrator neglects to tell us, for one Sunday in June 1952. This passage from *La place* is followed by a blank space on the page. While such spaces are common in Ernaux's later texts, which generally offer a series of fragments rather than a narrative per se, for those who have read *La honte*, this blank might be seen as particularly significant. In the retrospective light thrown by this later text, the blank in *La place* can be read as a kind of 'hole,' or more precisely, a *paralipsis*, in the story of her childhood that *La place*'s narrator supplies. As Genette has it, in a paralipsis, 'the narrative does not skip over a moment of time, as in an ellipsis, but it *sidesteps a given element*' (Genette's emphasis).[11] That is, the narrator conceals a certain part of a story (in Genette's sense of the word) while narrating, but only temporarily, for s/he reveals the 'missing' element later on in the narrative.[12] This blank space in *La place* can be read as a paralipsis not within that text itself (in which the scene is never recounted) but rather within Ernaux's œuvre as a whole since the publication of *La honte*.

In addition to this blank space, there are other textual clues in *La place* that suggest that something is missing in the narrator's account of her childhood there. Several pages after this space there appears a paragraph that is also set off by blank spaces. The narrator begins this paragraph using a demonstrative adjective to modify a Sunday ('*Ce* dimanche-là' [*That* Sunday]) that, curiously, has no discernable antecedent anywhere in the text preceding this paragraph. It is therefore not at all clear to the reader to which Sunday the narrator is referring. 'Ce dimanche-là [mon père] avait fait la sieste. Il passe devant la lucarne du grenier. Tient à la main un livre qu'il va remettre dans une caisse laissée en dépôt chez nous par [un] officier de marine. Un petit rire en m'apercevant dans la cour. C'est un livre obscène' (That Sunday, [my father] had had a nap. I get a glimpse of him as he walks past the attic window. He's holding a book which he returns to the crate that [a] naval officer has left in storage. He chuckles as he catches sight of me in the courtyard. It's a dirty book).[13] The referent is particularly difficult to pinpoint because *La place* adheres to no strict chronological order but rather follows what would seem to be the meanderings of the narrator's memory. The puzzled reader might initially think that the narrator is referring to the only specific Sunday mentioned in *La place*: the day of her father's death, which, like the scene in *La honte*, took place on a Sunday in June, only fifteen years later.[14] But the reader soon realizes that this explanation is impossible, because according to *La Place*'s narrator, on his final day her father lay incapacitated and semi-conscious all that morning until he died early in the afternoon.[15] In addition, in the passage from *La place* referring to 'ce dimanche-là,' the narrator also calls her parents' home 'chez nous' ([our] home), signalling most probably that she is speaking of a time when she was still living with her parents and not visiting them as an adult, as she was on the day of her father's death.

To what Sunday, then, could 'ce dimanche-là' refer? One explanation is that the Sunday enigmatically evoked in *La place* is in fact the Sunday on which the scene revealed in *La honte* took place, which the author of *La place* remembers while writing of her parents' bitter fights, but which she is either unwilling or unable to textualize at that time. In this passage in *La place*, in which the narrator (presumably as a child) sees her father through the attic window, the narration of signs of the father's usually hidden sexual desires – his concealment of a pornographic book after having taken a 'nap' and his guilty laugh at being caught red-handed – may be standing in for the narration of the terrifying signs – the sudden gestures of violence – of his usually equally stifled hostility towards his domineering wife. Both repressed desires – the one sexual, the other violent – perhaps revealed themselves on that same Sunday. The narrator of *La place*, however, narrates only the signs of the first, re/suppressing, in her turn, those of the second. 'Le déchiffrement de ces détails,' she says – such as that of her father through the attic window, and more generally those of her parents' behavior and lifestyle – 's'impose à moi maintenant, avec d'autant plus de nécessité que je les ai refoulés, sûre de leur insignifiance. Seule une mémoire humiliée avait pu me les faire conserver' (Now it is imperative that I unravel these memories, all the more so since I have long suppressed them, believing them to be of no consequence. If they have survived, it's solely because of the humiliation they caused) (72; 61). The shame she felt because of her parents' behaviour prompted at one and the same time, then, the indelible impression of certain details on her memory and the long-term repression of the most painful among them. Yet as my reading of these passages in *La place* indicates, the repression appears to backfire; for it is absence – the blank space and the missing referent – that 'gives away' the scene before the narrator is ready to reveal it.

In *Une femme* (*A Woman's Story*) (1988), a narrative of Ernaux's mother's life and final surrender to Alzheimer's disease, the text's narrator evokes another childhood scene of humiliation:

> Une veille de la Pentecôte, j'ai rencontré ma tante M... en revenant de classe. Comme tous les jours de repos, elle montait en ville avec son sac plein de bouteilles vides. Elle m'a embrassée sans pouvoir rien dire, oscillant sur place. Je crois que je ne pourrai jamais écrire comme si je n'avais pas rencontré ma tante, ce jour-là.

One year, on the day before Pentecost, I ran into my aunt M– on the way back from school. It was her day off, and as usual she was going into town with a shopping bag full of empty bottles. She kissed me on both cheeks, swaying slightly, incapable of uttering a single word. I don't think I could ever write as if I hadn't met my aunt that day, in that way.[16]

That is, she has not been nor will she ever be able to write as if she had been born a bourgeoise instead of having 'usurped' the role thanks to her academic and literary successes. On the other hand, Ernaux *was* able to write, for more than twenty years, as if she had not witnessed the scene of 15 June 1952 – as if her parents, though working-class, had not crossed a line that she seems to see as the boundary between respectability, however humble (as in the formula 'ce sont des gens simples mais braves' [they are simple but fine people]), and shameful coarseness, even criminality. What sets this particular scene of humiliation so far apart from the many others Ernaux reveals in her books? What about it drove her, an author scrupulously intent on discovering and exposing the 'truth' about her experiences, to be dishonest by omission?

The narrator of *Passion simple* offers some insight into the feelings that are roused by the act of revealing highly personal, often shameful, experiences in narrative. In the following passage she reflects on the imminent completion and publication of her narrative, in which she dissects her all-consuming passion for a man whose feelings towards her, she suspects, are considerably more measured:

Continuer [à écrire], c'est [...] repousser l'angoisse de donner ceci à lire aux autres. Tant que j'étais dans la nécessité d'écrire, je ne me souciais pas de cette éventualité. Maintenant que je suis allée au bout de cette nécessité, je regarde les pages écrites avec étonnement et une sorte de honte, jamais ressentie – au contraire – en vivant ma passion, pas davantage en la relatant ...

Quand je commencerai à taper ce texte à la machine, qu'il m'apparaîtra dans les caractères publics, mon innocence sera finie.

To go on [writing] is ... a means of delaying the trauma of giving this to others to read. I hadn't considered this eventuality while I still felt the need to write. But now that I have satisfied this need, I stare at the written pages with astonishment and something resembling shame, feelings I certainly never felt while I was living out my passion, nor while writing about it ...

Once I start typing out the text, once it appears before me in public characters, my innocence will be over.[17]

She felt no shame, then, while experiencing her passion, nor while speaking about it to friends, nor even while writing about it (at least in her own hand, as if in a diary). Shame arises, significantly, only when the narrator becomes a *reader* of her text. As the narrator of *Journal du dehors* (*Exteriors*) (1993) remarks, "'Je" fait honte au lecteur' ('I' embarrasses the reader),[18] even, the above passage from *Passion simple* suggests, when the textual 'je"'s reader is also its author. In reading her own text, *Passion simple*'s narrator becomes alienated from the 'I' inscribed there; it only refers to her while she is writing, just as the 'I' refers to a speaker only while he is speaking.[19] It is the exposure of her passion to an 'other' – even when that other is her reading- rather than her writing-self – and not the experience of passion itself that elicits shame.

This narrator's experience of her passion is fundamentally different, then, from the narrator of *La honte*'s experience of the scene, for this latter narrator makes it clear that she felt shame as well as terror *while living it out*. 'J'ai toujours eu envie d'écrire des livres dont il me soit ensuite impossible de parler, qui rendent le regard d'autrui insoutenable,' she writes at the end of her text, 'Mais quelle honte pourrait m'apporter l'écriture d'un livre qui soit à la hauteur de ce que j'ai éprouvé dans ma douzième année' (I have always wanted to write the sort of book that I find it impossible to talk about afterward, the sort of book that makes the gaze of other people on me unbearable. But what degree of shame could possibly be conveyed by the writing of a book which seeks to measure up to the events I experienced in my twelfth year).[20] Any shame a published account of the scene might cause her pales in comparison to that to which the actual experience gave birth. Moreover, not only did Ernaux's experience of the scene differ from her experience of her passion, but so also did the *writing* of the former differ from the writing of the latter: 'Lorsque j'ai commencé, en 1990, le texte que j'appellerai ultérieurement *La honte*,' she remarks in a 1997 interview, 'il s'agissait pour moi d'écrire ce qu'il serait le plus difficile et le plus "dangereux" d'écrire [...] [et] le plus honteux' (When I began, in 1990, the text that I would later call *Shame*, for me it was about writing what would be the most difficult and 'dangerous' thing to write ... [and] the most shameful).[21] Every stage of the evolution of the scene, then – the experience itself, the writing of it, then publishing the account – was not only shameful for Ernaux, but terrifying and even 'dangerous.' Once again, what set this scene apart?

As she thinks back to the months following the scene, it occurs to *La honte*'s narrator for the first time that her parents 'ont peut-être évoqué

entre eux la scène du dimanche, le geste de mon père, trouvé une explication, ou une excuse, et décidé de tout oublier' (perhaps discussed that
Sunday afternoon and my father's murderous gesture; they may have
arrived at an explanation or even an excuse and decided to forget the
whole thing).[22] 'Cette pensée,' however, 'comme toutes celles qu'on n'a
pas eues sur le moment, vient trop tard. Elle ne peut plus me servir,
sinon à mesurer par son absence la terreur sans mots qu'a été pour moi
ce dimanche' (This thought, like all those that elude one at the time,
comes too late. It can be of no help to me now; its absence only serves to
measure the indescribable terror [the terror without words] which that
Sunday has always meant to me) (21; 19). Here the narrator underscores
a key aspect of the scene: its wordlessness. It was an event that simply
defies language. Perhaps, as she suggests, her parents had talked later
and come up with a verbal explanation for it, but if so, they had never
communicated it to her. Even during the event itself, very little language
had apparently been used. The only words the narrator remembers are
her mother's 'Ma fille!' (My daughter!) and her own 'Au secours!'
(Help!); all else was 'sanglots' and 'cris' (sobs and cries) (15; 14). In her
narration of the scene, the narrator places much more emphasis on
action than on words: her father begins to tremble, he grabs her mother
and drags her to the basement, the narrator runs upstairs and throws
herself on her bed, and so on. While she does mention hearing a voice –
her father's – she describes it as 'inconnue' (unknown), and she does
not, moreover, tell us what it said, what words, if any, it spoke at this
moment. If her father did indeed speak, his words (which the narrator
has forgotten, repressed, or deliberately left out of the narrative) in no
way served as an explanation for the extraordinary violence that accompanied them.

This kind of exceptionally frightening experience, which the individual who lives it remembers vividly but cannot fully comprehend, can be
characterized as a traumatic experience. This scene may strike the
reader as trivial in comparison to some of the major, historical disasters
experienced and written about by other twentieth-century authors. But
in her introduction to *Trauma: Explorations in Memory* (1995), Cathy
Caruth reminds us that 'the pathology [of trauma] cannot be defined ...
by the event itself – which may or may not be catastrophic, and may not
traumatize everyone equally.'[23] Simplistically (or even tautologically)
speaking, a 'traumatic' event is any event that leaves a witness with symptoms of trauma, which I will define based on Caruth's as well as others'
definitions.

The narrator of *La honte* is in fact aware that psychologists would characterize the scene as a traumatic event for her. Yet 'dire "il s'agit d'un traumatisme familial" n'entame pas une scène que seule l'expression qui m'est venue alors pouvait rendre, *gagner malheur*. Les mots abstraits, ici, restent au-dessus de moi' (To say 'it was a childhood trauma' does nothing to explain a scene which could only be conveyed by the expression that came to me at the time: to *breathe disaster*. Here, abstract speech is beyond my reach) (Ernaux's emphasis).[24] This Norman expression ('Tu vas me faire gagner malheur,' literally, 'You're going to bring me misfortune/disaster'), which the narrator remembers repeating to her father immediately following the scene, offers a surprisingly accurate definition of the effects of trauma: in a footnote, the narrator explains that it means 'devenir fou et malheureux pour toujours à la suite d'un effroi' (to be driven crazy and to become miserable forever because of a scare) (15). This definition emphasizes both the depth and the permanence of the terror the experience leaves behind it. In describing the emotions felt by the eleven-year-old girl she once was, the narrator knows that above all she must avoid using vocabulary that was unknown to that girl – hence the expression 'gagner malheur.' 'Trauma' is nevertheless the term I will use here. Yet my objective is not simply to point out that the girl's experience was traumatic (which to contemporary readers is fairly obvious), but to explore how the narrative effectively reveals the peculiar workings of traumatic memory and the anxieties to which this kind of memory gives rise.

Of traumatic memory, Caruth writes that 'the literal registration of an event ... appears to be connected, in traumatic experience, precisely with the way it *escapes* full consciousness as it occurs' (Caruth's emphasis).[25] Caruth adds that the psychiatrist Pierre Janet, a contemporary of Freud, proposed that 'traumatic recall remains insistent and unchanged to the precise extent that it has never, from the beginning, been fully integrated into understanding' (153). A traumatic memory is an immediate 'etching into the brain' (153), a memory that stands apart from other memories for at least two reasons. The first is its extreme vividness and immutability: forty-five years after the event, *La honte*'s narrator is able to describe the scene in precise detail and remembers the exact date on which it took place (15 June 1952), a day she calls 'la première date précise et sûre de mon enfance' (the first date from my childhood that I remember with unerring accuracy).[26] In contrast to the narration of the actual scene, reproduced at the beginning of this chapter, the narration of what immediately preceded and followed it is much less precise. In these latter passages the narrator speaks only of what she 'most probably' did or of what 'must have' taken place. That morning, she says, 'j'étais allée à la messe de midi moins le quart comme d'habitude. J'avais dû rapporter des gâteaux du pâtissier installé dans la cité commerciale' (I had gone to Mass at a quarter to twelve as usual. I must have brought home some pastries from the bakery in the shopping center) (13; 13). Obviously the narrator remembers not that particular mass, only the fact that she always went to mass at that time ('comme d'habitude'). Similarly, she says she 'must have' picked up some pastries only because she knows that this is what she usually did on Sunday mornings. Expressions such as 'j'ai dû' (I must have), 'sans doute' (doubtless), and 'd'habitude' (usually) appear numerous times throughout the first fifteen pages of the text (13, 14, 15, 18, 23, 24, 27). In the short passage in which the scene itself is described, however, these suggestions of habit and normalcy disappear. Here the vocabulary (the adverbs in particular) and the verb tense (*le passé composé*, the simple past) signal that what is recounted is a singular and vividly remembered incident: 'D'un seul coup, [mon père] s'est mis à trembler convulsivement et à souffler. Il s'est levé et je l'ai vu empoigner ma mère,' etc. (All of a sudden, [my father] began to tremble convulsively and to wheeze. He stood up, and I saw him grab hold of my mother) (14; 14). The narrator's memory of these actions is not a composite of multiple memories left by recurring events, but rather a single, indelible impression. The second characteristic that sets traumatic memory apart from other memories is its power to frighten, disturb, and/or bewilder the rememberer long after the event it records is over. Indeed, a traumatic memory can leave the rememberer in a nearly constant state of anxiety, and psychologists categorize post-traumatic stress under the general heading of 'anxiety disorders.'[27]

Modern psychology and neurobiology have formulated hypotheses as to why certain experiences leave vivid, terrifying, and often inexplicable (and therefore unnarratable) impressions. Bessel A. van der Kolk and Onno van der Hart, contributors to Caruth's volume on trauma, discuss such research in their essay 'The Intrusive Past: The Flexibility of Memory and the Engraving of Trauma': 'When people are exposed to trauma, that is, a frightening event outside of ordinary human experience, they experience "speechless terror." The experience cannot be organized on a linguistic level, and this failure to arrange the memory in words and symbols leaves it to be organized on a somatosensory or iconic level: as somatic sensations, behavioral reenactments, nightmares, and flashbacks.'[28]

What the traumatized individual remembers especially, then, are images, colours, smells, sounds, textures, tastes, and also emotions – that is, physical as well as psychological *feelings*, the painful memories of which might be triggered later by similar feelings or sensations experienced in a different, non-traumatic, context. Specifically missing from these memories are words, which would render the event not only understandable – that is, accessible not just to the body but to the intellect as well – but also, and perhaps even more importantly, *communicable*.

These kinds of memories, physical and emotional memories (as opposed to intellectual and/or linguistic memories), seem to be primarily what the narrator has retained of the scene. She remembers, for example, the sensorial quality of her father's voice ('rauque et inconnue' [hoarse and unfamiliar/unknown]) registered by her ear, but not, as mentioned, what it said. It is the power of these mute but palpable memories that she attempts to overcome by transposing them into words and then narrative. In a summary of Pierre Janet's early insight into traumatic memory encodement, van der Kolk and van der Hart discuss Janet's notion of a very different kind of memory from somatic or sensory memory, which he terms 'narrative memory': 'Narrative memory consists of mental constructs, which people use to make sense out of experience (e.g., Janet, 1928).[29] Janet thought that the ease with which current experience is integrated into existing mental structures depends on the subjective assessment of what is happening; familiar and expectable experiences are automatically assimilated without much conscious awareness of details of the particulars, while frightening or novel experiences may not easily fit into existing cognitive schemes and either may be remembered with particular vividness or may totally resist integration.'[30]

Narrative memory is an individual's conscious awareness of his or her 'life story.' It does not just passively store individual (normal) memories, it actively evaluates and organizes them, then integrates them into a larger scheme of meaning. 'Psychodynamic psychiatry,' van der Kolk and van der Hart note, 'has always attached crucial importance to the capacity to reproduce memories in words and to integrate them in the totality of experience, i.e., to narrative memory' (167). In attempting finally to create a verbal narrative out of her wordless memories, *La honte*'s narrator hopes to accomplish the work that her mind was unable to do at the moment of the scene's occurrence. This work is to assign meaning to her impressions so that they may be integrated into the coherent store of past impressions that make up her life story.

Yet in recalling memories from the summer of 1952, the narrator is disturbed by a persistent feeling of what I will call dissociation. I base my use of the term somewhat loosely on the psychological definition, which describes dissociation as a mental disorder characterized by 'a disruption in the usually integrated functions of consciousness, memory, identity, or perception of the environment.'[31] Freud and Breuer defined dissociation as 'a splitting of the content of consciousness.'[32] The narrator's descriptions of her attempt to refamiliarize herself with her past in order to create the narrative point towards symptoms of such a disorder, which, according to van der Kolk and van der Hart, can be provoked, precisely, by trauma.

In order to begin telling her story, the narrator studies two photographs of herself taken during the summer of 1952. Initially, this strategy of refamiliarization fails, because when she looks at the photos, she is seized by the thought that the girl in them is an utter stranger: 'Si je ne les avais jamais vues, qu'on me les montre pour la première fois, je ne croirais pas qu'il s'agisse de moi. (Certitude que "c'est moi", impossibilité de me reconnaître, "ce n'est pas moi")' (if I had never seen them before, if I were shown them for the first time, I would never believe that it was me in them. [Absolute certainty – 'yes, that's me'; total disbelief – 'no, that's not me']).[33] She can therefore only refer to this girl in the third person: in one of the photos, a souvenir of her first communion, 'on voit une fille au visage plein, lisse, des pommettes marquées, un nez arrondi avec des narines larges [...] Un visage de petite fille sérieuse, faisant plus que son âge à cause de la permanente et des lunettes. Elle est agenouillée sur un prie-dieu' (there is a girl with a full, smooth face, prominent cheekbones, a rounded nose with large nostrils ... The face of a conscientious little girl, looking older than her age because of the glasses and permed hair. She is kneeling on a *prie-dieu*) (22; 20). Intellectually, the narrator knows very well that the photos indeed represent her as an eleven-year-old child, but missing from this knowledge is the memory, and the sensation, of actually *having been* her. In the communion photo, the girl holds a missal (a book containing the prayers and readings for Catholic mass) that the narrator still owns. 'De même que les photos constituent la preuve de mon corps de 52, le missel – dont la conservation au travers des déménagements n'est pas anodine – est la preuve matérielle irréfutable de l'univers religieux qui était le mien mais que je ne peux plus ressentir' (Just as the photographs are proof of my body in 1952, the missal – the fact that it has survived so many moves is in itself significant – provides indisputable evidence of the religious world to which I once belonged but which fails to move me today) (29; 25). The missal is significant to the narrator as a relic of the 'univers' it survives (the place and time in which she once lived, as well as the 'habitus,' in Bourdieu's terms, that was hers), but this is the only way in which it is still meaningful to her.[34] That is, the book holds for her none of the religious significance she knows it once held for the girl.

The narrator's profound lack of self-recognition and emotional attachment to the girl in the photographs can be explained in part by the vastly different temporal as well as social milieux in which the two of them (the woman and the girl she once was) live(d): 'La femme que je suis en 95 est incapable de se replacer dans la fille de 52 qui ne connaissait que sa petite ville, sa famille et son école privée, n'avait à sa disposition qu'un lexique réduit' (The woman I am in '95 is incapable of putting herself in the place of the girl of '52, who knew nothing beyond her little town, her family and her private school, and who had only a limited vocabulary at her disposal).[35] Yet it is the extraordinary and terrifying experience the girl underwent that summer – an experience which made her painfully aware of her shameful social status – that is at the heart of the narrator's sense of dissociation. While memory is 'the central organizing apparatus of the mind, which categorizes and integrates all aspects of experience and automatically integrates them into ever-enlarging and flexible meaning schemes,'[36] some experiences lie so far outside the realm of what an individual considers to be normal that they cannot fit into any of memory's preconceived categories.[37] Impressions made by these traumatic experiences stand apart from ordinary meaning schemes like faulty pieces of a jigsaw puzzle. The narrator's memories of the scene, because of their extreme irregularity, remain dissociated or detached from the careful and logical assemblage of other memories that has come to represent for her her life story. This lack of integration of certain memories, caused by their abnormality and incomprehensibility, only compounds their meaninglessness for their bearer, for, as structuralist theory suggests, individual elements of any structure (one's life story in memory, for example) possess no meaning in and of themselves; rather, they acquire meaning only through their position within the structure. Traumatic impressions can find no appropriate place in the structure of memory and so remain agonizingly unintelligible (just as was the original experience) to their bearer.

On a literary level, the narrator's sense of estrangement when looking at the girl in the photographs resembles to some extent that experienced by the narrator of Proust's À la recherche du temps perdu (*In Search of Lost Time*) as he reflects on his past.[38] For him, as Leo Bersani points out, the individual is not a monolith but rather a series of multiple and disparate selves whose consciousnesses are normally as separate and mutually inaccessible to one another as if they were contained in what Proust's narrator calls 'mille vases clos' (a thousand sealed vessels).[39] Most of these multiple selves succeed one another throughout his lifetime; some of them coexist during the same period, yet still remain separate and mutually exclusive. Intellectually, he is aware of the states of mind of many of his multiple current and past selves: he knows, for example, that whereas he seeks independence from his mother during the daytime, he longs for her comforting presence at night, and that while he once desperately loved Gilberte, he now finds her banal. Yet what he cannot do while he is experiencing one particular self is truly *live* or *feel* as any of the others do or did. For him, this kind of 'dissociation' (this is my term, not his) is not provoked by any event but rather is a normal and inevitable aspect of the human condition. The realization of his own multiplicity is nevertheless a source of profound distress for Proust's narrator, and it is in part this realization, Bersani maintains, that incites him to begin the narrative that will lend some kind of unity, he believes, to all of these ephemeral and disparate selves.[40] Such is one of the goals, I want to suggest, of the narrator of *La honte*, whose author, as I will point out, makes multiple references to *La recherche* throughout her work.

While going through the 'traces matérielles,' like the missal, that remain of her life at the time of the scene, the narrator comes upon the score of a song, 'Voyage à Cuba,' that had been popular during the summer of 1952.[41] The song strikes her as much less foreign than the missal, and in humming it she begins to feel a connection with the girl in the photos. The song can produce such an effect, she concludes, because '[elle] parle d'amour et de voyage, deux désirs toujours actuels dans ma vie' ([it] talks about love and travel, two desires still present in my life) (29; 25). These desires are (to adopt the Proustian metaphoric spirit) like unbroken strings that stretch from the narrator's current self all the way back to the self in the photographs and that vibrate along with the music the narrator hums. The narrator notes that it is more the melody of the song than its lyrics that offers her this emotional (rather than solely intellectual) glimpse into her past. Yet in a reference to Proust later in the narrative, she seems to forget the role that this song has played in allowing her to establish a link between her present and her past, a project that Lyn Thomas affirms is 'fundamental to Ernaux's writing and identity.'[42]

Proust écrit à peu près ceci que notre mémoire est hors de nous, dans un souffle pluvieux du temps, l'odeur de la première flambée de l'automne,

etc. Des choses de la nature qui rassurent, par leur retour, sur la permanence de la personne. À moi – et peut-être à tous ceux de mon époque –
dont les souvenirs sont attachés à un tube d'été, une ceinture en vogue, à
des choses vouées à la disparition, la mémoire n'apporte aucune preuve de
ma permanence ou de mon identité. Elle me fait sentir et me confirme ma
fragmentation et mon historicité.

In his writings, Proust suggests that our memory is outside of us, residing in
a gust of rainy wind or the smells of early autumn – things linked to nature
that recur periodically, confirming the permanence of mankind. For me
and no doubt many of my contemporaries, whose memories are connected
to ephemeral things such as a fashionable belt or a summer hit, the act of
remembering can do nothing to reaffirm my sense of identity or continuity.
It can only confirm the fragmented nature of my life and my historicity.
(95–6; 81)

If the narrator underscores here the fundamental sameness of her
project and that of Proust's narrator – to discover through narrative a
hidden continuity of the self – she also points out what she sees as an
important difference between his experiences and her own. Because
eternal and cyclical nature functions as a kind of storage site for his
memories, Marcel is assured a permanence of self that the narrator of *La
honte*, with her mnemonic reliance on objects of fad, is not. When these
ephemeral objects disappear, she implies, they take with them her memories of her past selves. Yet hit pop songs are not as subject to collective
oblivion as she suggests, and when she hears one in a supermarket,
although it does not generate, like the Hawthorn bush, thousands of
pages of detailed reminiscences, it does arouse in her emotions and
desires that she recognizes as identical to those she felt when listening to
the song as a child. Songs therefore *do* provide her with proof, however
fugitive, of what *La recherche*'s narrator calls a 'moi permanent, qui se prolonge pendant toute la durée de notre vie' (a permanent self, which
endures throughout our life).[43]

The narrator of *Journal du dehors* comes to this conclusion about the
emotive power of music when she compares the emotions she experiences while listening to pop songs from her past to those she feels while
rereading books from that same past:

À l'hypermarché Leclerc, au milieu des courses, j'entends 'Voyage.'[44] Je me
demande si mon émotion, mon plaisir, cette angoisse que la chanson

finisse, ont quelque chose de commun avec l'impression violente que m'ont faite des livres. L'émotion provoquée par la chanson de Desireless est aiguë, presque douloureuse, une insatisfaction que la répétition ne comble pas [...] Il y a plus de délivrance dans un livre, d'échappée, de résolution du désir. On ne sort pas du désir dans la chanson (où les paroles comptent très peu, seule la mélodie).

While shopping at the supermarket Leclerc, I hear 'Voyage.' I wonder if the emotion and the pleasure I experience, as well as the feeling of panic that the song will end, have anything to do with the violent impression left by certain books, such as *Bella estate* by Pavese, or Faulkner's *Sanctuary*. The feelings aroused by Desireless's song are intense, almost painful, leading to a form of frustration which does not fade with repetition ... A book offers more deliverance, more escape, more fulfillment of desire. In songs one remains locked in desire. (The lyrics are not that important, only the melody matters).[45]

Books provide *Journal*'s narrator with a resolution of desire that songs do not (how ironic that a song which incites yet refuses to satiate desire is sung by an artist named Desireless!). Yet she goes on to say that, precisely because of this resolution of desire, books do not have the same mnemonic effects as songs. In songs, there are

ni lieux, ni scènes, ni personnes, rien que soi-même et son désir. Pourtant, c'est cette brutalité et cette pauvreté qui me permettent, peut-être, de faire affluer toute une période de ma vie et la fille que j'étais en entendant, trente ans après, 'I'm just another dancing partner'.[46] Alors que la richesse et la beauté du *Bel été*, de la *Recherche du temps perdu*, relus deux trois fois, ne me redonnent jamais ma vie.

no places, no scenes, no characters, only oneself and one's longing. Yet the very starkness and paucity of music allow me to recall a whole episode of my life and the girl I used to be when I listen to 'I'm Just Another Dancing Partner' thirty years later. Whereas the beauty and fullness of *Bella Estate* and *A la recherche du temps perdu*, which I have reread two or three times, can never give me back my life. (62–3; 55)

Appropriately enough, considering this reference to *La recherche*, listening to a song from her past affords *Journal*'s narrator a true Proustian moment, a moment in which involuntary memory grants her access to one of her past selves.[47] Proust's involuntary memory indeed shares qualities with what I have been referring to in this study as sense memory.[48] Involuntary memory is aroused by sensory stimuli, such as the taste of the madeleine, the feel of the uneven paving stone, the sound of the spoon against a plate. A present stimulus similar to a past one calls forth memories of the events and emotions – for Proust's narrator, generally felicitous rather than traumatic emotions – associated with that past sensation. For *Journal*'s narrator, the catalyst for this resurgence is neither high literature (like *La recherche* itself) nor classical music (like Vinteuil's sonata for Swann). Rather, it is a pop song heard in a *hypermarché*. Both of these phenomena are products of the only kind of culture – popular culture – the narrator knew as a girl. The pop song in *Journal* evokes for that text's narrator no *specific* memory – no precise place, event, or person ('ni lieux, ni scènes, ni personnes') – but it does elicit, like the madeleine, emotion. The emotion the song evokes is desire – not a particular desire (for a particular man or object) but rather, to think in Proustian terms, an 'essential' desire. This is an enduring, overarching desire that has accompanied the narrator throughout the permutations of all her successive selves and that she is able to recognize instantly, at any time and in any place, as uniquely her own.

The failure of books, as well as of the lyrics of songs (unlike their melodies), to 'give back' to *Journal*'s narrator her life points in part to the limitations inherent in the project of attempting to recapture the past through words. Yet this failure is doubtless also due to the *kinds* of books – 'high' literature, products of *la classe dominante* – that she cites. On this subject, the narrator of *La place* remarks in turn, 'Quand je lis Proust ou Mauriac, je ne crois pas qu'ils évoquent le temps où mon père était enfant. Son cadre à lui c'est le Moyen Âge' (When I read Proust or Mauriac, I cannot believe that the time period evoked in these books is the same one during which my father was a child. In his milieu, it was more like the Middle Ages).[49] There are no teacakes, opera outings, or indoor toilets in her father's story. In yet another reference to Proust, *La place*'s narrator makes mention of the malapropisms of Marcel's servant Françoise, to which Duras makes indirect reference in her story 'Madame Dodin,' discussed in chapter 1.[50] Like the narrator of 'Madame Dodin,' the narrator of *La place* concludes that while the literary portrayal of such a *rustre* may arouse indulgence and nostalgia in the reader, the real thing provokes only distaste: 'Proust relevait avec ravissement les incorrections et les mots anciens de Françoise. Seule l'esthétique lui importe' – and not the *sociologique*, as for Ernaux's narrators – 'parce que Françoise est sa bonne et non sa mère' (Proust took delight in pointing out the mistakes and the old-fashioned words used by Françoise. His concern, however, was purely aesthetic, because Françoise was not his mother but his maid).[51] Françoise's grammatical and lexical errors are only charming, she concludes, to those who have never had to make a conscious effort to avoid such linguistic faux pas themselves. So while, finally, Ernaux's narrators participate like Proust's in a search for lost selves, and while, as for him, certain places, objects, and sensations help her recapture them by triggering involuntary memory, these places, objects, and sensations belong to a social milieu that – aside from the ironic portrayal of servants there – is unrepresented in Proust's novel.[52]

This dissociation of the self textualized in *La honte* is accompanied by another quintessentially Proustian dissociation: that of linear time. Throughout *La honte*, the narrator speaks of her life as if it were divided into periods ('temps'), to which she gives specific names. Referring to her parents, she remarks, 'Quand il leur arrivait de montrer qu'ils avaient de l'affection l'un pour l'autre, par un sourire ou un rire complices, une plaisanterie, je croyais être revenue *au temps d'avant la scène*' (When they did show signs of affection for each other – joking, sharing a laugh or a smile – I imagined I had gone back to *the time before that scene*) (emphasis mine).[53] On the other hand, the second photo she studies, an image of her father and herself on a pilgrimage to Lourdes in August 1952, inaugurates, she writes, 'le temps où je ne cesserai plus d'avoir honte' (the time/era during which I would never cease to feel ashamed) (25; 22). The scene has thus irrevocably cleaved her life into two periods, which have since remained inassimilable.

Similarly, the narrators of several of Ernaux's other texts divide their lives into temporal periods, each marked by a particular emotional state and each disconnected from the others. The narrator of *Passion simple* refers to the period of her obsession as 'le temps de la passion' (the time of passion).[54] She realizes she is no longer living in this period when 'tout cela [her affair] commence à m'être aussi étranger que s'il s'agissait d'une autre femme' (all this is beginning to seem as strange to me as if it concerned another woman) (76; 63). For her part, the narrator of *Une femme* evokes 'le temps où [ma mère] vivait encore' (the time when [my mother] was still alive), implicitly opposing this period to the period after her mother's death, a time during which she herself no longer feels alive and in which all she can do is mourn and relive the 'time of her mother' through its narration.[55] Although these narrators are aware of and can describe the emotional states corresponding to each of these different 'times,' they no longer live or feel them, for these periods are, once again, as if sealed away in 'mille vases clos.'

Time in *La honte* is also divided in more complicated ways than through simple slashes on a timeline. When describing her Catholic school years, the narrator speaks of 'le temps scolaire' (school time).[56] This designation does not refer to the period of years she spent going to school, but rather to the time she spent each day at the private, bourgeois school she attended. She opposes this time to the radically different time she spent during this same period at home with her working-class family and neighbours. 'Le temps' in 'le temps scolaire' could thus be read as something like 'atmosphere' or 'milieu.' It is as much spatial as temporal, signifying a distinctive 'place-time' in which certain kinds of clothing, behaviors, beliefs, preferences, and language were acceptable and others were clearly not. This radical break between the two *temps* of school and home is a guiding problematic in much of Ernaux's work.

In *La honte*, the narrator goes on to say that this 'temps scolaire' is itself 'inscrit dans un autre temps, celui du missel et de l'évangile' (is embedded within another time, that of the missal and the gospel) (78; 67). This latter *temps* does not refer to a discrete section of a timeline either, but rather to an ahistorical, cyclical time containing within it '[le] temps de l'Avent, de Noël ... du Carême ... de Pâques ... D'année en année, chaque jour, l'école privée nous fait revivre la même histoire' (the time of Advent, Christmas ... Lent ... Easter ... Day after day, year after year, the private school makes us relive the same story over and over again) (78–9; 67). These are times that, unlike 'le temps de la passion' for the narrator of *Passion simple*, are never lost but continually return and reinsert themselves into the present. The missal the girl in the photo holds and that the narrator still owns is dated 1951 to 1968 and thus covers a delimited period of time. Yet these are 'dates étranges, tant le livre est *hors du temps*' (strange dates, since the book is so *immune to time*) (28; 25 – emphasis mine). The temporal period of the narrator's late childhood and adolescence – included within the dates of the missal – was a period when religion regulated or at least cast a shadow over the narrator's every thought and action. Because of the scene in 1952 in particular, this period seems to her narrator to have taken on the timelessness of the missal ('un livre [...] hors du temps') that now serves as a sign for it. The period of her childhood and adolescence seems itself 'hors du temps': 'Je ne peux énoncer et décrire les règles de cet univers qu'au présent, comme si elles continuaient d'être aussi immuables qu'elles l'étaient pour moi à douze ans' (I can only list and describe the rules of this universe in the present tense, as if they were still as immutable today as they were for me when I was twelve) (79; 68). As Lawrence Langer writes in reference to the Holocaust, trauma 'stops the chronological clock and fixes the moment permanently in memory and imagination, immune to the vicissitudes of time.'[57] Indeed, the narrator of *La honte* does describe the scene as 'figée depuis des années' (frozen for all these years).[58] Yet it is not just the particular moment of the scene, but also the broader *temps* (in the sense of atmosphere or milieu as well as period) in which it occurred that seems to have become timeless. Her memories of this *temps* remain unchanged and undampened by the passage of linear time, as if they were not memories at all but fresh perceptions of a constantly current and recurring event. Resistant to insertion at a fixed place along the narrator's personal timeline, this *temps* slides alongside it, always catching up with the present and continuing to affect (always negatively, it would seem) the narrator's interpretation of current experiences. The effect of the scene's perpetual presentness, while still strong enough in Ernaux's fifties to incite her finally to write about it, was especially powerful throughout the rest of her adolescence: 'Après, ce dimanche-là s'est interposé entre moi et tout ce que je vivais comme un filtre. Je jouais, je lisais, j'agissais comme d'habitude mais je n'étais dans rien. Tout était devenu artificiel' (From then on, that Sunday was like a filter that came between me and everything I did. I would play, I would read, I would behave normally, but somehow I wasn't there) (18; 17). The filter of which she speaks is made up of her memories of the scene, which cannot be stored with other memories. They seem therefore to float somewhere in her brain, acting as a filter between perception and cognition – between her apprehension of present events and her interpretation of them. These kinds of homeless memories, as van der Hart and van der Kolk point out, are often revived in situations that are similar in some way to the situation in which the trauma originally occurred, and they often determine the subject's interpretation of these present situations, however benign they may be in reality.[59] For a long time after the scene, the narrator says, she was hypersensitive to environmental stimuli resembling those she had perceived during it. Instead of evoking desire or pleasure, certain popular songs from that period incited anxiety:

> A cette époque passait souvent à la radio une chanson bizarre qui évoquait et mimait une bagarre surgissant brusquement dans un saloon: il y avait une période de silence, où une voix chuchotait juste 'on entendrait une

mouche voler' puis une explosion de cris, de phrases confuses. À chaque fois, j'étais saisie d'angoisse.

Around that time a strange song often played on the radio, mimicking a fight that suddenly breaks out in a saloon; there was a pause, a voice whispered, 'you could have heard a pin drop,' followed by a cacophony of shouts and jumbled sentences. Every time I heard it I was seized with panic.[60]

The girl also became highly conscious of the slightest disagreement between her parents, fearing that what had always been, up to the moment of the scene, insignificant quibbles would escalate into a second scene, perhaps with more serious consequences than the first (19; 17–18). Years later, the experience continues to affect the way the adult narrator perceives her past. The town of her childhood, 'Y.,' is for her 'le lieu d'origine sans nom où, quand j'y retourne, je suis aussitôt saisie par une torpeur qui m'ôte toute pensée, presque tout souvenir précis, comme s'il allait m'engloutir de nouveau' (the nameless place of origin: as soon as I go back, I succumb to a state of lethargy that prevents me from thinking or even remembering, as if the place were going to swallow me up once again) (43–4; 38). Thoughts and words are swept away in this place, and, to borrow Charlotte Delbo's vocabulary, intellectual memory ('tout souvenir précis') is supplanted by sense memory, whose domain is the body and not the mind. While in 'Y.,' the narrator changes from a being who thinks, analyses, and speaks (and who therefore can narrate) to one who can do nothing but feel; and what she feels, primarily, is paralysis, like that which the girl experienced during the scene.

In addition to those of self and of time, the narrator complains of living yet a third kind of dissociation: that of self from others. She says that the text we are reading is her first attempt at a written account of the scene; but then she adds that she had previously tried to communicate it orally: 'À quelques hommes, plus tard, j'ai dit: "Mon père a voulu tuer ma mère quand j'allais avoir douze ans." Avoir envie de dire cette phrase signifiait que je les avais dans la peau. Tous se sont tus après l'avoir entendue. Je voyais que j'avais commis une faute, qu'ils ne pouvaient recevoir cette chose-là' (Later on, I would say to certain men: 'My father tried to kill my mother just before I turned twelve.' The fact that I wanted to tell them this meant that I was crazy about them. All were quiet after hearing the sentence. I realized I had made a mistake, that they were not able to accept such a thing) (16; 15). Attempts to verbalize her experience had thus proved fruitless, their only effect being to aggravate the solitude and mutism in which the scene's memory had left her. 'Cela ne pouvait se dire à personne, dans aucun des deux mondes qui étaient les miens' (I couldn't tell it to anyone, not in either of the two worlds in which I lived) (108; 91), that is, neither in the working-class world of her parents, where the scene was simply 'forgotten,' nor in the narrator's adoptive, bourgeois world, where such behaviour was simply too sordid to discuss. The scene is not only difficult to speak, then, but also, as the men's reaction attests, difficult to hear. 'Le pire dans la honte,' the narrator remarks, 'c'est qu'on croit être seul à la ressentir' (The worst thing about shame is that we believe we are the only ones to experience it) (109; 92), and this feeling of isolation is indeed another common effect of trauma. The conversion of lived experience into intellectual or *narrative* memory not only serves the individual's need for clarity and order, but 'fundamentally serves a social function' as well.[61] The communication of narrative memory has the potential to bring teller and listener together and reinforce their sense of mutual understanding and commonalty. Traumatic memory, in contrast, 'has no social component; it is not addressed to anybody, the patient does not respond to anybody; it is a solitary activity.'[62] The events it has recorded are most often *un*common experiences, experiences that most potential listeners do not share. Were the rememberer to try to communicate them, she would most likely find her listener, as *La honte*'s narrator indeed does, at a loss.

Many, then, are the difficulties this narrator encounters in attempting to carry out her narrative project. Why, then, does she persist? In *Une femme*, that text's narrator makes a revealing comment about the impetus behind her own narrative drive: 'Je sais que je ne peux pas vivre sans *unir par l'écriture* la femme démente qu[e ma mère] est devenue, à celle forte et lumineuse qu'elle avait été' (I know that I can't live without *reuniting through writing* the demented woman [my mother] became with the strong and radiant woman she had once been) (emphasis mine).[63] 'Unir par l'écriture' (to unite through writing) the disparate images she has of her mother (her mother's different 'selves' as she sees them) is thus an essential goal of her narrative. At the end of her text, she claims success: 'Maintenant, tout est lié' (Now, everything is linked/tied together) (103; 89). Yet this assertion seems paradoxical when the reader notes that the sentence that expresses it is broken off from the rest of the text. The entire text, moreover, is disjointed, riddled throughout with blank spaces of varying sizes. Like all of Ernaux's later texts, as noted, *Une femme* is not a linear, teleological narrative but a collection of impressions – an 'inventory of signs' as *Passion simple*'s narrator puts it – of the particular reality being explored.[64] *Une femme*'s narrator's claim that she has been able to link through this highly fragmentary text 'everything' – presumably every 'significant' element of her mother's story, all the different traits that made her who she was – is obviously open to question. It seems doubly so in light of Ernaux's later production of a second text about her mother and her disease (*Je ne suis pas sortie de ma nuit [I Remain in Darkness]*),[65] which suggests that she later concluded that the first text had in fact not told the 'whole' story. Presumably the drive to link disparate memories and images of her mother had not been satisfied.[66] While the project of *Une femme*'s narrator is to unite various images of her mother into a coherent portrait that would reveal her mother's essence or reality, the narrative concerns not just the mother, for the daughter inevitably figures in such a portrait as well: 'C'est [ma mère], et ses paroles, ses mains, ses gestes, sa manière de rire et de marcher, qui unissaient la femme que je suis à l'enfant que j'ai été' (It was [my mother], and her words, her hands, her gestures, her manner of laughing and walking, that linked the woman I am with the child I once was).[67] While she lived, the mother was the seemingly unchanging *point de repère* for all the daughter's successive selves (carefree child, shame-filled adolescent, conflicted student, 'bourgeois' wife and mother, successful writer, and so on). Upon her mother's death, *Une femme*'s narrator writes, 'j'ai perdu le dernier lien avec le monde dont je suis issue' (I lost the last link with the world from which I came) (106; 92), the working-class world she had abandoned and of which almost no trace – aside from her memories – remains in her present life.

This same drive to *link* lies behind the narration of *La honte* as well, and it also has several facets. The first, already discussed, is a Proustian desire to unseal the 'vases' that contain the narrator's past selves and to lend them coherence. The second, touched upon in the discussion above of the narrator's attempts to tell others about the scene, is a wish to destroy the barriers that her traumatic memories and the shame they generate have raised between herself and others. The isolation against which *La honte*'s narrator struggles, provoked by both her shame and her social displacement, looms large in almost all of Ernaux's texts. The narrator of *Une femme*, for example, wants to translate her mother's life into text – to bring her mother with her into the world of the intellect to which she herself had gained access – in order to feel 'moins seule et factice' (less alone and artificial) in this still foreign world.[68] The narrator of *Passion simple* carries on an intimate relationship with a man, but lives her passion alone. Perhaps because her lover is literally a foreigner, she is cognizant throughout the affair of what she maintains most women only discover at the end – that 'l'homme qu'on aime est un étranger' (the man we love is a stranger) – and she is certain that her lover neither shares her obsession nor is even aware of it ('lui-même aurait été stupéfait d'apprendre qu'il ne quittait pas ma tête du matin au soir' [he himself would have been stupefied to learn that I thought about him day and night]).[69] She longs to tell someone about her passion, but fears eliciting from her interlocutor only embarrassed silence, as the woman next to her at the hairdresser's does when she announces that 'on [la] soigne pour les nerfs' (she is being treated for her nerves), or as *La honte*'s narrator does when she tries to tell her lovers about the scene.[70] In the end it is in written rather than oral discourse – in a deferred but ultimately much more far-reaching way – that she finally reveals her passion and manages, she hopes, to link herself to others: 'Je me demande si je n'écris pas pour savoir si les autres n'ont pas fait ou ressenti des choses identiques, sinon, pour qu'ils trouvent normal de les ressentir' (I wonder if I'm not writing in order to find out if others have done or felt the same things, or at least think it's normal to feel them).[71] Writing seems to allow her to communicate what she had not been able to without the physical intermediaries of paper and pen, or without the comforting delay between narration and reception that writing entails. Writing has helped her discover, in unexpected ways, a connection between herself and others, a connection that had been lacking between her and her lover. It has done so by making her acutely aware of her own fragile, even pathetic, humanity: 'J'ai découvert de quoi on peut être capable, autant dire de tout. Désirs sublimes ou mortels, absence de dignité, croyances et conduites que je trouvais insensées chez les autres tant que je n'y avais pas moi-même recours. À son insu,' she says of her oblivious lover, 'il m'a *reliée* davantage au monde' (I learned what one is capable of – that is, everything: sublime or deadly desires, lack of dignity, attitudes and beliefs I had found absurd in others until I myself turned to them. Without knowing it, he *reconnected* me to the world) (emphasis mine).[72]

The narrator of *La honte* also expresses her need to open herself to others, like most of Ernaux's narrators, by creating a narrative of *exposure*. This need can be understood as a consequence of the degree to which, during her childhood, everything – her body, possessions, beliefs, desires, and certainly her shame – was to be kept hidden. In the third section of *La honte* (71–107; 69–90), for example, the narrator provides a detailed description of the stifling architecture and atmosphere of the private, all-girls Catholic school she attended as a child: 'La grande bâtisse de brique rouge foncé du pensionnat occupait tout un côté d'une rue silencieuse et sombre du centre d'Y. [...] Aucune fenêtre au rez-de-chaussée,' just 'quelques ouvertures rondes haut situées pour le jour et deux portes toujours closes' (The large building in dark red brick that was the boarding school took up the whole side of a quiet, somber street in the center of Y. ... No windows on the first floor, only a few circular openings high up to let in the daylight and two doors, always closed).[73] The school was as if hermetically sealed so as to 'protect' its pupils from the gaze of (especially male) outsiders. 'Les seuls hommes qui avaient le droit de pénétrer ordinairement et de circuler dans l'école privée,' the narrator pointedly notes, 'étaient les prêtres et le jardinier, cantonné dans les caves ou dans le jardin' (Ordinarily the only men who could penetrate and circulate within the private school were the priests and the gardener, who were confined to the cellars and the grounds) (74; 63). 'À la différence de l'école publique, plus décentrée, où on voyait jouer les élèves dans une immense cour, derrière les grilles, rien du pensionnat n'était visible du dehors' (Unlike the public school on the outskirts of town, where children could be seen playing in huge courtyards behind closed gates, nothing that went on in the private school was visible from outside) (72; 62). Yet it was not only the inward but also the *outward* gaze that the school's high walls were built to obstruct: 'Il était interdit de regarder depuis n'importe quelle fenêtre dans la rue' (It was forbidden to look out onto the street from any window), 'la rue' (the street) signifying all that was public, profane, and therefore prohibited (72; 62). Although as a girl she was constantly encircled by classmates and teachers inside these walls, the narrator states that she had no friends there and felt no sense of community (98; 83). Her social status (inferior to that of most of the other pupils), along with her memories of the scene (which painfully confirmed this inferiority), prevented her from feeling at home during this first stage – the first of many – of a journey that would definitively separate her from her place of origin.

Yet just as the narrator's existence at school was to be contained and hidden from others, as if, very literally, in one of Proust's 'mille vases clos,' so was her life at home, which was paradoxically much more public than her life at school. At home the family was perpetually surrounded by the customers of her parents' *café-épicerie* and subject to an 'exposition continuelle qui oblige à offrir une conduite respectable (ne pas s'injurier, dire des gros mots, du mal d'autrui), à ne manifester aucune émotion, colère ou chagrin, à dissimuler tout ce qui pourrait être objet d'envie, de curiosité, ou *rapporté* (a constant exposure that obliged us to display respectable behaviour [no insults, no rude words, no gossip], to contain our emotions, whether anger or sadness, and to hide anything that might excite envy or curiosity, anything likely to be *talked about*) (67; 56 – Ernaux's emphasis). The golden rule of social intercourse was to discover as much as possible about others' lives while revealing as little as possible of one's own (62; 52). At home, then, the young girl had to construct around herself an emotional and behavioural facade every bit as impenetrable as the brick and mortar of her school building.

In a 1988 interview, Ernaux says that one of the most valuable aspects of writing for her is its 'fonction de dénonciation' (denunciatory function), in particular its potential to denounce social injustice.[74] Related to this verbal function is the visual one I have been exploring: writing's potential to *expose*, to open what is closed and to make visible what is hidden. Writing can render the private public, as Ernaux's work certainly illustrates. 'Associer pour toujours le mot *privé* au manque et à la peur, la fermeture,' *La honte*'s narrator remarks, 'Même dans *vie privée*. Écrire est une chose publique' (I will always associate the word 'private' with deprivation, fear, and lack of openness. Even in the expression 'private life.' Writing is something public) (Ernaux's emphasis).[75] Through her public (to be published) narrative, she attempts to dismantle the walls of this very private school so that her reader may join her in this *lieu sacré*, or at least in her memories of it.

Related to these first two manifestations of the narrator of *La honte*'s drive to *link* – her struggles first to unite her disparate selves into a coherent whole, and second to connect herself to others – is yet a third and even more significant one: her efforts to link her personal history – that which she hopes to reconstruct through her narrative – to collective history. To do this, she will undertake the kind of 'ethnobiography' that the narrators of *La place* and *Une femme* construct.[76] To create their stories of the mother and father, these narrators explore not just their personal memories of them but also the social, economic, and historical forces that shaped their lives. *Une femme*, Laurence Mall suggests, has '[une] nature délibérément hybride [qui] doit être rapportée à la forte structure dichotomique du projet d'Ernaux, où le personnel et l'objectivité, l'affectif et le politique, le singulier et la généralité, l'individuel et le social, le privé et le public sont sans cesse contrastés et fondus' (a deliberately hybrid nature [that] derives from the dichotomous structure of Ernaux's project, in which the personal and the objective, the affective and the political, the singular and the general, the individual and the social, the private and the public are constantly contrasted and confounded).[77] *Une femme*'s narrator makes a sometimes painful effort to see her mother both as a unique individual and as a product (and to some extent victim) of historical circumstances. Both *Une femme* and *La place* offer complex portraits of their subjects, but also pointed critiques of the relations of power that made them permanent members of *la classe dominée* (the dominated class).

The objectives and methods of *La honte*'s narrator will be much the same; the subject of her text, however, will be herself rather than her parents ('être en somme ethnologue de moi-même' [to carry out in short an ethnological study of myself]).[78] In her self-portrait, this narrator also attempts to close the gap between the terms of the binary oppositions Mall cites above. In order to link her personal experience with a collective one, she visits the city archives in Rouen to study the 1952 editions of a daily newspaper (*Paris-Normandie*) that her parents read when she was young. She begins with January: 'Je voulais retarder le moment d'arriver au 15 juin, me remettre dans la succession innocente des jours qui était la mienne avant cette date' (I wanted to delay the moment when I would reach June 15, to place myself back in the innocent succession of days I had known before that date) (32; 28). Yet finding a familiar world within this text proves more difficult than she had anticipated:

> Je connaissais la plupart des événements évoqués, la guerre d'Indochine, de Corée, les émeutes d'Orléansville, le plan Pinay, mais je ne les aurais pas situés spécialement en 52, les ayant sans doute mémorisés dans une période ultérieure de ma vie. Je ne pouvais relier 'Six bicyclettes à plastic font explosion à Saïgon' et 'Duclos est écroué à Fresnes pour atteinte à la sûreté de l'État' à aucune image de moi en 52 [...] Je ne reconnaissais rien. C'était comme si je n'avais pas déjà vécu en ce temps-là.

> I knew of most of the events mentioned, the war in Indochina, the Korean War, the riots at Orléansville, the Pinay Plan, but I would not have necessarily situated them in 1952, having doubtless memorized them at a later time in my life. I couldn't connect 'Six bicycles loaded with plastic explosives blow up in Saigon' or 'Jacques Duclos imprisoned at Fresnes and indicted on charges of plotting against security of the state' with the images I had of myself in 1952 ... I recognized nothing. It was if I hadn't lived at that time. (32–3; 28)[79]

To her disappointment, the narrator is unable to draw any connection whatsoever ('Je ne pouvais *relier* [...]') between these headlines and her own memories. She *knows* ('Je connaissais') the historical events cited in the newspaper, but she *recognizes* none of them ('Je ne reconnaissais rien'). That is to say, she knows the events through intellectual memory – through having learned and memorized them from books – but she cannot connect them to personal experience. One of the definitions of 'reconnaître' is indeed 'saisir (un objet) par la pensée, *en reliant entre elles des images, des perceptions*' (to grasp [an object] through thought, *by linking together images and perceptions*) (emphasis mine).[80] The words 'perception' and 'image' suggest that 'reconnaître' involves the senses as well as the intellect; one meaning of 'reconnaître' would thus be to sense or to feel again what one once sensed or felt in the past. The events described in the newspaper were never a part of the girl's perceptual experience, and therefore they evoke no sense memories. They cannot then help her recapture the past that she herself lived.

Still, what troubles the narrator in conducting her research is less the unfamiliarity of the events reported in this newspaper than the absence of a single, all-too familiar one. After reading the edition of 15 June, 'Je n'ai pas eu envie,' she says,

de poursuivre plus avant la lecture des journaux. En descendant les escaliers des Archives, je me suis rendu compte que j'étais venue là comme si j'allais trouver la scène dans le journal de 52 [...] Aucun des milliards de faits qui s'étaient produits dans le monde ce dimanche-là ne pourrait être placé à côté de la scène sans me remplir de stupeur. Elle seule a été réelle.

I didn't feel like reading any further. Walking downstairs, I realized that I had gone to the archives thinking I might actually find some record of what had happened to me in the 1952 newspaper ... I couldn't place any of the billions of events that had happened somewhere in the world that Sunday afternoon alongside the scene without feeling stupefied. Only the scene I had witnessed was real to me. (35–6; 30–1)

It was to verify somehow the truth of her troubling memories, the narrator realizes, that she had consulted this historical record. 'Sur les différences entre les époques,' she learns, however, 'les journaux ne fournissent que des signes collectifs' (When it comes to illustrating social change, newspapers can only provide collective signs) (37; 31), signs whose reality, though verified in the newspaper, pales in comparison to the vividness of her memories of the scene. The 'objective' reality in which she had tried to anchor her subjective experience had curiously proved to be made of much less solid material than the latter.

The newspaper accounts of these contemporary events, which were as foreign to the girl as if they had happened in another country or in the Middle Ages, cannot, then, help the narrator 'recognize' herself in the photos of her. At the end of the first section of *La honte*, she therefore redefines her project: 'Pour atteindre ma réalité d'alors, je n'ai pas d'autre moyen sûr que de rechercher les lois et les rites, les croyances, et les valeurs qui définissaient les milieux, l'école, la famille, la province, où j'étais prise et qui dirigeaient, sans que j'en perçoive les contradictions, ma vie' (To convey what my life was like at that time, the only reliable method I have is to explore the laws, rites, beliefs and references that defined the circles in which I was caught up – school, family, small-town life – and which governed my existence, without my even noticing its contradictions) (37; 32). She will conduct this 'research' by consulting not newspapers and history books, but the archives of her own mind. Moreover, the process by which she will begin to recognize her past will be not reading, but *writing*.

In a 1995 interview, Ernaux states that her texts 'sont une recherche sur la réalité' (are an inquiry into reality).[81] This last word appears repeatedly throughout her own œuvre and in numerous other interviews. Her texts do not themselves constitute the reality she is seeking, she says elsewhere, for 'le réel, c'est quelque chose qui est sans mot' (the real is something without words).[82] The epigraph to *La honte*, a translation of a quote from Paul Auster's *The Invention of Solitude*, confirms this contention: 'Language is not truth. It is the way we exist in the world.'[83] This epigraph serves as a *caveat lector*, a warning to the reader who places too much faith in the author's ability to recreate reality through words. Consistent with Ernaux's insistence that the reality she seeks to examine in her texts lies outside those texts is her preoccupation with the *material*. In *La honte*, for example, the narrator begins the search for her past self, the girl of 1952, by drawing up a list of '[les] traces matérielles de cette année-là' (the material traces of that year),[84] personal possessions, like the missal, that she still owns as an adult.[85] Lyn Thomas argues that 'unlike great writers of the French canon such as Marcel Proust, for whom the discovery of truth through writing involved a turning inwards, a focusing on the inner life, the truth sought by Ernaux is primarily social,' and indeed the buildings, food, clothing, household objects, and other exterior *things* that Ernaux minutely describes in her work represent for her wordless signs of social class.[86] The problem for the writer, of course, is that material objects can only appear in literary texts in the form of the words that signify them. Yet even though words cannot replace the real, the author's lexical choices, Ernaux insists, can determine how accurately or truthfully the text represents it: 'Il faut que les mots soient collés au plus près du réel. Il y a tout de même des mots qui coïncident plus que d'autres avec le réel' (Words have to stick as closely as possible to the real. There are, after all, words that coincide better than others with the real).[87] For Ernaux, these words are neither poetic nor abstract; they are primarily the everyday words used by the people represented in her texts to designate objects and ideas common to their milieu.

Although for Ernaux, once again, the words of a text cannot replace or reproduce the realities to which they refer, some words, the narrator of *La honte* suggests, *function themselves as objects*. Such words seem to share the same nature as the objects, events, and emotions she must work to recall and retrieve ('retrouver') from her past. They are not the kind of words the narrator uses in the present to represent the past, but words that were themselves elements of or 'objects' within the past she is examining. One of her strategies in conducting her investigation into the past is the following:

> Mettre au jour les langages qui me constituaient, les mots de la religion, ceux de mes parents liés aux gestes et aux choses, des romans que je lisais dans *Le Petit écho de la mode* ou dans *Les Veillées des chaumières*.[88] Me servir de ces mots, dont certains exercent encore sur moi leur pesanteur, pour décomposer et remonter, autour de la scène du dimanche de juin, le texte du monde où j'ai eu douze ans et cru devenir folle.

> Bring to light the languages I was made of, the words of religion, those of my parents that were linked to gestures and things, those of the novels I read in *Le Petit écho de la mode* and *Les Veillées des chaumières*. Use those words, some of which I still find oppressive, to take apart and reassemble, around that Sunday in June, the text of the world when I turned twelve and thought I was going mad.[89]

These words seem to the narrator to be ontologically indistinguishable from the gestures and things to which they are 'liés.' Their 'pesanteur' underscores their materiality, as does their function here as metaphorical building blocks that the narrator uses to take apart and put back together ('décomposer et remonter') her text. The reality for which *La honte*'s narrator searches, then, is not entirely 'sans mots,' in that words constitute a concrete part of that reality.

The narrator soon discovers, however, that she cannot realize her narrative project using such object-words alone. Although they are part of the real she is seeking, they are

> opaques, des pierres impossibles à bouger. Dépourvus d'image précise. Dépourvus de sens même, celui que pourrait me fournir un dictionnaire. Sans transcendance ni rêve autour: comme de la matière. Des mots d'usage indissolublement unis aux choses et aux gens de mon enfance, que je ne peux pas faire jouer.

> opaque, stones too heavy to move. Devoid of any precise image. Devoid of meaning even, the kind of meaning a dictionary could provide. There is no transcendance, no dreaming with these words: they are like matter. Familiar words inextricably linked to people and things from my childhood, words I can't budge. (69; 58)

As things themselves ('des pierres [...] comme de la matière'), these words, while signifiers of social class, no longer function for her as *linguistic* signifiers. That is, they do not refer to other signifiers, and they therefore put an abrupt end to Derrida's eternal chain. Like the objects that the narrator lists as material proof of her past ('les traces matérielles'), these words cannot 'speak for themselves,' so to speak. The narrator must then explicate them for the reader, using not an abstract or lyrical language, but an analytical language that is nevertheless foreign to the milieu evoked in the narrative. 'Il me semble,' she reflects, 'que je cherche toujours à écrire dans cette langue matérielle d'alors et non avec des mots et une syntaxe qui ne me sont pas venus, qui ne me seraient pas venus alors' (It seems to me that I'm always trying to write in that material language of my past, and not with a vocabulary and syntax I didn't possess, that I wouldn't have come up with, at that time) (69; 58).

Siobhán McIlvanney, however, demonstrates that Ernaux does not always follow her own narrative precepts: 'Une tension subsiste chez Annie Ernaux entre son désir de rester fidèle à ses origines en employant les mots de sa classe et de sa famille et la manière consciente et consciencieuse avec laquelle elle entreprend la transcription de ce langage' (A tension persists in Ernaux's writing between her desire to remain faithful to her origins by using the words of her social class and family, and the conscious and conscientious way in which she undertakes the transcription of that language).[90] For one thing, objects and people are not presented in her texts as if by a camera, with no narrative commentary, in the style of Hemingway or Robbe-Grillet in certain of their texts. Ernaux holds that the 'reality' of an event or period cannot be captured solely by 'objective' description and a simple notation of the 'facts' (if such things were even possible). Rather, what she has determined she must do to try to grasp the reality of an event or period is submit its traces to a narrative examination, which she carries out with the various instruments – linguistic, intellectual, experiential, or other – she has acquired since it occurred. An understanding of the reality of the scene in *La honte* (or its 'truth,' a word that Ernaux often uses in conjunction with 'reality' and that seems to mean for her the 'true meaning' of a reality, would thus demand not just a knowledge of the sequence of events but also a grasp of the meanings, causes, and effects of these events.[91] The most salient of these effects is the eleven-year-old's shame, which *La honte*'s narrator now knows was not a natural and inevitable response to the sudden manifestation of an intrinsic defect within her family, but rather a response conditioned by living in a social system that designates, according to the relations of power in place, certain behaviours as shameful. In order to try to attain such truths, Ernaux's narrators narrate in a self-conscious manner, frequently questioning, testing, and adjusting their narrative procedures. In *La honte*, in the end, it is through a synthesis of both the narrator's and the girl's understandings and vocabularies that the narrator is able to approach, although perhaps not attain, the truth of the scene and of the period of her life in which it occurred. I add this caution, because in *L'écriture comme un couteau* Ernaux gives her own 'definition' of the word 'vérité' (truth), a definition that does not really tell us what the word means to her, but that does inform us of her feelings about the possibility of arriving at truth, through narrative or other means: 'Pour moi, la vérité est simplement le nom donné à ce qu'on cherche et qui se dérobe sans cesse' (For me, truth is simply the name we give to that which we seek and which always eludes us).[92] The narrative search for truth, then, is in some sense an exercise in frustration.

I have argued that in *La honte*, the narrator's memories of the scene resist integration into a coherent narrative. These memories, which hold for the most part images, sensations, and emotions, do not readily lend themselves to verbalization, and what words the narrator does find to communicate them do not always render them comprehensible to her. Yet the resistance of the memories themselves to integration is not the only resistance perceptible in the text. As noted above, one of the narrator's goals is to comprehend the scene by seeing it, as well as the 'authors' of it, her parents, as inevitable products of certain social, economic, historical, and linguistic laws: 'Je vise peut-être à dissoudre la scène indicible de mes douze ans dans la généralité des lois et du langage' (My aim is perhaps to dissolve the unspeakable scene of my twelfth year in the general social laws and language [of the time]).[93] The narrators of *La place* and *Une femme*, as I have also pointed out, have similar projects. In subordinating the personal to the collective (indeed to the political), Ernaux's narrators try to ensure that their narratives will be received not as narcissistic revelations but rather as pointed critiques of social injustice grounded in personal experience.[94]

Yet linking the personal to the collective in such a way proves, like all the other kinds of linking attempted in Ernaux's narratives, to be painful for her narrators and thus induces resistance on their part. As Mall notes, seeing her mother as a product of social conditions rather than as a unique, inimitable individual diminishes the pleasure that the narrator of *Une femme* derives from certain memories: 'Le devoir de l'explication objective s'oppose à l'abandon – coupable – au plaisir de l'image libre' (Assuming the duty of explaining things objectively stands in direct opposition to giving in to the guilty pleasure of the image).[95] She aims at demystification but finds that such stripping away of illusion – her own, most of all – is indeed an agonizing process. In a frequently quoted passage from *La place*, that text's narrator also speaks of feeling such a resistance while constructing the 'ethnobiography' of her father:

En m'efforçant de révéler la trame significative d'une vie dans un ensemble de faits et de choix, j'ai l'impression de perdre au fur et à mesure la figure particulière de mon père [...] Si au contraire je laisse glisser les images du souvenir, je le revois tel qu'il était, son rire, sa démarche, il me conduit par la main à la foire et les manèges me terrifient, tous les signes d'une condition partagée avec d'autres me deviennent indifférents. A chaque fois, je m'arrache du piège de l'individuel.

In trying to expose the web of his life through a number of selected facts and details, I feel that I am gradually moving away from the figure of my father ... If on the other hand I indulge in personal reminiscence, I remember him as he was, with his way of laughing and walking, taking me by the hand to the fair to see the huge, frightening merry-go-rounds, and I forget about everything that ties him to his own social class. Each time I face this dilemma, I have to tear myself from the subjective point of view.[96]

By perceiving the mark of her father's social condition on his character traits, speech, beliefs, and behaviours, the narrator gains a certain, objective knowledge (*connaissance*) about the man, but loses her affective recognition (*reconnaissance*) of him as her father. The 'souvenir' of which she speaks belongs to sense and not intellectual memory, and intuitively, she suspects that in this 'guilty' memory nevertheless lies a certain truth about her father that cannot be apprehended solely through an ethnographic approach.

La honte's narrator is equally distressed by the demystification – this time, that of her *own* presumed uniqueness – that her narrative effects:

> Décrire pour la première fois, sans autre règle que la précision, des rues que je n'ai jamais pensées mais seulement parcourues durant mon enfance, c'est rendre lisible la hiérarchie sociale qu'elles contenaient. Sensation, presque, de sacrilège: remplacer la topographie douce des souvenirs, toute en impressions, couleurs, images [...] par une autre aux lignes dures qui la désenchante, mais dont l'évidente vérité n'est pas discutable par la mémoire elle-même.

> To describe for the very first time, with no criterion other than accuracy, streets along which I used to walk as a child without ever thinking about them, is to expose the social hierarchy they implied. I almost feel I am committing a sacrilege: replacing the sweet landscape of memory – a whirl of impressions, colors and images ... – by a far harsher one that strips it of all magic, but whose truth cannot be questioned, not even by memory.[97]

'Sensation de sacrilège' indeed, because by exposing in narrative the social factors behind the scene in particular, the narrator manages to strip it, as she had in fact wanted to do, of its 'caractère sacré d'icône' (sacred aura of an icon) (30). In the process, however, pleasurable sense memories ('impressions, couleurs, images') are abruptly replaced by the black and white of text. This serves to explicate the mechanisms of the social alienation into which the scene initiates the adolescent but which she does not yet understand.

Yet there is something even more disturbing to *La honte*'s narrator about the narrative she has produced. Narrated, the scene becomes knowable to others, and in this way the isolation into which it had plunged her is mitigated. The scene becomes knowable to others, however, only at the price of becoming unrecognizable to her: 'Depuis que j'ai réussi à faire ce récit, j'ai l'impression qu'il s'agit d'un événement banal, plus fréquent dans les familles que je ne l'avais imaginé [...] Les mots que j'ai employés pour la décrire me paraissent étrangers, presque incongrus. Elle est devenue une scène pour les autres' (Now that I have managed to write this narrative, I have the impression that it describes a banal event, one more common among families than I had imagined ... The words I have used to describe it seem foreign to me, almost incongruous. It has become a scene destined for others) (16–17; 16). Like unique, personal possessions traded for common currency, her private memories are exchanged for (necessarily collective) words that conjure not '*la* scène' but '*une* scène,' a scene like those one reads about in a newspaper or hears recounted on a television talk show. With the publication, or as Lacan has it, the 'poubellication,' of her text (that is, its inevitable profanation and alienation from its author as a result of its publication), the narrator, like that of Duras's 'Madame Dodin,' knows she will be relinquishing the exclusive 'rights' to her story.[98] Yet at the same time, this realization – that the written narrative separates itself from its author and becomes autonomous – indeed makes it *possible* for the narrator of *Passion simple* to expose her story: 'C'est [...] par erreur qu'on assimile celui qui écrit sur sa vie à un exhibitioniste, puisque ce dernier n'a qu'un désir, se montrer et être vu dans le même instant' (It's ... a mistake to compare someone writing about his own life to an exhibitionist, since the latter has only one desire: to show himself and to be seen at the same time).[99] In the temporal delay between writing and reading and the spatial separation between writer and reader there is freedom, but there is also alienation and loss.

As the narration of *La honte* advances, gains are made but unexpected losses occur in the narrator's pursuit of both an understanding of the scene and release from its enduring grip on her. Locked within her mind, the scene remains maddeningly inexplicable. Once explicated in narrative, it seems not only comprehensible, but also banal, just another story of working-class domestic violence. As long as it is kept private, the memory of the scene creates a barrier of secrecy between the narrator and others. Once shared with these others, it becomes vulnerable to their misinterpretation and appropriation. While still a wordless memory, the scene retains a terrifying vividness and presentness that haunts the adult narrator. Its transposition into narrative results in a dissolution not just of its horror but of its truth as well. Is the exposure and banalization of personal experience a fair price to pay for relief from the anxiety and shame it produces? Does this exposure even secure such relief? Can the rational, ordered elaboration of memory in language ever be truly faithful to that memory? And even if it can be, is memory ever truly faithful to the reality of the experience in the first place? These are all questions that the narrator of *La honte* raises but that she does not – cannot, surely – answer definitively.

The narrator is aware of the 'explanation' of the scene that a psycho-therapist would likely offer her: 'Je n'attends rien de la psychanalyse ni d'une psychologie familiale dont je n'ai pas eu de peine à établir les con-clusions rudimentaires depuis longtemps, mère dominatrice, père qui pulvérise sa soumission en un geste mortel, etc.' (I expect nothing from psychoanalysis or therapy, whose rudimentary conclusions became clear to me a long time ago – a domineering mother, a father whose submis-siveness is shattered by a murderous gesture, etc.).[100] Yet a sociohistorical explanation, the one she attempts to discover through her auto-ethno-biography, proves equally unsatisfactory to her for the reasons given above. Yet in the end, are not the *effects* of such an experience more sig-nificant than its causes, whether psychological, social, economic, or other?

One of the most obvious of the incident's effects on the narrator of *La honte* is that it saddled her with an unshakable sense of shame. Yet per-haps an even more significant effect is the narrative drive it gave her. 'Cette scène figée depuis des années,' she declares, 'je veux la faire bouger pour lui enlever son caractère sacré d'icône à l'intérieur de moi (dont témoigne, par exemple, cette croyance qu'elle me faisait écrire, que c'est elle qui est au fond de mes livres)' (That scene frozen within me for all these years – I would like to bring it out and strip it of its sacred aura [which long made me believe that it was responsible for my writing, that it lies somewhere at the heart of all my books]) (30–1; 26–7). Assum-ing in this reference to other books the role of author, the narrator maintains here that the scene is not only the seed of *La honte* but the impetus of all her other narrations as well. Part of her long-held reluc-tance to narrate the scene, she says, was an underlying anxiety that doing so would bring upon her a punishment – that, precisely, 'de ne plus pou-voir écrire quoi que ce soit ensuite' (of not being able to write anything else afterward) (16; 16), as if revealing the source of her creativity would destroy it. It is with relief – relief mixed with disappointment, however – that she realizes that no such mystical punishment has befallen her for setting the scene to words. There is disappointment because, while the persistence of her narrative drive is productive, it is also troublesome, for it is a desire never quite satisfied by the texts – *La honte* included, it would seem – that it produces.

In an interview about the writing of *La honte*, Ernaux states:

J'ai écrit d'une traite la scène du dimanche 15 juin 1952 [...] Pendant qua-tre ans, j'ai laissé de côté ces pages, j'ai 'tourné' autour de la honte, comme d'une matière dans laquelle il faudrait plonger un jour ou l'autre [...] Tout

se passe comme si (disant cela, j'abdique une grande part de choix con-
scient dans l'écriture), j'avais besoin de (re)prendre un thème, une période, déjà présents dans mes textes et de les soumettre à une autre
approche, constamment. Comme si la 'vérité' ne pouvait être obtenue que
dans ces mouvements 'tournants.'

I wrote the scene of Sunday, June 15, 1952 all at once ... For four years, I put
those pages aside and I 'turned about' shame, like a material into which I
knew I would have to plunge one day or another ... Everything happened as
if (saying this, I relinquish a great deal of conscious choice in writing), as if
I needed to take up again a theme, a period, already present in my texts,
and to submit them constantly to another approach. As if the 'truth'
couldn't be obtained except through these 'turning' movements.[101]

Like Duras with her initial draft of 'Monsieur X.,' Ernaux brooded
over this narrative sketch for several years before the desire for communication overrode the anxiety of disclosure. Many years before *La honte*'s
publication, Ernaux had already suspected that the exploration of childhood and family she had begun in *Les armoires vides* would not soon be
exhausted: 'L'écriture n'est pas une psychanalyse. Au bout de quatre
livres, je ne suis pas débarrassée de ce qui est fondamental. Peut-être vais-
je trouver d'autres biais pour évoquer cette coupure [between her parents and herself] de façon différente' (Writing is not psychoanalytic
therapy. Even after four books, I have still not shaken off what is fundamental. Perhaps I will find other ways to evoke that rupture [between her
parents and herself] in a different way).[102] As Claire-Lise Tondeur writes,
'inculture et honte sociale peuvent être surmontées mais la honte psy-
chique primordiale reste irréductible' (Lack of culture and social shame
can be surmounted, but psychic, primordial shame remains intractable);
that is, while social shame can be overcome – and considering the
increasing frankness of Ernaux's publications, it seems to have been in
her case – the psychic effects of *trauma* cannot.[103] Ernaux must therefore
constantly return, be it explicitly or furtively, to the site of her trauma. Yet
like Duras's multiple literary returns to Indochina, the site of that
author's own childhood trauma, Ernaux's journeys to Y. are never exact
repetitions. With *La honte*, she indeed finds yet another way to evoke the
'coupure' (rupture) of which she speaks. And although, as its narrator's
comments above imply, *La honte* does not satiate narrative desire, it does
go the furthest towards mending this rupture, towards reconnecting
(*relier*) that which had been divided by it (herself and her parents, her

past and her present selves). *La honte* does not just rework previous texts, it fills in the blank spaces within them and also links them together, thereby unifying these texts, as well as the memories and selves inscribed in them, as never before.

La honte is in fact the last text (as of this writing) in which Ernaux revisits her childhood, which suggests that it did bring some sense of closure, however imperfect, to the scene of her twelfth year, around which the earlier texts had turned ('tourner autour') without ever touching it. Some of the texts that have followed continue to evoke instances of shame, but these are instances that she endured as an adult and that therefore left less of an impression, presumably. Also like Duras's texts, Ernaux's have become more and more revelatory, or even, some critics have suggested, exhibitionist. *Se perdre* retells the story of the author's affair with a Russian diplomat already recounted in *Passion simple*, but in it, more of the nature of the couple's sexual relationship is exposed, as is more of the real identity of the lover. *L'événement* reprises the story of the abortion first told, in novel form, in *Les armoires vides*, but it tells it in greater and more graphic detail. In *L'occupation* (2002), Ernaux writes explicitly of a different but equally obsessional love affair, this one with a man thirty years her junior, a man to whom *La honte* is dedicated and whose identity was never really kept a secret.[104] *L'Usage de la photo* (The Use of the Photo) with Marc Marie (2005) impressionistically chronicles her relationship with Marie through the presentation of photos the couple took of the disposition of the clothing they discarded before each of their sexual encounters and the commentary on these photos each of them subsequently wrote.[105] Judging by the progression of genres in Ernaux's œuvre, from novel to 'auto-ethnography' to 'journal intime' (personal diary) (as she herself has labelled *Se perdre*),[106] and by the increasing frankness with which the author recounts highly personal experiences (precisely because, she argues, collective history is implicated and reflected in them), in Ernaux's case as in Duras's, narrative desire seems to have soundly overridden narrative anxiety. Although Duras and Ernaux have vastly different styles and personas, there are more similarities between them than Ernaux acknowledges when she charges Frédéric-Yves Jeannet with comparing them simply because they are both women writers.[107] As I argued in the introduction to this book, the social displacements they both underwent doubtless inform their (however disparate) formal choices, and representations of these displacements also make their way into the content of many of their texts. The movement in Duras's œuvre from auto-fiction to explicit autobiography, from *Les impudents* and *Un barrage contre le Pacifique* to *L'amant* and *La douleur,* is echoed in Ernaux's tortuous journey of self-revelation from *Les armoires vides* to *La honte* and beyond.[108] And each of these two literary evolutions echoes the real-life evolution each author underwent from social subordination and lack (more material in Duras's case, more cultural in Ernaux's) to fame, fortune, and prestige. Along their journeys through different geographical and social spaces and literary phases, both women appear to have shed some 'baggage' (inhibitions, anxieties, and for Ernaux in particular, a great deal of shame) and to have acquired new, much more desirable possessions, the most salient of which is the cultural capital that French society confers on successful writers.[109] Over the course of their long careers (fifty years for Duras, thirty for Ernaux so far), they have used their autobiographical writing to confirm the feminist, as well as sociological, credo that the personal *is* the political. As Ernaux writes in a short text about her first sexual advances towards the young lover in *L'occupation,* for example, 'j'ai senti que, pour une femme, la liberté d'écrire sans honte passe par celle de toucher la première, avec désir, le corps d'un homme' (I felt that, for a woman, the freedom to write without shame comes only after [attaining] the freedom to make the first move and to touch, with desire, a man's body).[110] There is more at stake in both Ernaux's and Duras's writings than 'just' the creation of 'realistic' self-portraits, that is, portraits whose fragmentation and multiplicity faithfully reflect those of the real self. Duras and Ernaux do succeed in this first endeavour, but what they also portray in their writing are the often violent forces (in *La douleur,* that of military, political, and psychic domination, in *La honte,* that of cultural and social domination) that shape both the self and others.

In chapter 3, the domination against which the writer in Sarraute's *Entre la vie et la mort* (*Between Life and Death*) struggles is of a very different, but for him no less weighty, nature. This is a creative domination exercised on him by his literary forefathers and contemporaries, the latter of whom spend much of their time jockeying for a position within a literary hierarchy that the former seem already to have fully colonized. When he is not himself swept up into this fierce competition among poetic egos, one of his primary objectives (which he shares with the narrator of *La honte*) is to create a text that represents as faithfully as possible a non-textual reality. The difficulty of this task will prove Herculean, and the writer will despair of, alternately, his competence at and the very possibility of such representation. During the writing process, he will find himself cast in the role of physician who must constantly take the pulse of the patient on whom he is performing a procedure of the utmost delicacy. He must constantly ask of his text, is it living or dead? Does it convey the spirit of the reality it is meant to reveal, or does it smother it under cliché and literary luxuriance? Although the tone of Sarraute's text is deeply ironic and the writer's anxieties most often portrayed as comical, his concerns about maintaining a lifeline (a link, in Ernaux's terms) between reality and language are nevertheless shared, in all seriousness, with the writer who gave birth to him.

PART TWO:
NARRATING LIFE, NARRATING DEATH

3 The Anxiety of Influence and the Urge to Originate: Nathalie Sarraute's *Entre la vie et la mort*

Is it living or dead? This is the crucial question that the writer in Nathalie Sarraute's *Entre la vie et la mort* (1968) obsessively poses about the text he is attempting to create.[1] What he desperately wishes to know but cannot decide is whether his text grasps the essence of reality as he perceives it, in all its organic flux, or whether it simply dissects, describes, and catalogues that reality post mortem, as a medical student does her cadaver. This uncertainty is the source of the writer's greatest anxiety, which he experiences most acutely when alone at work, facing 'la page blanche ... que sa blancheur défend' (the white page ... which its whiteness defends) (126; 129).[2] When he is out in society, however, doing all the worldly things that writers do when they are not writing, his anxieties multiply. In his social circle, he has his image to promote and to defend against the constant attacks of others, mostly fellow writers, who are jealous, inwardly insecure, and outwardly arrogant; who are, in short, just like him.

But before unpacking much more of Sarraute's novel, I must point out some important differences between it and the texts discussed in chapters 1 and 2. First, the writer in *Entre la vie et la mort* is not properly speaking the novel's narrator. In this text, as in most of Sarraute's later novels, the narrator is hardly discernible. If there can be said to be some kind of heterodiegetic narrator or narrative voice, then it conveys information almost exclusively through direct and indirect 'discourse' (I will explain my quotation marks below). The novel thus seems to be narrated from multiple perspectives, and shifts in perspective occur without warning.[3] Perspective belongs alternately to the writer, to his editor, to each of his parents, and to a multitude of nameless, indeterminate *ils* (male 'they') and *elles* (female 'they') who people the narrative. In addition, from time to time these *ils* and *elles* suddenly become *je* (I) or *nous* (we), as if these characters had decided to take over the narration of their stories. The *ils* and *elles* quickly return, however, the disembodied, heterodiegetic narrative voice apparently having reasserted its authority.

Trying to describe Sarraute's narrative techniques using standard narratological terminology is a frustrating endeavour. Over the course of her career, Sarraute increasingly dispensed with such notions as 'narrator,' 'character,' and 'plot' and deliberately made it difficult for the reader to determine at any given moment exactly whose perspective is being presented, and by whom. As for the concept of character, while I speak of 'the writer' in *Entre la vie et la mort*, like all the other 'characters' in the novel, he has no proper name.[4] He is never even referred to in the novel as 'l'écrivain' (the writer); rather he is designated simply by the pronoun *il* (or occasionally by *je*). His profession only becomes apparent through his actions and his interactions with others. As Sarraute states on the inside cover of the original Gallimard edition, this *il* is not meant to represent a unified character; rather he is a *trompe-l'œil*, 'un héros fait de pièces disparates, qui peut difficilement tenir debout' (a hero made of disparate parts who holds together only with difficulty). Valerie Minogue reproduces this quote in *Nathalie Sarraute and the War of the Words* and notes that this *il* appears to refer at different moments to writers at very different stages in their careers.[5] In the first scene in the text, he is an established and manifestly pompous writer – the description of his words and gestures is laden with irony – speaking before a group of admirers about the tortuous manner in which he creates his masterpieces: 'Non, décidément non, ça ne va pas [...] J'arrache la page [...] Je jette. Je prends une autre feuille. Je tape' (No, definitely no, that won't do ... I tear out the page ... I throw it away. I take another sheet. I type).[6] Later on, this *il* is a young man whose first book has just been accepted for publication (77; 77), and in yet another scene, he circulates among the literati but has himself not yet written, much less published, anything at all ('Mais pourquoi n'écrivez-vous pas?' questions an impatient *elle*, 'Vous ne faites qu'en parler ... ' [But why don't you write? All you do is talk about it ...] [60; 58]). The *il* also has varying writing habits and family backgrounds, as Minogue points out.[7] While early on, for example, the *il* states that he writes only on a typewriter, a bit later we find him using a pen and still later, a pencil.[8] Nevertheless, there is enough *psychological* coherence within this writing *il* (in a text and indeed an œuvre that constantly challenges coherence of any kind) that for practical purposes, I, like other commentators of the text, will refer to this chameleon *il* as 'the writer.'

Although *Entre la vie et la mort* is not the first or the only of Sarraute's texts in which there is a *mise en abyme* of the act of writing, in it this *mise en abyme* is more profound and more prolonged than elsewhere. The homodiegetic, first-person narrators of two earlier novels, *Portrait d'un inconnu* (*Portrait of a Man Unknown*) (1947) and *Martereau* (1953), are contemplative observers of the people around them and harbour secret ambitions, the reader gathers, of embarking on literary careers. In *Le planétarium* (*The Planetarium*) (1959), young Alain Guimier is struggling to write a doctoral thesis but is too mesmerized by visions of future literary grandeur to finish it.[9] *Les fruits d'or* (*The Golden Fruits*) (1963) is a novel about various critics' and writers' impressions of an eponymous novel (the one Sarraute's reader has in hand, presumably), and it explores some of the same relationships (those between writer and text, critic and text, writer and critic, and so on) that are foregrounded in *Entre la vie et la mort*.[10]

So while the *il* in *Entre la vie et la mort* is neither a conventional character nor a conventional narrator, because he is a writer who frequently and anxiously reflects on the act of writing, he has much in common with the two narrators studied in chapters 1 and 2. And although I have said that the *il* in *Entre la vie* does not appear to be its narrator, there is some suggestion in the novel that he might in fact be its *author*, or at least the author of parts of it.[11] Given Sarraute's penchant for *mise en abyme*, this supposition, which would make the *il* if not the narrator then the narrator's creator, is not unreasonable. In any case, the task of setting down his vision of reality in writing makes the *il* just as anxious as – or probably more anxious than, as will become apparent – the narrators examined earlier.

There is, nevertheless, still one obvious difference between this *il* and these other narrators, and that is his gender. Sarraute has maintained, however, that her more frequent use of male 'protagonists' (if her books can be said to contain any such thing) reflects only a desire on her part to maintain a certain gender 'neutrality' (the masculine being for her the 'unmarked' gender). Because she contends that her conception of the human psyche and its tropisms holds equally true for men and women, her characters, she says, are most often no more than 'un groupe désigné par "ils" ou "elles" [...] où l'emploi du masculin ou du féminin est quelquefois déterminé seulement par un souci de phonétique ou de diversité' (a group designated as 'ils' or 'elles' ... where the use of the masculine or feminine is sometimes determined by a concern for sound or variety).[12] Minogue affirms that, aside from the simple pronouns used to designate them, there is a lack of any gender distinction among the characters in *Tu ne t'aimes pas* (*You Don't Love You*) (1989) in particular, but also in most of the rest of Sarraute's œuvre.[13] It would seem that for Sarraute, then, male writers are just as anxious as female writers – or, alternately, that female writers are just as anxious as male writers, since, she maintains, there is no difference in the tropismic activity of the two genders. The anxieties inscribed in *Entre la vie et la mort* are therefore only 'feminine' insofar as the author of this book is a female. Yet whatever their gender or lack thereof, anxieties do loom large in this book. While Sarraute's treatment of her characters' anxieties is often ironic, the fact that she mines the subject so thoroughly (not just here but in all her examinations of the human psyche) suggests that it has significance for her. Later in this chapter, I will look more closely at gender in *Entre la vie et la mort* – that not only of the words designating characters but also of the words designating objects – in order to see whether, despite Sarraute's comments, it might in fact bring something to bear on the kinds of anxieties manifested in the text.

As in all of Sarraute's texts, *Entre la vie et la mort*'s 'characters' (these anonymous and seemingly incorporeal entities designated exclusively by pronouns) are constantly traversed by what Sarraute calls *tropismes*.[14] Tropisms are tiny, barely perceptible, and largely involuntary psychological movements of attraction and repulsion, aggression and defence, that are common to all human beings and whose elaboration was Sarraute's literary objective from her very first text, appropriately titled *Tropismes* (1939),[15] to her very last (*Ouvrez* [*Open*] [1997]).[16] Most of the tropisms the reader witnesses (as if through a strange and powerful microscope) are negative ones, movements of repulsion and defence. The writer in *Entre la vie et la mort*, who is not unlike most of the other *ils* and *elles* who inhabit Sarraute's world, is frequently preoccupied with warding off a seemingly immanent danger. On each occasion that he perceives such a threat, its source appears to him to be one or more of the outwardly supportive members of his entourage – an 'intimate' friend or an 'admiring' fellow writer. The reader of the novel has difficulty discerning whether those surrounding the writer really are as despicably double-faced as he presumes them to be, or whether the writer is paranoid. That is, the reader is often uncertain whether the 'threats' that stimulate defensive tropismic activity in the writer are real or imagined.

The primary reason for this ambiguity is that passages in the text that are not direct discourse (real dialogue set off by quotation marks or dashes) are presented in what might be called free indirect 'discourse' (which is produced by the narrator speaking from the perspective and in the tone of one of the characters). Yet such a designation is imprecise, because passages that are not actual dialogue are not in fact *discourse*, nor are they even what we normally define as 'thoughts.' Rather, these passages represent what Sarraute calls 'sous-conversation' (sub-conversation). Actual tropisms, according to Sarraute, are non-verbal, or 'prelinguistic'; but because she is a writer, her representation of tropisms is necessarily verbal. She designates her verbal (textual) representations of tropisms as 'sous-*conversation*' because, although non-verbal in reality, tropisms are exchanged, like words, among individuals, only at a barely perceptible level (if they are perceived at all, it is through the senses rather than the intellect).[17] Sarraute's narratives are often confusing to the reader because, first, what seems like dialogue is often not dialogue (rather it is *sous-conversation*, an exchange of tropisms), and second, it is often unclear exactly which character or characters are experiencing the tropisms represented by these pseudo-dialogues. When a tropismic put-down appears in the text (and they frequently do), is it really directed by one character towards another? Or is it only imagined – put in the mind if not the mouth of another – by its supposed victim? For as Celia Britton remarks of Sarraute's characters, 'X's interest in Y is not so much for Y's own sake as to find out what Y thinks of X.'[18] An *apparent* change of perspective in the text is therefore often deceptive.

Yet whether the threats Sarraute's characters perceive are actually issued (tropismically) by their antagonists (who at other moments appear as kindred spirits), or whether they simply invent them, their *effects* on their psyches are very real. Most of Sarraute's characters, including the writer, are therefore hopelessly anxiety-ridden. It must be noted that Sarraute herself would probably be loathe to attach such a ready-made label ('anxiety' in this case) to an ephemeral psychological state provoked, like all states or emotions, by ever-vacillating tropisms. 'Ces choses ténues' – not just obscure psychological states but *any* shadowy reality the author is trying to point out – 'ne se laissent pas prendre par la définition et par les grosses désignations du langage déjà utilisé,' she maintains. 'Elles sont si fines qu'elles passent au travers de ce filet' (These tenuous things don't let themselves be captured by definitions or by broad labels taken from ready-made language. They are so fine they pass through this net).[19] In another metaphor, Sarraute insists that using a prefabricated term to describe an obscure reality would be like throwing a blanket over a fire: 'tout s'éteindrait' (it would all go out/die).[20] That is, the life of the phenomenon designated (whatever it may be) would be extinguished. I will return to this notion of the 'lethality' of language below. In the meantime, in order to avoid having to invent as extensive a collection of metaphors as Sarraute herself and thereby trying my own readers' patience, I will continue to use the term 'anxiety' to speak about the very particular movements of fearful defence or retraction that Sarraute's beings so frequently endure. And despite Sarraute's warnings about such labelling, 'anxiety' seems an especially apt label for these movements, because they occur under the *apprehension* or the *expectation* of danger rather than under certain and present danger.

In *Entre la vie et la mort*, the writer's anxiety is double-sided, for he harbours two pressing but incompatible desires. Competing with a desire to forge and maintain a certain notoriety for himself in the literary world (and the accompanying anxiety that he will be incapable of doing so) is his desire (and its accompanying anxiety of failure) to create an original, 'living' work of art. While these desires coexist within the writer, he feels that the fulfilment of one of them would render the fulfilment of the other impossible, for the artist cannot preoccupy himself with mundane social ambitions without compromising the vitality, and therefore the value, of his work. It is the often comical tension between these two desires (and their concomitant anxieties) that drives the narrative the writer struggles to create to its tentative and ambiguous conclusion. For example, when an anonymous *il* brings up the writer's latest book, the writer immediately panics, expecting a critical assault: 'Il [the writer] lève la main comme pour se protéger... il s'écarte comme pour ne pas être éclaboussé... "Oh non, je vous en prie..."' (He raises his hand as if to protect himself ... he draws aside as though to avoid being spattered ... 'Oh, no, I beg of you ... ').[21] The *il*'s comments are positive, however: 'vous savez que c'est excellent' (You know, it's excellent) (96; 97). Yet even when, in a later scene, others tell the writer they also like his book, his tropisms remain defensive:

Il sent comme une peur légère, une inquiétude... Et si c'était une méprise? Une erreur? S'ils la découvraient tout à coup? S'ils voyaient en lui un imposteur? Il détourne les yeux, il se replie, il a envie de se cacher... Comme il est touchant, attendrissant de modestie, d'innocence... Ils lui tendent les bras comme à un enfant qui va faire en titubant ses premiers pas...

He feels a sort of mild fear, a certain disquiet ... And if there were a misunderstanding? A mistake? If they should discover it all of a sudden? If they were to regard him as an impostor? He looks away, he withdraws within himself, he feels like hiding ... How touching he is, how moving in his modesty, his innocence ... They hold out their arms to him as they would to a tottering baby just learning to walk... (141; 146–7)

It is possible that in this passage we have an example of the sudden shifts in perspective discussed above. The first part of the passage appears to present the writer's perspective (his tropismic 'thoughts'), and the part beginning with 'Comme il est touchant' (How touching he is) seems to offer the others' perspective. The patronizing child metaphor is either their actual image of the writer, or the writer's *conception* of their image of him (in which case the passage presents his perspective alone). Certainty might be necessary in order to gauge the writer's level of paranoia, but it is not in order to gauge the level – extremely high – of his anxiety. The child metaphor, whether theirs or his, effectively conveys the subordinate status the writer feels he has before these imposing *ils*, whose every pronouncement he anticipates with 'peur' (fear) and 'inquiétude' (worry).

Yet within every Sarrautean being, the tropismic tide can and frequently does turn (from defensiveness to aggression, from self-assertion to self-loathing, and so on).[22] In another scene, the writer seems to be riding a wave of confidence as he expounds on the profession, or rather the vocation, of writing: 'À ne jamais oublier,' he commands his salon audience. 'Il ne faut jamais tenir compte de personne. Aucun avis ne doit compter [...] Que de ça ... Il pose sur sa poitrine sa main grande ouverte ...' (We should pay attention to no one. No opinion should matter ... Except to this ... He lays his hand flat on his chest ...).[23] The irony of this statement emerges when the writer suddenly recognizes in his audience a certain *elle* '[qui] n'a pas besoin de lever le petit doigt pour le faire aussitôt se ratatiner, occuper le moins d'espace possible, pour lui donner envie de se cacher, de s'enfuir, l'échine basse...' ([who] doesn't have to lift a finger to make him shrivel right up, take up as little room as possible, to make him feel he wants to hide, to flee, his tail between his legs ...) (152; 159). He feels he has been caught playing the role of the great writer, for she, a writer herself, is not as easily duped as the others. To her, he feels certain,

Il était comme le petit garçon emporté par l'ardeur du jeu, revêtu de sa panoplie de général, brandissant son sabre, éperonnant son cheval, entraînant ses troupes à l'assaut... et qui, apercevant du coin de l'œil sa gouvernante apparue derrière la fenêtre, sait, sans qu'elle ait besoin de

l'appeler, que le moment est venu pour lui d'aller se déshabiller et prendre
son bain ...

He was like a little boy carried away by the excitement of play, dressed in his
general's outfit, brandishing his saber, setting spurs to his horse, leading his
troops into battle ... and who, out of the corner of one eye, having seen his
governess through the window, knows, without her having to call him, that
the time has come for him to go undress and take his bath ... (153; 160)

This elaborate image, saturated with both comedy and pathos, is typical of Sarrautean metaphor. Despite his bravado, in reality the writer is
desperately dependent on what others think of him. His gestures, however – both the real one of thumping his heart and the imaginary one of
brandishing his sword – do attest to a desire to *appear* self-assured.
Although Sarraute's characters share many of the anxieties of Kafka's
tormented souls, they would never allow themselves to be as unremit-
tingly harassed as these latter. They resemble more closely Michaux's
persecuted and perpetually self-excusing Plume, who exacts revenge on
his aggressors through unexpected fits of violence.[24] Attacks may make
Sarraute's *ils* waver, but like 'ces poupées lestées de plomb' (those dolls
weighted with lead), they can never be beaten down entirely.[25]
     Most of the anxieties and desires that assail Sarraute's writer are com-
mon to all of her characters, who must carefully navigate their way
through a churning sea of collective and most often threatening tropisms, but some are indeed specific to writers. A less worldly desire than
that for the recognition and approval of his fellow writers, but one that is
equally anxiety-provoking, is, as noted, a desire to capture alive in his
writing a reality that remains unnoticed by others. Although the writer is
able to enjoy only brief intimations of this evasive reality, he is certain of
its existence and is desperate to show it to others without perverting or
killing it. Other writers, those like the celebrity Germaine Lemaire in *Le
planétarium*, appear to be confident that they can seize reality with ordinary words: 'Sur ce qui bouge dans les recoins ombreux, flageole, frémit,
se dérobe... informe, mou, vaguement inquiétant... dans ce qui suinte,
coule, saigne, palpite, ils lancent ces mots... ils les plantent dedans ... ils
harponnent cela et ils le tirent à eux...' (Upon all that moves in shadowy
corners, wavers, trembles, slips away ... formless, flabby, vaguely disturbing ... into all that seeps, trickles, bleeds, palpitates, they hurl these words
... they plant them in it ... they harpoon it and pull it towards them ...)
(36; 31). But what they reel in, the writer knows, is nothing but a carcass:

'Ils regardent cela, étendu à leur pieds... comme une charogne gro-tesquement étalée sur le dos, le ventre ouvert, les pattes écartées [...] cela se dessèche et durcit au soleil' (they look at it, lying at their feet ... like a carrion, stretched out grotesquely on its back, with its belly open, its legs spread wide apart ... it dries and hardens in the sun) (36; 31). He alone seems to understand that the hunt must be carried out with prudence and deftness. To multiply metaphors (as Sarraute so often does), nor-mal, everyday words are instruments much too blunt to be useful in the delicate operation the writer must perform on the reality he perceives.

'Reality' is a word Sarraute uses abundantly in her essays and lectures, as the title of one of these latter, 'Nouveau roman et réalité' (1963), attests.[26] In this lecture, Sarraute maintains that the work of a writer, at least that of a good one, consists of searching out and exposing 'une réal-ité inconnue' (an unknown reality) (432). Aware of the ambiguity of this term and also that she is living in an 'ère du soupçon' (age of suspicion) – an era in which not only the representation but also the very existence of phenomena has been called into question – Sarraute anticipates her suspicious audience's objections: 'Les philosophes vont m'arrêter auss-itôt. De quelle réalité parlez-vous? Et qu'appelez-vous la Réalité?' (The philosophers are going to stop me immediately. What reality are you talk-ing about? And what do you call Reality?) (432).[27] In the initial, some-what coy answer she gives to her own questions, she affirms the creative writer's prerogative to avoid defining, at least explicitly or didactically, the sense she gives to the words she uses: 'Je ne suis pas philosophe ... Je refuserai de me transporter sur leur terrain. Sur mon terrain à moi, qui est celui du romancier, le mot réalité représente quelque chose d'assez clair. Chaque romancier, quand on prononce le mot de réalité, sait auss-itôt ce qu'on veut dire' (I'm not a philosopher ... I refuse to venture into their territory. In my own, which is that of the novelist, the word 'reality' represents something quite simple. Each novelist, when the word 'reality' is pronounced, immediately knows what is meant) (432). Yet since *readers* may not know what she means by 'reality,' Sarraute does elaborate: it is not, she emphatically maintains, 'la réalité que tout le monde voit, que tout le monde, autour de soi, perçoit du premier coup d'œil' (the reality that we all see, that we all discern, all around us, at first glance), for this reality is nothing but 'un trompe-l'œil' (432). 'La réalité pour le roman-cier, c'est l'inconnu, l'invisible' (Reality for the novelist is the unknown, the invisible) (432). It is 'faite d'éléments épars perdus dans la masse infinie des virtualités, des possibilités, emprisonnés dans la gangue du vis-ible, étouffés sous le déjà vu, sous la banalité et la convention' (made up of scattered elements lost in the infinite mass of virtualities, possibilities, imprisoned behind the veneer of the visible, suffocated under the already seen, under banality and convention) (432). Significantly, this description is almost entirely negative, that is, non-descriptive: Sarraute's reality is unknown, invisible, lost, imprisoned, and stifled! If she is vague, in part it is because she purports to define not just the reality she explores in her own work but those which other writers explore in theirs. This is not to say that reality for her is subjective, that it is whatever each writer wants it to be. Rather, each writer chooses one small part ('une parcelle') of the same collective reality to examine in his work.[28] The *parcelle* that Sarraute has claimed for herself is the phenomenon of tropisms.

Intentionally imprecise, Sarraute's use of the word 'reality,' like Ernaux's, also seems contradictory at times, or at least ambiguous. At a colloquium on the *nouveau roman* at Cerisy-la-Salle in 1971, Sarraute gave a lecture titled 'Ce que je cherche à faire' ('What I Am Trying to Do'), some lines of which have already been reproduced above. During the discussion that followed this lecture, Alain Robbe-Grillet 'accused' Sarraute of the heresy, for many of the novelists and theorists present, of believing in 'une sorte d'antériorité' (a sort of anteriority), that is, a reality that exists before and outside of language.[29] Sarraute responded that indeed for her, 'il y a un pré-langage: une sensation, une perception' (there is a pre-language: a sensation, a perception).[30] The human being, Sarraute maintains, can sense or perceive certain realities before she thinks or speaks them, before she recognizes, categorizes, and names them with language. Yet Sarraute adds that this sensation or perception is 'quelque chose qui va à la recherche du langage, qui ne peut pas exister sans langage, c'est ça, sans langage, cela n'existe pas, je suis d'accord' (something that seeks out language, that cannot exist without language, yes, that's right; without language, it cannot exist, I agree) (50). Curiously, then, for Sarraute there is a 'pré-language,' but there is no 'sans langage' (without language). Or perhaps the distinction is that, while this 'pré-langage' *is* ('*il y a* un pré-langage'), it does not *exist* ('ça n'*existe* pas'), in which case there is for her an important semantic difference between these two verbal constructions. Perhaps 'exister' connotes for her activity or active-ness, for the reality in question (*ça*) is the subject of the sentence rather than the object, as in the passive and impersonal 'il y a.' 'Exister,' moreover, means not only 'avoir une réalité' but 'vivre' as well (to have a reality, to live), a definition which 'il y a' does not share. As the title of the novel in question suggests, for Sarraute, the writer's primary objective is to uncover ('dévoiler') hidden realities and to make them 'live' to the fullest extent possible in her work. So while it would seem that the realities of which Sarraute speaks can 'be' without language, it is only through language that they can 'exist' or live.

This distinction might help explain the ambiguity in an earlier talk, cited above, in which Sarraute says that the writer's work 'tend à dévoiler, à faire exister une réalité inconnue' (tends to uncover, to make exist an unknown reality).[31] The comma between these last two verbal constructions implies that they are equivalents, but they obviously are not. Whether language unveils reality or makes it exist is precisely the point in question, both here and at the 1971 colloquium. Once again, Sarraute's insistence on the verb 'exister' may signify that it has for her a meaning beyond that of 'il y a' or 'être.'[32] What is certain, in any case, is that Sarraute does insist on a reality that the human being senses before he conceptualizes or names: 'Cette réalité, qui n'est pas immédiatement perceptible, est faite d'éléments épars que nous devinons, pressentons très vaguement, d'éléments mêlés en un magma confus, qui gisent, privés d'existence et de vie' (This reality, which is not immediately perceptible, is made up of scattered elements that we divine, that we sense only vaguely, elements lost in an indistinct magma, that lie there, deprived of existence and life).[33] Here, Sarraute explicitly associates the notion of 'existence' with that of 'life' and suggests that it is language that lends these 'qualities' to a vague and as yet indeterminate reality – a reality that, nevertheless, already *is*.

How does the writer in *Entre la vie et la mort* describe the particular 'parcel' of reality he hopes to unveil in *his* work? An examination of many of the metaphors the writer uses (he is as fond of this rhetorical figure as his creator) to evoke that reality in the book he is writing reawakens the question of the role of gender in Sarraute's work. Like Minogue, Sheila M. Bell argues that gender is 'played down' in Sarraute's novels and that

in a number of cases – though not all – the 'elle' [designating a person] derives from a grammatically feminine noun. There is at least one occasion where the text [*Tu ne t'aimes pas*] appears to play with the reader's expectations in these matters: 'une présence... / —Mais comme à l'écart... très effacée...' (p. 97; feminine?) becomes on next mention 'cette présence effacée... mais stimulante... un témoin' (p. 99; masculine?). Even if the 'elle' comes without an alibi and is there simply for the sake of variety or as a convenient and minimally 'characterizing' way to distinguish between speakers, the presence of such devices tends to discourage the reader from attaching too much significance to the gender of the pronoun.[34]

When discussing gender in Sarraute's work, Bell, Minogue, and the author herself all speak of the characters, and they all maintain that their gender is irrelevant. Yet a careful reading of *Entre la vie et la mort* reveals a significant predominance of feminine pronouns in a number of passages. In these passages, feminine pronouns refer not to characters, however, but to things. These things are different manifestations of the reality that the writer pursues and that the other 'genderless' characters help him (usually without knowing it) discover. The feminine gender of the word 'réalité' does not explain this recurrent femininity, for this word never once appears in the passages in question. Unlike in her more didactic essays, in her novels Sarraute would be loathe to employ such a broad label to designate 'ce qui bouge dans les recoins ombreux, flageole, frémit, se dérobe' (that which moves in shadowy corners, wavers, trembles, slips away).[35] Such a blanket-word, once again, would only stifle or kill the reality that it is the writer's duty, precisely, to animate ('faire exister').

Despite the absence of a feminine antecedent such as 'réalité,' *Entre la vie et la mort*'s writer nevertheless clearly favours feminine pronouns when evoking the reality that interests him. When the writer's editor suggests that he tweak the style, that he clean up the 'vulgarity' he sees in the manuscript that has just been accepted for publication, the writer replies, 'Oui, vous avez raison. Je l'aurais déjà fait... mais alors, elle disparaît, elle se durcit, se dessèche...' (Yes, you're right. I would have done it already ... but then, it/she disappears, it/she hardens, dries up). 'Qui elle?' (What is this 'it'/Who is this 'she'?), the editor queries, for there has been no mention in the conversation of either a woman or a feminine object. The writer responds, 'Cette chose, là, qui bouge, se propulse... elle s'arrête, elle ne passe pas... Quand on la cherche, on trouve des mots...' (That thing there, that moves, propels itself/herself along ... it/she stops, it/she doesn't come across ... When you look for it/her, you find words) (79; 78). The writer's use of the feminine word 'chose' (thing) could perhaps help explain his earlier choice of a feminine pronoun; but 'chose' appears in his speech only after 'elle,' as if it were just an afterthought, a catch-all word that will make do to signify precisely what the writer has difficulty describing. The editor's question, 'Qui elle?' also attests to even a francophone's tendency to assume that an 'elle' that acts ('elle s'arrête, elle ne passe pas') is a 'qui' – a person and not a thing. And indeed, the metaphors the writer uses throughout the novel to evoke 'cette chose' are most often images not just of feminine objects, but of *different kinds of women*.

In another scene, for example, the first in which we see the writer at work, he is desperately trying to invoke 'cette chose, vibrante, tremblante' (that thing that vibrates, trembles), for he knows that it is the only source from which he will be able to draw a living text (74; 74). Suddenly, it appears before him:

> Longtemps il la contemple... elle est bien telle qu'il l'avait aperçue quand elle lui était apparue pour la première fois, telle qu'il l'avait pressentie, et pourtant différente... pareille à la divinité qui s'entoure d'une lumière plus vive et parle à celui qu'elle revient visiter plus clairement et à plus haute voix...

> He looks at her for a long time ... she is just as he had perceived her when she had appeared to him for the first time, just as he had sensed her, and yet different ... like the divinity who surrounds herself with a brighter light and speaks to those to whom she reappears more clearly and in a louder voice ... (75; 74).

Grammatically speaking, each 'elle' in this passage could be translated into English as 'it,' but the personification is so patent here that such a translation hardly makes sense.[36] In this passage, 'cette chose' is a kind of Virgin Mother visiting the writer as if he were Bernadette at Lourdes. The humble writer gazes up at the glowing figure he had at first not believed was real, and listens in awe to her prophetic words. He feverishly transcribes them, having apparently been chosen by divine prerogative to transmit them to those incapable of seeing her or hearing her message. To the writer's dismay, however, when transcribed, the divinity's words seems to lack the power and life they had possessed when she had first pronounced them. As reproduced in his text, is her voice ('sa voix') not 'Trop haute? Trop claire? Ne dirait-on pas qu'on perçoit par moments en elle comme des claquements métalliques? Ne dirait-on pas par moments qu'elle est transmise par un haut-parleur ou bien enregistrée sur un disque?' (Too loud? Too clear? Doesn't it seem as though, at times, one can perceive in it a sort of metallic clinking? Doesn't it seem at times that it is being transmitted over a loudspeaker, or else recorded?) (75; 74). 'Canned' as it is inside the writer's hackneyed prose, the feminine voice of this goddess sounds no more divine than that of a Sunday morning televangelist.

In a third scene, the *cela* (that/it) the writer initially uses to designate his elusive reality once again metamorphoses into an *elle*, this time in a radically different guise. She does begin as a thing, as 'cette petite chose impalpable, timide, tremblante, qui chemine, progresse doucement, propulsant les mots, les faisant vibrer...' (that little, intangible, timid, trembling thing that plods steadily along, progresses gently, propelling the words, making them vibrate ...), a mysterious, unnamable object that somehow infuses itself into the writer's text and animates his otherwise moribund writing (154; 162). This *elle* then begins once again to take on womanly features; she becomes here an Eliza Doolittle of sorts, a somewhat vulgar but enchanting scamp whom the writer tries to dress up in finery. In this scene the writer has mistreated her through the academic overmanipulation of the text that is supposed to 'clothe' (represent) her, and so she has hidden herself from him in order to avoid further manhandling: 'qu'elle daigne juste se montrer' (that she would only deign to make an appearance), the writer tropismically implores,

> tout sera mis en œuvre pour la servir... il a essayé de la dresser, de lui apprendre les bonnes façons, il l'a obligée à surveiller sa ligne, à se faire toute mince pour bien porter ces modèles de grand couturier, ces phrases qu'avec tant de soins, d'efforts il a dessinées, sobrement élégantes ou savamment désordonnées, ou brochées et chamarrées de mots somptueux... il lui a appris, lui aussi, comme tant d'autres, à s'effacer pour mieux les présenter, les mettre en valeur [...] elle doit avoir fini par acquérir la grâce anonyme et grêle, la désinvolture appliquée des mannequins.

> everything will be done to serve her ... and he had tried to train her, to teach her good manners, he made her watch her figure, become slender so as to look good in the models of the *grands couturiers*, in these sentences he designed with such care, such effort, soberly elegant or cleverly disordered, or brocaded and embroidered with sumptuous words ... he also taught her, like so many others, to be self-effacing, the better to present them, to show, them off ... she must have ended up acquiring the anonymous, haughty grace, the studied offhandedness of models... (154–5; 162)

Like so many writers before him, the writer had become caught up in the profligate play of weaving words into more and more elaborate, more and more outlandish outfits until the wisp of a woman buried beneath them, whose delicate charms they were only meant to enhance, topples under their weight. His writing has become *forme* (form) without *fond* (content), an ornate shell grown too cumbersome for its dainty inhabitant.

Aware that he has driven the *elle* away, the writer knows he must

s'arracher d'ici, courir, revenir vers cela... Vers elle qui se tient là avec en elle
ce vacillement, ce louche flageolement ... il sent, tandis qu'il s'approche
d'elle cette avidité d'autrefois, cette humilité, cette tendresse... 'Il y a des
éternités... Je suis si content ... Pourquoi ne se voit-on plus jamais? quand
pourrait-on se revoir?'

tear himself away from here, hurry, return to that [*cela*] ... To she (*elle*) who
is waiting there, bearing in herself that wavering, that suggestive trembling
... he feels, as he approaches her, the old avidity, the humility, the tender-
ness ... 'It's been ages ... I'm so glad ... Why do we never see each other anymore? When shall we meet again?] (155–6; 163)

Although the 'cela' is still personified as a woman here, her persona
has changed yet again. The writer's has as well, for he speaks of having
lost sight of his objective of creating real ('living') art. His wish to reas-
sert that objective is figured as a desire to rekindle a passion for a former,
and it would appear somewhat sleazy, lover ('avec en elle [...] ce louche
flageolement' [within her ... that suggestive trembling]). Creative and
sexual drive ('cette avidité') are fused in the writer's fervid imagination
as he struggles at his writing table, tormented by the knowledge that
without his mistress, his writing will die. It will become nothing more
than a string of clichés that countless writers before him have used to
trace the outlines of a stable, familiar, and ultimately inauthentic world.

The writer therefore continues to invoke this *elle* throughout the
novel. She answers his call several more times, sometimes incarnating
just the reality the writer seeks to know, at other times slipping on for size
the text he is creating as well. What is consistent is that each time she
appears, it is in a new guise. In one passage in which she emerges, the
tension between the writer's literary ambitions and anxieties is so high
that it provokes a doubling of his consciousness, a doubling which the
anxious narrator of Sarraute's *Enfance* (1983) also experiences.[37] Lacking confidence in his own judgment, the writer asks his more critical
double to evaluate what he has just written, a task which the double
undertakes with more enthusiasm than the writer had perhaps bar-
gained for: 'Beau résultat. C'est mort' (Nice job. It's dead), the double
coldly pronounces.[38] Despite his deference to this exacting double, the
wounded writer cannot help but attempt to defend his work. In one sentence of his text in particular, he asserts, 'Il y a, vous me direz ce que vous

voudrez, une certaine force et, pardonnez-moi... comme une grâce ingénue' (You can say what you like, there exists in its movement a certain force and, you'll forgive me ... a sort of ingenuous grace ...) (71; 70). 'Ingénue!' sputters the double, 'vous ne voyez donc pas qu'elle est grotesque? Des mièvreries. Des clins d'œil de vieille coquette du répertoire...' (Ingenuous! Don't you see that she's grotesque? Affectations. Winks from an aging stock-company coquette...) (71; 70). On a grammatical level, the *elle* in the double's retort refers back to the sentence, *la phrase*, in question ('cette phrase qui sinue' [that sentence that meanders] [71; 70]). The metaphor that immediately follows this pronoun, however, breathes human – and more specifically feminine – life into it (at least in Sarraute's text, if not in her poor writer's). According to the double, the writer's *elle* is most emphatically not (an) 'ingénue'; on the contrary, she is an old hussy (her hackneyed words suggest that she has 'been around') whose attempts at seduction (with her 'mièvreries,' her flowery, poetic style) are pathetic, indeed grotesque. The writer's innocent waif is for his disabused double a painted whore.

There are still more scenes in the novel in which this woman-reality makes an appearance. In one, she is even a 'dompteuse,' a lion tamer who domesticates the 'bêtes féroces' (ferocious beasts) that constantly threaten to overrun the writer's text: 'la platitude, la naïveté, la simplicité, la mièvrerie, l'indigence, l'ostentation, la grossièreté' (platitude, naïveté, simplicity, affectation, indigence, ostentation, boorishness) (170–1; 179). What multiple talents this *elle* possesses! By far the most important of these talents for the writer is her ability, whenever she favours him with a visit, to calm his artistic anxieties, which she does by infusing his perpetually ailing text with some of the life she so abundantly possesses. I will return later to this chameleon *elle* in order to look even more closely at her nature and the important role she plays in the creative process documented in *Entre la vie et la mort*. But for now I would like to return to a discussion of the particular anxieties that plague this novel's writer.

As already noted, much of the writer's anxiety is generated by his concern for how others, especially other writers, judge his literary abilities. In one anxiety-provoking scene, the anonymous entities who make up the writer's social circle (represented in this passage as *elles* 'for variety') accuse him of using people and objects from real life – people and objects with which they are all familiar – as models for the characters and objects in his book. One of these *elles* is the first to discover this 'dirty' secret about the writer, who had previously claimed, apparently, to rely entirely on his own imagination in his writing: 'Ah le coquin, le chapardeur,' the *elle* tropismically 'thinks' (or is it the writer imagining her thoughts?), 'c'est donc ici, tout près, dans ce qui lui appartient à elle aussi, dans leur stock commun qu'on a en catimini été chiper cela... on a essayé de le camoufler et de l'écouler, ni vu ni connu... mais elle l'a reconnu aussitôt...' (Ah, the rascal, the scrounger, it was here then, quite nearby, in what belongs to her as well, in their common stockpile, that he had slyly pinched it ... he had made an effort to camouflage it and dispose of it, with no one the wiser ... but she had recognized it right away ...) (104; 105). Such filching from the real world is unbecoming of a writer of real imaginative talent, the *elle* implies. 'Allons, ne niez pas,' she goads the writer, 'Ces doigts grassouillets aux bouts pointus qui se redressent. Je sais où vous les avez pris ... Ce sont les doigts de Mme Jacquet' (Come on, don't deny it ... Those plump fingers with their pointed, upturned tips. I know where you took them from ... Those fingers belong to Mme Jacquet) (104; 105). The writer denies the allegation that makes of him a lowly copyist of a reality accessible to all, rather than the visionary he aspires to be. 'Quelle Mme Jacquet?' he sputters. 'Je n'ai pris ça nulle part. Je l'ai pris n'importe où. Quel besoin j'avais, je vous le demande un peu, d'aller chercher Mme Jacquet [...] Je veux bien être pendu si j'ai jamais pensé à votre Mme Jacquet' (What Mme. Jacquet? I didn't take them from anywhere. I took them from nowhere. Why would I need, I ask you, to go after Mme. Jacquet ... I'll be hung if I ever thought of your Mme Jacquet) (104–5; 106). The vehemence of his denial both betrays his espousal of the *elle*'s view that a truly original writer need take nothing from real life and belies his assertion that he came up with those pudgy fingers all on his own: 'Voilà... il est prêt à avouer... C'est vrai qu'il a pris ça ici, dans leur monde familier...' (There ... he's ready to confess ... It's true that he took that from here, from their familiar world ...) (106; 107).

Still, the writer is not willing to concede victory to this *elle* just yet, because those fingers, he insists, do not belong to 'their' Mme Jacquet. Instead he has drawn them from his own private, and therefore original, collection of memories and images:

> Cela aurait pu, c'est vrai, leur appartenir aussi, mais il se trouve que c'est à lui. Cela fait partie de son stock à lui, chacun a le sien, de ses réserves faites, comme les leurs, de petites choses de toutes sortes, de la pire camelote parfois... c'est dans son pécule amassé au cours de toute sa vie qu'il a pris cela... Mais rien chez elles, il ne leur a rien pris. Pas touché à leur Mme Jacquet.

That could have belonged to them too, that's true, but it just so happens that it's his. It's part of his stock, everyone has his own, his own reserves, composed, like theirs, of all kinds of little things, sometimes of the worst kind of trash ... he took that from the nest egg he has accumulated over an entire lifetime ... But nothing from them, from them he has taken nothing. Didn't touch their Mme Jacquet. (106; 107)

But the others reject the writer's claim to originality on such grounds, insisting that *any* reference to lived experience, whether theirs or his, violates the rules of authentic artistic creation. They change tactics by examining the writer's characters and searching not just for traces of themselves and of the writer's other acquaintances (which they find in abundance) but for traces of the writer himself. Borrowing from one's *own* life, they assert, is even less becoming of an artist than borrowing from those of others:

Retroussant leurs manches, hardiment elles fouillent... plus loin, encore plus loin... là, dans ce tréfonds où quelque chose de vivant tressaille et se rétracte... elles plongent jusque-là leur bras et elles détachent, elles tirent et ramènent au jour ce paquet de chairs sanguinolentes... elles le montrent... 'Toute votre enfance. Je l'ai vue... camouflée, c'est entendu, mais elle y est.'

rolling up their sleeves, boldly they dig ... further, still further ... there, in the depths where something living startles and draws back ... they plunge in up to their shoulders and detach it, pull on it and bring into the light this bundle of blood-streaked flesh ... they hold it up ... 'Your entire childhood. I saw it ... camouflaged, of course, but here it is.' (108; 110)

This marvellously graphic image demonstrates the very literal way in which these *elles* rip a mass of living tissue from writer's book and label it like an organ destined for a jar of formaldehyde: 'votre enfance' (your childhood). The examination has become an autopsy. The *elles*' lethal objective has been to deny the writer's originality and to make him one of their *nous*: 'Il a été attrapé,' affirms one of them, offering a brand new metaphor. 'J'ai réussi à le saisir par une touffe de sa longue barbe blanche et à le tirer ici, à le faire descendre ici parmi nous. Regardez-le [...] Tout pareil à nous. Rien, je vous assure, de miraculeux' (He was caught ... I managed to grab him by a tuft of his long white beard and drag him here, make him come down here among us ... He's just like us. Nothing miraculous, I assure you) (108–9; 110).

Predictably, jealous of his autonomy and certain (at least at fleeting moments) of his originality, the writer resists their efforts to envelope him in their *nous*. In the literary circles in which he manoeuvres, he is acutely sensitive to any suggestion that his work is like anyone else's. When his editor brings up the name of a fellow writer (a certain 'Régier') and asks the writer if he likes his work, the writer is at first anxious to please: 'Si, je l'aime, bien sûr que si. Je l'admire' (Oh, yes, I like him, of course. I admire him) (77; 76). His initial tropismic desire to be agreeable, however, is quickly overcome by a stronger need to assert his individuality: 'Mais si vous croyez à une influence, là, je ne pense pas, je l'ai lu très tard, j'avais déjà commencé...' (But if you see an influence there, I don't think so, I read him quite late. I had already begun ...) (77; 76). At this point, this real conversation, in quotation marks, is replaced by a *sous-conversation*, an exchange of wordless tropisms in which the normally timorous writer bristles with indignation at the editor's implication: 'Il fait un mouvement, sa main se tend vers le mince paquet de feuilles posé sur la table ... Ce qui est là existe si fort que tous vos Régiers seront morts depuis longtemps ... Pourquoi Régier? Mieux que tous les Régiers passés, futurs, présents...' (He makes a move, his hand reaches out for the slender manuscript lying on the table ... What is in there exists so intensely that all your Régiers will be long dead ... Why Régier? Better than all the Régiers, past, present and future ...) (78; 77). Once again, the haste and vehemence of this tropismic denial reveals more than the writer intends. What is revealed here, specifically, is an acute anxiety about the issue of *influence*.

According to Harold Bloom, every 'strong' poet (that is, any poet worth remembering) since Shakespeare has been afflicted with what Bloom calls, in his eponymous book, the 'anxiety of influence.'[39] The strong poet desires to break away from his precursors and to create an original œuvre that owes nothing to those that preceded it. I use the masculine possessive in paraphrasing Bloom, because for him almost all the 'strong' poets are men (although he does mention the sexually ambiguous Emily Dickinson, as well as Christina Rossetti).[40] The strong poet's relationship with his precursors, usually one in particular, is like Freud's conception of the relationship between Oedipus and Laius (8–11). The poet suffers because, unlike the mentally healthy but morally weak 'normal' man, he never learns to submit to the father's law; that is, he never learns to accept the father's poetic (or as Lacan has it, linguistic) priority. Indeed, the poet must not accept this priority, for if he does he will be reduced to poetic impotence. Rather than allowing the poet, like normal

men, to avoid castration, submitting to the father's/precursor's authority would only bring castration upon him. Were he to succumb to the
precursor's influence, his pen, so to speak, would run dry.

It certainly appears that, whether he writes poetry or prose (it is not
clear which), the writer in *Entre la vie et la mort* suffers from the literary
anxiety of influence that Bloom describes. This anxiety is betrayed not
only in the way he bristles at the mention of a contemporary but in his
reaction to the frequent references his fellow writers make to 'les
grands,' the great writers who came before them.[41] Anxious preoccupation with celebrated precursors is presented in the novel as a characteristic of all writers. Multiple references are made by various *ils* and *elles* to
such 'grands' as Baudelaire (59, 60, 125, 132), Balzac (59, 60, 118, 132),
Kafka (78, 113, 123), Flaubert (59, 60, 118), Proust (61, 125), Nerval
(125), and Jarry (79). The angst-ridden Mallarmé is also paraphrased
twice – without attribution – by members of the writer's circle (31 and
126).[42] The 'castrating' fathers and stepfathers of the Brontës, Kafka,
and Baudelaire are also given a quick nod (113), reinforcing Bloom's
claim that even the greats – indeed, especially the greats – had to struggle against fatherly influence.[43] Even the writer's own flesh-and-blood
father, from whom the despotic fathers above could have learned a trick
or two, makes an anxiety-provoking appearance in the text (113). It
seems that he has little use for writers ('ces "créateurs", ces "artistes", ces
"poètes"'... les guillemets rigides et lourds comme les fers des condam-
nés sonnent'), especially modern ones ('Vous savez que ces "génies"
n'ont même plus besoin de savoir rimer' [these 'creators,' these 'artists,'
these 'poets'... the rigid quotation marks rattle like the irons of condemned men... You know that these 'geniuses' don't even have to know
how to rhyme anymore] [119; 122]). Upon hearing the news that his
son's book is going to be published, he promptly asks him how much he
had to pay the press for the honour (116; 119).

When the writer and those in his circle mention their precursors, it is
nearly always to compare themselves to them. But making such comparisons, the initiated know, can be dangerous business. The writer gets into
trouble when he suggests that he is a particularly sensitive observer, even
of the most banal or profane scenes from life, and that this talent is what
makes him capable of transforming elements of lived experience into
art. The others immediately suspect him of claiming the parentage of a
Flaubert or a Baudelaire, 'qui ont raconté comment ils se sont gorgés
aussi jusqu'à l'écœurement de platitudes, de vulgarité[, e]n véritable
martyres' (who have told how they too have been gorged to the point of

nausea with platitudes, vulgarity[, l]ike real martyrs) in order to have the raw material necessary for their art (59; 56). For the writer's hubris, 'il faudra,' the others decide, 'que quelqu'un le rappelle à l'ordre, lui coupe l'herbe sous le pied' (someone will have to call him to order, cut the grass from under his feet) (60; 57). He is not a real martyr for art, he is only playing the role of one, just as he had tried to play that of the *enfant prédestiné* (predestined child) in an earlier scene (18).[44] A certain amount of humility (but not *too* much) is necessary when invoking the names of these forefathers, the others warn the writer. In a hilarious display of neurosis doubtless common among moderately successful artists, the others patiently explain to the writer their place in the literary hierarchy:

> Bien sûr, nous sommes les petits. Enfin pas les petits exactement. Car parmi les petits nous sommes les plus grands. Nous sommes les moyens, devrait-on dire, ce serait plus juste. Mais un pareil classement entre petits, moyens et grands pourrait indisposer nos maîtres [...] Les grands sont sourcilleux. Ils se méfient même de notre admiration. Elle suppose que nous les regardons, et cela, déjà, est insolent... Ce qui convient à leur égard, c'est le silence.

> Of course, we are the little ones. Well, not exactly the little ones, because among the little ones we are the biggest. Or rather, we are the middle ones, that would be more accurate. But such a classification of little, middle, and big might antagonize our masters ... The big ones are supercilious. They are wary even of our admiration. It implies that we observe them, and that alone is insolent... With regard to them, the proper thing is silence. (83; 82)

How these literary lightweights differ from Bloom's 'strong' poets, who employ every defence mechanism conceivable to shake off their anxiety and repudiate their precursors' emasculating influence![45] What the writer in *Entre la vie et la mort* deplores most in these *moyens* (who insultingly include him in their *nous*) is their fear of trespassing on what they consider to be their masters' domains, that is, of taking on in their own writing some of the essential questions and problems with which their masters grappled. For them, 'tout est dit, tout a été prospecté, tout est occupé. Il n'y a pas un buisson d'aubépine, pas un rosier, pas un caillou qui ne soit interdit' (everything has been said, everything has been prospected, every territory is occupied. There's not a single hawthorn bush, rose bush, or pebble that is not off limits).[46] Rather than seize fertile lands that *les grands* once held, these spineless *moyens* think they must 'se dépêcher de retourner chez eux, de se réfugier là où les puissants, les grands n'ont pas daigné pénétrer, sur ces parcelles exiguës qu'avec la largesse de gens bien nantis ils ont négligées, qu'ils ont traversées à la hâte poussés, pressés, qu'ils étaient par leurs vastes desseins' (hurry home, take refuge there where the powerful, the great have not deigned to enter, on those narrow plots which, with the liberality of the well-provided, they have neglected, which they have passed over hastily, driven, spurred on as they were by their vast projects) (145–6; 152).

When he is feeling self-assured, the writer despises the others' cowardly surrender to the overwhelming force of their anxiety of influence. He is of course subject to that anxiety himself, but manages from time to time to adopt a Balzacian confidence in his ability to wrestle with any subject matter – Society, Love, Truth – he chooses: 'Lui, il peut s'emparer de n'importe quoi sans crainte, sans vergogne. Tout est à lui, puisqu'il est assez fort pour le prendre [...] / Chaque chose maniée par lui renaît, transfigurée, devient sa chose à lui, créée par lui, portant sa marque' (He, on the other hand, can take possession of anything without fear, shamelessly. Everything is his, since he is strong enough to take it ... / Everything he touches is reborn, transfigured, becomes his thing, created by him, bearing his trademark) (146; 152–3). In order to maintain this virile *élan* in the face of mounting anxieties, however, the writer needs assistance. This assistance, as we have already begun to see, comes in the shape of a woman.

In order to assert his own literary vigour, Bloom's poet must also enlist the help of a woman: the Muse. Poets need Muses, Bloom writes, because they are diviners; that is, they can read the heavens and attain a knowledge of the future inaccessible to mortals.[47] 'Poetic anxiety,' Bloom maintains, 'implores the Muse for aid in divination, which means to foretell and put off as long as possible the poet's own death, as poet and (perhaps secondarily) as man' (61). Potential sources of the dangers the Muse can foresee are nature, the gods, ordinary men – but also, and more importantly, rival poets (59). Yet while the Muse helps alleviate some of the poet's anxieties about threats to his mortal and poetic life, she is the *cause* of others – most notably, anxieties about her fidelity. The poet fears that his Muse, his source of poetic/prophetic knowledge, 'has whored with many before him' (61). If she shares with others the secrets she reveals to him, how can his poetry, the medium through which he communicates this divine knowledge to lesser men, be unique? The Muse does offer the poet both protection and inspiration, but because of her femininity (which man has always associated with sexual inconstancy, indeed treachery), she also saddles him with a significant dose of masculine anxiety.

In *Entre la vie et la mort*, the writer's encounters with the mysterious and versatile *elle* discussed earlier have much in common with Bloom's depiction of the relationship between a poet and his Muse. Like that of the Muses, the principal function of Sarraute's *elle* seems to be revelation, that of the hidden realities the writer wants to 'faire exister' (make exist) in his book. Since the Muses divine – they have access to knowledge only the gods have – , they can properly be called divine (and indeed, they are the daughters of Jove).[48] In a passage already reproduced above, when the writer first meets the *elle*, she appears to him, precisely, '*pareille à la divinité* qui s'entoure d'une lumière plus vive et parle à celui qu'elle revient visiter plus clairement et à plus haute voix...' (*like the divinity* who surrounds herself with a brighter light and speaks to those to whom she reappears more clearly and in a louder voice...) (emphasis mine).[49] In this scene, the *elle* verbally communicates her knowledge to the writer ('[elle] *parle*' [she speaks]), just as the Muses communicate theirs to their poets.

When his *elle* is not with him, like Bloom's jealous poet the writer experiences the acute anxiety of a lover uncertain (and suspicious) of his mistress's whereabouts: 'Je la cherche, agité, anxieux, partout où il est possible qu'elle se montre, qu'elle me fasse signe... de ces petits signes entre nous que personne d'autre, semble-t-il, ne perçoit' (Agitated, distressed, I look for her everywhere she might possibly appear, might give me a sign... those little signs between us that no one else, it seems, perceives) (173; 182). The writer wants to believe that his relationship with his 'Muse' is exclusive and that the two share a language of non-verbal signs incomprehensible to others. But the suspicion that she has been unfaithful to him, whether with his precursors or his contemporaries, is never far from his mind. His anxiety of influence is thus exacerbated by a related anxiety about the possibility that the reality his Muse shows him and on which he has staked his claim has already, like the sluttish Muse herself, been 'taken.'

In his book, Bloom argues that the strong poet attempts to overcome his anxiety of influence by misreading the poetry of his precursor. He calls this misreading 'misprision' and suggests that the poet can perform it on his precursor's work in a variety of ways. For example, he can read the previous poet's work in such a way as to suggest that it is accurate or valuable only 'up to a certain point, but then should have swerved, precisely in the direction that the [later poet's] poem moves.'[50] Or, the later poet can suggest that the precursor failed to take his ideas far enough. In this second manoeuvre, the later poet will borrow some of the precursor's terms, change their meanings, then employ them to 'complete' – antithetically, that is – the precursor's supposedly 'unfinished' poem (14). Through these and other defence mechanisms, or 'revisionary ratios' as Bloom calls them, the later poet attempts to diminish the value of the precursor's work and to enhance that of his own. 'Every major aesthetic consciousness,' Bloom maintains, 'seems peculiarly more gifted at denying obligation as the hungry generations' – from Shakespeare's 'sons' to the Romantics to the Modernists – 'go on treading one another down' (6). Indeed, according to Bloom this is the only attitude a poet can adopt if he is to have any hope of emerging from his precursor's artistic shadow and creating an original œuvre. The strong poet's ultimate goal is to make it appear not as if his work were an improvement on the precursor's, but rather as if the precursor's work were somehow a poor imitation of his own (15–16)!

Like her writer in *Entre la vie et la mort*, in her critical writings, Sarraute herself demonstrates quite a preoccupation with her poetic predecessors. She frequently invokes the likes of Flaubert, Proust, Kafka, Mallarmé, Baudelaire, and Woolf, among others. Also like her writer, she places a premium on originality, on being the first to 'discover' a new reality and to reveal it to the reader through the invention of a new literary form. The writer who is truly engaged in his work ('his' because Sarraute's hypothetical writer is always male) and who is likely to come up with something worthwhile (the 'strong' writer in Bloom's vocabulary)

s'acharne à débarrasser ce qu'il observe de toute la gangue d'idées préconçues et d'images toute faites qui l'enveloppent, de toute cette réalité de surface que tout le monde perçoit sans effort et dont chacun se sert, faute de mieux, et il arrive parfois à atteindre quelque chose d'encore inconnu qu'il lui semble être le premier à voir. Il s'aperçoit souvent, quand il cherche à mettre au jour cette parcelle de réalité qui est la sienne, que les méthodes de ses prédécesseurs, créées par eux pour leurs propres fins, ne peuvent plus lui servir. Il les rejette alors sans hésiter et s'efforce d'en trouver de nouvelles, destinées à son propre usage.

works to rid what he observes of the matrix of preconceived ideas and ready-made images that encase it, of the surface reality everyone can easily see and which, for want of anything better, everyone uses; and occasionally he succeeds in attaining something that is thus far unknown, which it seems to him he is the first to have seen. When he tries to bring to light this fragment of reality that is his own, he frequently notices that the methods of his predecessors, which were created by them for their own ends, can no longer serve his purpose. He therefore rejects them without hesitation and applies himself to finding new ones for his own use.[51]

The kind of reality Sarraute means, as I have noted, is not what is visible to everyone and what has already been analysed, classed, and catalogued; rather, 'c'est l'inconnu, l'invisible. Ce qu[e l'écrivain] est seul à voir. Ce qu'il est, lui semble-t-il, le premier à saisir' (it's the unknown, the invisible. What [the writer] alone sees. What he is the first, it seems to him, to grasp).[52] Following the haughty Flaubert, Sarraute maintains that the writer can commit no worse crime than to rehash the discoveries of his predecessors, to reinvent the literary wheel, so to speak.[53] Like Bloom's strong poet, and also like herself, Sarraute's ideal writer is well versed in his predecessors' work and thoroughly aware of their accomplishments. He seeks, however, not to imitate their style and to reproduce more images of 'their' realities, however skilfully, but to surpass their understanding of the world and to reveal a previously unseen aspect of it. Of course, writers who subscribe to this 'progressive' understanding of the literary tradition usually forget that it implies their own eventual obsolescence, for future writers try to and most certainly will surpass them. But the strong writer focuses on those who have come before him rather than on those who will follow, for his primary interest lies in being *first*.

Not surprisingly, the kind of writing Sarraute's ideal writer does is precisely the kind in which she herself, she maintained, had always been engaged. At the 1971 colloquium at Cerisy, Sarraute insisted on what made her different from the other so-called *nouveaux romanciers* (most of them present) while they, like the smothering group of *moyens* in *Entre la vie et la mort*, attempted to convince her that she was really just one of them. In essays and at previous colloquia, she had already tried to point out differences between their objectives and hers, but it was at this colloquium – which she attended only reluctantly and only for one day – that she managed to irritate most thoroughly her colleagues. This is no wonder, considering that at one point in her address she implied that if there were similarities between her work and theirs, it was only because they had adopted her innovations:

Ce qui me rapproche des écrivains qui appartiennent à ce qu'on a appelé le Nouveau Roman c'est, vous le savez, l'emploi de certaines formes. Des

formes que j'ai été amenées à élaborer il y a bien longtemps. Il y aura
bientôt quarante ans ... La plupart de ces formes sont aujourd'hui très
répandues, constamment employées.

What I have in common with the writers who belong to what has been called
the New Novel movement is, as you know, the use of certain forms – forms
that I came to develop a long time ago, almost forty years ago ... Most of
these forms are common today and are used constantly.[54]

The formal innovations to which Sarraute refers include the paring
down of characters to colorless *figurants* and that of plot to a loose collection of scenes that follow no temporal order and/or that are repeated
with variations (26). While many readers (myself included) do find Sarraute's work extraordinarily innovative, the implication that she single-
handedly *invented* these departures from the traditional novel is somewhat dubious. What is certain, at any rate, is her poetic desire – indeed,
her need – to affirm her originality before this group of contemporaries.
She furthermore speaks of being 'dans un certain isolement' (in a certain isolation), which she did not deliberately seek, she maintains, but of
which she cannot complain. 'Il m'a probablement été nécessaire' (it was
probably necessary for me), she says – necessary, that is, for her to have
produced the truly original œuvre she has (25).

In a 1965 essay on Flaubert that she titles, significantly, 'Flaubert le
précurseur?' (Flaubert the Precursor?), Sarraute questions what she says
has become an indisputable fact for her contemporaries: that Flaubert is
'notre maître à tous' (the master of us all), the precursor of all modern
(and therefore the New) novelists.[55] In this essay, the general question of
whether Flaubert is the father of modern French novelists evolves into
the more personal one of whether he is *Sarraute's* literary father; what
she is really pondering here is, to what extent is she herself indebted to
Flaubert for her discovery and revelation of the reality of tropisms in particular? If Flaubert has been unanimously adopted by her contemporaries as their precursor, it is because, Sarraute writes, 'il est le premier pour
qui la forme joue le rôle prédominant' (he is the first for whom form
takes precedence) (62). Flaubert's ambition, she maintains, was to create in his novels '[un] langage qui ne renvoie à rien d'autre qu'à lui-
même' ([a] language which refers to nothing other than itself) (63), and
indeed, he himself wrote that *Madame Bovary* would be 'un livre sur rien,
un livre sans attache extérieure' (a book about nothing, completely
detached from the outside world).[56] During the 1950s and 1960s, such

was the stated objective of several of the *nouveaux romanciers*, and it was an objective that Sarraute never shared.[57] It was precisely Flaubert's hyperpreoccupation with form and his attempt to divorce language from its referential function, Sarraute contends, that led him astray from what should be the true mission of the modern novelist: the discovery and revelation of new realities.

It is in Flaubert's *Salammbô* 'plus que dans aucune de ses autres œuvres,' Sarraute argues, 'que la psychologie est inexistante, que la description occupe toute la place et que s'affirme le pur souci du style' (more than in any of his other works, that psychology is inexistent, that there is only description, and that what is affirmed here is a pure concern for style).[58] During her talk at Cerisy as well, she maintained that Flaubert 'n'est pas moderne parce que précisément, les modernes cherchent ce qui n'est pas définissable. Un moderne décrit quelque chose sans le nommer' (is not modern precisely because modern writers seek out what is not definable. A modern writer describes something without naming it), either because he wants the reader to see a banal object in a new way (as in Sartre's *La nausée* [1938] or Robbe-Grillet's *La jalousie* [1957]) or because the 'object' has no name, indeed is not an object before the writer begins describing it (like Sarraute's ubiquitous *cela*).[59] The modern writer's duty is to create for the reader 'des impressions neuves. Impressions qui ne servent qu'une fois, qui grossiront plus tard notre stock de réminiscences et qu'il sera dangereux pour tout écrivain de l'avenir de nous obliger à faire surgir' (new impressions. Impressions that only work once, that we will add to our stock of reminiscences and that it would be dangerous for any writer in the future to make us pull out again).[60] This last, rather menacing line makes evident Sarraute's conception of the rules of the literary game: in short, each new writer had better keep off his precursors' terrain, or else risk literary oblivion. Originality is the writer's greatest obligation, then, and in *Salammbô* at least, Flaubert the presumed 'maître des modernes' failed to fulfil this obligation.

In *Madame Bovary*, on the other hand,

> les défauts de Flaubert deviennent [...] des qualités. Quelque chose maintenant les transforme, qui a l'importance des plus grandes découvertes. Un aspect neuf du monde, une substance inconnue a fait irruption dans le roman [...] Cet élément neuf, cette réalité inconnue dont Flaubert, le premier, a fait la substance de son œuvre, c'est ce qu'on a nommé depuis l'inauthentique.

Flaubert's faults become ... qualities. Something now transforms them, something that has the importance of the greatest of discoveries. A new aspect of the world, an unknown substance irrupts in the novel ... This new element, this unknown reality which Flaubert was the first to make the substance of his work, it's what we have since named the authentic. (76–7)

In *Bovary*, Flaubert still plucks images from stockpiles accessible to everyone, but now he makes the banality of Emma's and others' sentiments, acts, and speech *the very subject of his novel.* Irony, of which Sarraute herself is a master, pervades Flaubert's text and informs the reader that the beauty found in it is hollow. Instead of springing from an authentic self, every one of Emma's thoughts and words has been pilfered from a pulp novel. *Bovary* partially redeems Flaubert for Sarraute, because in it, 'l'apparence est démasquée et cette percée qui la révèle change la belle forme de qualité douteuse en forme d'art' (appearance is unmasked, and that crack which allows one to see through it changes the beautiful form of dubious quality into an art form) (82).

What Sarraute argues, then, is that Flaubert was himself inauthentic when he said that form alone matters and that a novel should be about nothing (63). Whether he realized it or not, his true goal was the revelation of a certain psychological reality (inauthenticity), which has much in common with the psychological reality that Sarraute strives to reveal in her work. In *Le planétarium*, for example, Tante Berthe's romantic desire to recreate the sombre elegance of a Gothic cathedral in her Passy apartment by installing a certain kind of door is not unlike Emma's attempt to create for herself a home and a life like that of the characters in the romantic novels she reads. In the end, Sarraute concludes that Flaubert is indeed the moderns' master – but not for the reasons they think he is. He was not obsessed, as they are, with *forme* over *fond*; rather, he did what they *ought* to be doing and what she herself, she makes clear, has always been doing: searching out unrecognized realities and giving them life through language.

Whatever the validity of Sarraute's interpretation of Flaubert's work, it is significant that what she essentially does in this essay is recreate Flaubert in her own image. She is of course not the first writer to perform this trick. As Bloom points out, literary history teems with 'strong' writers who have insisted that their precursors achieved not what they thought they did, but rather something else, something that only they, their poetic progeny, could fully accomplish. Bloom calls this anxious manoeuvre a *tessera*, one of the six defence mechanisms that writers seeking filial freedom have at their disposal. Through it, a younger writer 'antithetically "completes" his precursor, by so reading the parent-poem as to retain its terms but to mean them in another sense, as though the precursor had failed to go far enough.'[61] In her *tessera*, Sarraute maintains that Flaubert's preoccupation with *forme* was really a preoccupation with *fond*, because, as she said on many occasions, *forme* and *fond* are inextricable rather than antithetical.[62] Sarraute thus 'completes' Flaubert's work for him through both her criticism, which reveals the *real* value of the work, and her own creative writing, which explores more forcefully a reality that Flaubert had stumbled upon (despite himself, it would seem) in *Bovary*. In her essay 'Conversation et sous-conversation,' Sarraute appears to perform a kind of *tessera* on Proust as well when she dreams of 'une technique qui parviendrait à plonger le lecteur dans le flot de ces drames souterrains que *Proust n'a eu le temps que de survoler et dont il n'a observé et reproduit que les grandes lignes immobiles*' (a technique that could plunge the reader into the waves and eddies of those underlying dramas that *Proust only had time to view from above and of which he only observed and reproduced the broad, motionless lines*) (emphasis mine).[63] What might he have accomplished, Sarraute seems to be asking, had he had both her insight and her longevity?[64]

Let it be clear, however, that Sarraute's exquisite irony is not lost on me. Minogue notes that many readers took seriously Sarraute's ironic characterizations, in 'Conversation et sous-conversation,' of Woolf as 'naïve' (79; 98) and of Proust and Joyce as *dépassés* (93; 104).[65] In this essay and elsewhere, Sarraute mocks not these writers but rather those of her contemporaries who claim that 'psychology' can no longer be the subject matter of the modern novel, as it was for the above writers. In her book, Minogue reprints a letter written by Sarraute in response to such misunderstandings of her attitude towards her predecessors.[66] In it, Sarraute asserts her 'grande et très sincère' (great and very sincere) admiration for them, which she also expresses elsewhere and which she undoubtedly felt. Nevertheless, the specific comments about Flaubert and Proust I quoted earlier contain not the slightest hint of irony: neither Flaubert nor Proust, Sarraute unequivocally contends, explored deeply enough the territories they had staked out for themselves. She acknowledges that this is in part the fault of their place on the literary timeline (thus rejecting the assumption that anteriority means advantage): to reproach Proust for not going further, as she says Gide did, 'n'est-ce pas là reprocher à Christophe Colomb de n'avoir pas construit le port de New York?' (isn't this like reproaching Christopher Columbus for not having constructed the port of New York?).[67] By focusing on what she sees as these writers' shortcomings and by suggesting that the paths they should have taken are those she herself has blazed, Sarraute is simply asserting herself as a 'strong poet.' Her drive to claim originality and creative if not temporal priority mirrors not only that of Bloom's assertive creatures, but also that of her own literary progeny – the writer in *Entre la vie et la mort*.

If Sarraute shared the ambition of Bloom's strong poets, it seems likely that she also shared some of their anxieties. Elsewhere, I have written about the way Sarraute bristled each time she was compared to another writer and how she fiercely defended her originality.[68] To an interviewer questioning her about her relationship with Sartre, for example, she unequivocally rejects the suggestion that he was a literary mentor (just as her writer does in regards to 'Régier'): 'il est [...] absolument impossible et aberrant de parler d'une influence quelle qu'elle soit de Sartre sur moi. C'est tout à fait faux' (it is ... absolutely impossible and aberrant to say that Sartre had some kind of influence on me. This is totally false).[69] The title of another interview makes clear her feelings about comparisons between her and Sartre's companion: 'Nathalie Sarraute ne veut rien avoir de commun avec Simone de Beauvoir' (Nathalie Sarraute wants to have nothing in common with Simone de Beauvoir). 'Toutes les comparaisons,' she tells yet another interviewer, 'me paraissent [...] insupportables. Surtout cette manie qu'on a' – present in this book – 'de comparer les femmes entre elles' (All comparisons seem insufferable to me. Especially that mania people have of comparing women among themselves).[70] As a 'first-generation feminist,'[71] Sarraute dismissed any claims about essential differences between men and women (ironically, this is one conviction she *did* have in common with Beauvoir). Her theory of tropisms, after all, is that they are a universal human phenomenon. In resisting comparisons to other women writers, it is also likely that she was anxious to avoid the relegation of her work to the 'subgenre' of 'women's literature,' a category thoroughly maligned by male modernist writers in particular.[72]

Despite the desires and anxieties that I have argued Sarraute shared with Bloom's 'strong' poet, there nevertheless remain important differences between their conceptions of artistic creation. In *The Anxiety of Influence*, Bloom depicts the romantic tradition and its literary offspring, modernism, as being populated by ruthless artists interested first and foremost in proving the superiority of their work over that of others. Literature for them is not the search for reality or truth, but rather a forum in which competitive, 'manly' artists jostle for places of priority in the literary hierarchy. In his critique of Bloom's theory, Frank Lentricchia warns that Bloom presents

> a demonic version of the ideal of originality. In the end, he manages to draw out every bit of malevolent potential from the late Enlightenment and romantic fascination with originality: anarchism, radical relativism, solipsistic subjectivism, morbid and paralyzing self-consciousness, gnosticism and Manichaeism – all are consequences of Bloom's celebration of the ideal of originality.[73]

By equating the relationship between poet and precursor to that between father and son in the Freudian family romance, Bloom lends the former an air of violence that Lentricchia finds difficult to reconcile with his knowledge of the romantic tradition. Lentricchia questions

> this view of romanticism as the search for the unique and irreplaceable self which wants to articulate a uniquely original language. The preponderance of testimony of romantic poets and theorists since Wordsworth has claimed rather the opposite. Wordsworth overtly rejects the idea of the private self because he wishes to speak the natural language of natural men, and by so doing reach through to interior universals, 'general passions.' (329–30)

Originality for originality's sake, Lentricchia maintains, is not a romantic value; the romantics' objective was instead to discover and reveal an inner reality common to us all. While such a universalizing view of 'human nature' (which is not unlike Sarraute's) is at the very least suspect to the twenty-first-century reader, it is not the egomaniacal attitude that Bloom, in his own quest for theoretical originality, ascribes to these poets (326). For the romantics, morose contemplation of the self and anxious assertions of one's uniqueness and superiority were hazards rather than obligations of the trade.

Sarraute's writer in *Entre la vie et la mort* is certainly not immune to these hazards. The other writers' perpetual comparisons among themselves, between themselves and him, and between themselves and their precursors leave him feeling disgusted by his own smallness at certain moments, and maniacally confident in his superiority at others. Neither attitude serves the true task at hand. 'Qu'on l'oublie,' he tropismically implores his antagonists when he sits down to write, 'qu'on le laisse, qu'on l'abandonne ici jusqu'où ne songent pas à s'introduire sur les traces des enfants prédestinés les mères aimantes' (they should forget him [...] leave him, abandon him here where doting mothers following the tracks of predestined children wouldn't think to enter).[74] Yet even when left alone to write, he finds himself lured by a Flaubertian 'pur souci du style' (pure concern for style), which risks destroying any of the life he might have managed to preserve in his text. He recites to himself, then, his own self-imposed duty: 'ne pas laisser par inadvertance, par un souci frivole d'élégance, de beauté, se glisser ici rien d'inutile, aucun futile ornement... tout ici doit servir à faire se déployer, s'affirmer, quoi donc? Ce mouvement d'une parcelle de substance vivante?' (not to allow anything useless, no trivial ornament to slip in here through inadvertence, through a frivolous concern for elegance or beauty ... here everything must serve the unfolding and assertion, of what, exactly? This movement of a particle of living substance?) (73; 72).

He poses this last line as a question, because his encounters with the Muse who leads him to this 'substance vivante,' and who also often embodies it so as better to call his attention to it, are so fleeting that he cannot help but begin to doubt her existence. The Muse reappears, however, this time in the unlikeliest of guises. During a conversation with members of his circle, the writer feels assaulted by the strange accent of one of his interlocutors: 'Les molles voyelles graisseuses impitoyablement sur lui s'étirent, s'étalent, se vautrent... Ces vaaacances... la courte consonne finale apporte un bref répit, et puis on va recommencer... le soooleil... laaa meeer...' (Pitilessly the lazy, unctuous vowels stretch themselves, spread themselves, wallow over him ... this vacaaation ... the short final consonant gives a brief respite, and then it'll start up again ... the suhhn ... the seeea ...) (39; 34). Suspecting that the man's 'popular' accent is in fact an affectation, the writer tropismically attempts to make him abandon this phonetic fraudulence. But

> autant essayer de faire revenir à lui avec des tapes fraternelles sur le dos, des rires moqueurs, un sadique en train de s'acharner sur sa victime. Rien ne peut le contraindre à la lâcher... Les vaaacances... elle est traînée, toute défigurée, grotesque, avilie, prostituée, un objet dont la brute se sert pour exécuter ses louches desseins...

> you might as well try to bring to his senses with friendly back-slaps and mocking laughter a sadist in the act of assaulting his victim. Nothing can make him let go of her ... Vacaaation ... she is dragged about, entirely disfigured, ludicrous, debased, prostituted, an object the brute uses to carry out his shady designs ... (40–1; 36)

The disfigured vowel becomes here 'la victime,' a feminine noun that can refer to either a man or a woman. That this personified *elle* is 'prostituée' by the mispronouncing *il*, however, certainly lends her femininity. It would thus seem that the writer's Muse has selflessly metamorphosed herself once again, this time into a battered and violated vowel in order to reveal to the writer yet another 'parcelle de réalité': that of the mispronouncing man's fundamental inauthenticity.[75]

Heroically, the writer attempts to rescue his Muse from the sadist and nurse her back to health by pronouncing correctly each vowel into which she has infused herself: 'Les vacances. La mer. La pêche... Voyez comme elle est belle quand on la traite ainsi [...] Comme elle se dresse, toute droite et légère, naturellement discrète, modeste et fière' (Vacation. Sea. Fishing ... See how pleasing she is when treated this way ... How she stands there, straight and light, naturally discreet, modest and proud) (41; 36). Yet by adjusting her in such a way, is not the writer only participating in her brutalization, just as when he had tried to starve her and train her for the runway? Was it not, after all, the distorted form she was willing to take on that led the writer to the truth about this man? Is he not here frivolously concerned with her formal beauty, like 'ce poète agonisant' who, 'en entendant la bonne sœur qui le soignait dire: collidor [...] s'est dressé sur son lit, et rassemblant ses dernières forces [...] a articulé très distinctement: cor-ridor. Et puis [...] est retombé. Mort' (a certain poet on his death bed [who], upon hearing the nun nursing him say 'collidor,' sat up in bed, and gathering all his strength, articulated very distinctly: 'cor-ridor.' And who then fell back on his pillow. Dead) (41; 36–7). The writer realizes that in attempting to make the man pronounce his vowels in the fashion of the bourgeois he really is, he has been trying to reattach the signifier to its conventional signified (popular accent to popular origins, bourgeois accent to bourgeois origins). In these moments of weakness the writer forgets that it is precisely the ill fit of certain surfaces that creates the gaps ('les fentes' [56]) through which he is able to see the realities hidden underneath.

Words that are 'tout lisses, rigides et droits' (smooth, rigid, and straight), the ones the writer is tempted to choose when on his own, are particularly unsuitable for embodying the feminine reality he glimpses throughout the novel. This is because this reality has quite the opposite form: it is *liquid* rather than solid.[76] The fugitive *cela* 'ruisselle avec un naturel parfait, comme une source, comme une eau vive qui suit sa pente' (flows with perfect naturalness, like a spring, like running water that follows its fall) (74; 73). The vowels the affected *il* pronounces are 'molles' and 'graisseuses' (lax and unctuous or greasy), and they expel a liquid that sprays the writer.[77] When he surreptitiously scratches at the now-hardened coating – the word *vulgarité* – that the others had hastily spread over the *il*'s vowels, 'cela coule' (it streams forth) (63; 61). In a different but equally leaky metaphor, when the writer suggests to the others that the reality underneath the mispronouncing man's vowels is not what they think it is, 'comme on recouvre de sel pour l'absorber la vilaine tache de vin qu'un maladroit a faite sur la nappe blanche, eux aussitôt se dépêchent de jeter là-dessus les mots qui vont résorber cela... "Sorti d'un milieu modeste. N'en a que plus de mérite"' (just as one covers with salt to soak it up an ugly wine stain that some clumsy person has made on the white tablecloth, they hurry to throw over that the words that will absorb it ... 'He comes from a modest background. All the more to his credit') (39–40; 35). They are uninterested in, indeed are frightened of, 'ce qui suinte, coule, saigne' (what seeps, flows, bleeds) underneath the solid surfaces of everyday words (36; 31). In her essays, Sarraute constantly stresses that the reality under her own microscope, tropisms, are made up of a 'substance fluide qui circule chez tous, passe des uns aux autres, franchissant des frontières arbitrairement tracées' (fluid substance that circulates in everyone, flows from one person to the next, crossing arbitrarily drawn borders), and that conventional language exercises upon this liquid reality 'une action pétrifiante, asséchante' (a petrifying, drying action).[78]

In her well-known essay 'La "Mécanique" des fluides' ('The "Mechanics" of Fluids'), Luce Irigaray associates – as has Western culture in general, she argues – the fluid with the feminine.[79] Physicists, Irigaray writes, have never been able to understand fully the mechanics of fluids, and since they cannot account for all of the properties of fluids, they cannot adequately symbolize them in mathematical formulae. On the other hand, they have long understood and delineated the mechanics of solids. In order to 'cover up' their ignorance of the mechanics of fluids, men of science have put forward the mechanics of solids as *the* mechanics of objects – all objects – in the world. For Irigaray, fluid is like woman, whom 'solid' man purports to understand and whom he insists on symbolizing with the same formulae, the same language, he uses to symbolize himself. But feminine fluid is 'toujours en excès, ou en défaut, par rapport à l'unité. Il se soustrait au "Tu es cela". Soit à toute identification arrêtée' (always in excess, or else lacking, in relation to unity. It eludes the 'You are that.' That is, any definite identification).[80] Sarraute's fluid reality, represented in *Entre la vie et la mort* by a constantly evolving, fluid feminine persona, only stops flowing when it is violently contained or solidified by conventional language. Thus solidified, the reality is no longer itself, just as woman, for Irigaray, is no longer herself when she is 'solidified' – symbolized – by man.[81]

Sarraute, it must be acknowledged, had little patience for avant-garde feminist theory. Her conception of human nature, as we have seen, was that it was genderless and universal. Nevertheless, the flagrant femininity of the fluid reality the writer seeks in *Entre la vie et la mort* cannot be ignored. Throughout the novel, the fluidity of this feminine reality is contrasted with the impenetrable – and symbolically masculine – solidity of language (note, however, that it is just as often the *elles* as the *ils* who frantically attempt to wipe up the spills or stop up the leaks the *male* writer causes by his refusal to accept solid appearances). While language, when not manipulated properly, has a destructive, coagulating effect on the feminine and fluid reality depicted in the novel, it is of course the only tool the writer, indeed any writer, has at his disposal. Sarraute tells us that

entre ce non-nommé et le langage qui n'est qu'un système de conventions, extrêmement simplifié, un code grossièrement établi pour la commodité de la communication, il faudra qu'une fusion se fasse pour que, patinant l'un contre l'autre, se confondant et s'étreignant dans une union toujours menacée, ils produisent un texte.

between this un-named thing and language, which is nothing but an extremely simplified system of conventions, a code roughly constructed to facilitate communication, a fusion must occur so that, brushing one against the other, merging and embracing in a constantly threatened union, they produce a text.[82]

This passage offers perhaps the raciest imagery in all of Sarraute's chaste œuvre. In it, *la réalité*, delicate and capricious, and *le langage*, her clumsy but determined pursuer, must come together in a tenuous union in order for a living text to be born. The two are equally essential to this creation. While on the surface the use of a female muse-figure as source of inspiration for a male writer (however androgynous) may appear to reinforce traditional, patriarchal representations of literary production, Sarraute's superbly ironic treatment of her neurotic writer and his relationship with his co-dependent Muse prevents us from viewing this model with romantic seriousness. Besides, Sarraute's Muse is much more than a pretty face; through her superheroine fluidity, she thwarts the 'masculine' drive (which does not belong exclusively to men) to define, categorize, name, and control. She plays an active – indeed exhausting – rather than passive role in the generation of the writer's text.

Throughout the novel, however, the writer's noble desire to know and reveal reality just as 'she' is collides periodically with two baser needs: to dress her up in fine apparel (inflated, 'poetic' language) that shows off his skills (but disfigures her), and to achieve poetic priority over other writers past and present. In Bloom's depiction of it, this last desire is clearly marked as masculine: it is a desire to kill the proverbial father in order to avoid 'castration,' which in the case of a writer means literary oblivion. Of course, this does not mean, despite the bias of Bloom's examples, that women do not experience this drive. I have argued that it is present not only in the writers in Sarraute's novels, but also in the writer *of* these novels. At the same time, however, Sarraute self-consciously caricatures and mocks this drive in her fiction. In *Entre la vie et la mort*, she sanctions her writer's desire to explore new terrain, but she makes him the object of her biting irony when it is his ego that motivates him to do so. When he preoccupies himself too much with the style and appearance of his text, he is punished by feeling it go limp in his arms. When his concern is to transmit faithfully his messianic visions and not simply to enhance his reputation, he is rewarded with both an enchanting visit from his Muse and the production of a text that, when held next to a mirror, leaves upon it the 'fine buée' (fine mist) that confirms its vitality.[83]

Yet just as, according to Sarraute, it is the uneasy marriage between language and a reality that already 'is' that reveals a reality that now 'exists,' perhaps in the end it is the union of these two desires that produces a living work of art. If the writer lets his anxieties overpower his ambition to become 'the first' and 'the only,' he risks ending up among *Entre la vie*'s 'moyens' who, like faithful but dull-witted disciples, go about reciting only what their masters have taught them. But if his ambition leads him to mistreat his Muse, to attempt to reverse roles and become her master rather than her servant, then his work will languish. For Sarraute's writer, then, proceeding with humility may not be 'the natural and only mode of pursuing truth.'[84] Perhaps, rather, it is with a careful mixture of 'feminine' humility and 'masculine' arrogance – a mixture that Sarraute apparently negotiated with success during her life[85] – that the anxious writer must approach his (or her) work if its pulse is to be heard.

In chapter 4, the two narrators whose anxieties I examine are also men, but they are exponentially 'more' male than Sarraute's incorporeal *il.*

This is because, unlike him, they both have robust, virile bodies, and more significantly, they are firmly situated in a historical context – a context, moreover, that is profoundly patriarchal and misogynist. In this society, the biological maleness of these two narrators has determined the attitude they adopt towards women, which is a dangerous mixture of desire, contempt, and dread. Like the narrator of Duras's 'Monsieur X.,' both of these narrators find themselves driven, after forty years of silence, to narrate painful memories of a summer they would prefer to forget. The violence they perpetrate against the women who serve, perversely, as the Muses who inspire their narratives is brutally real rather than comically metaphorical. These men share with the narrators already discussed a desire to relieve certain anxieties by narrating feelings, memories, events, and encounters with others that they do not understand. As I will show, despite the vast differences between these men and Sarraute's *il*, the realities they manage to unveil through their narratives turn out to be, like that which this latter discovers, decidedly feminine. Yet instead of enchanting them, the feminine quality of what is revealed to them, not surprisingly, repulses them both. They apply their efforts, then, not towards carefully preserving the life of these feminine realities, but towards wilfully destroying them.

4 The Sound of the Semiotic: Anne Hébert's *Les fous de Bassan*

Anne Hébert's *Les fous de Bassan* (1982) is a sort of postmodern mystery tale in which several narrators tell their version of the events leading up to and following the murder of two adolescent girls.[1] The novel might be characterized as postmodern in that the 'same' story is narrated several times from different perspectives, a narrative technique that calls attention to the subjectivity or relativity of truth. One way in which it is perhaps *not* postmodern (and the reader is grateful for this) is that the question posed throughout the narrative – the identity of the murderer – is answered in the end.[2] The novel is comprised of six narratives by five different homodiegetic, first-person narrators. I have chosen to focus my attention, in this study on anxiety in women's writing, on the narratives of two of the three male narrators; I have done so because it is in these narratives that anxiety is the most palpable. While the narratives of the two female narrators – the two murder victims – are saturated with desire, anxiety is for the most part absent from them. This absence might be explained in part by the fact that the girls' narratives appear in the form of personal diaries (although one is apparently narrated from the grave). Presumably, then, the girls do not suffer from the anxiety of authorship felt so keenly by Ernaux's and Sarraute's narrators in particular. The three narratives by the two male narrators I examine, on the other hand, belong (either explicitly or implicitly) to genres that are destined to be read: two of them are letters, and the third, as well as one of the letters, have all the hallmarks of the confession (a point to which I will return later in the chapter). Another explanation for the relative lack of anxiety in the feminine narratives may be that, while these girls are 'guilty' of sexual curiosity and longing, they are innocent, unlike their male counterparts, of crimes of violence, the memory of which provokes in these latter the anxious dread of potential discovery and punishment. This is the primary anxiety that both propels and hinders these men's narratives.

This chapter will therefore differ from the previous three, because it will focus not on the anxieties of a female narrator, nor on those of a 'vaguely' male or androgynous narrator, but on those of two 'emphatically' male narrators (for these men are deeply despotic and misogynist). It will also differ from the others in that, though it examines the narratives of male narrators, the principal issues it raises are specifically feminist issues. *Les fous de Bassan* is in fact the only one of the four literary texts I analyse in this study in which misogyny and women's oppression are primary concerns. Although the Gestapo agent's sadistic manipulation of the female narrator in Duras's 'Monsieur X. dit ici Pierre Rabier' (discussed in chapter 1) is certainly an example of male aggression towards women, we must not forget that Rabier exercises this same kind of sadism against men as well, as the story he tells the narrator about the German deserter he befriended and then had executed demonstrates.[3] He is also responsible for the deportation and/or execution of countless resistants and Jews, most of whom are male (like the narrator's husband). In Ernaux's *La honte* (discussed in chapter 2), the shameful memory evoked is that of a violent scene between the narrator's parents during which the father holds the blade of a billhook to the mother's throat, but it is precisely the extraordinary nature of the father's action that makes the narrator's memory of it so indelible. Throughout Ernaux's œuvre, the father is portrayed on the contrary as gentle and meek, and the mother as powerful and dominating. So while misogyny and violence against women are present in these texts, and while Duras and Ernaux are certainly known as feminist writers, 'Monsieur X.' and *La honte* target for the most part other social, intellectual, and emotional issues, such as collaboration, resistance, social mobility, shame, and of course, anxiety.[4]

On the other hand, there is one essential similarity between these two texts and Hébert's: all three works are examinations of memory (whether real or fictional) and its capacity both to stimulate and to stall narrative. In fact, memory's (usually inopportune) resurgence into the present is a fundamental theme throughout Hébert's œuvre, from her earliest prose texts (such as 'Le torrent' and *Kamouraska*) to her latest (such as *Le premier jardin* and *L'enfant chargé de songes*).[5] The anxiety to which this unwelcome resurgence gives birth will be, as it is in chapters 1 and 2, one of this chapter's main concerns.

In my reading of *Les fous de Bassan*, I make use of a linguistic notion conceived by Julia Kristeva, a philosopher and psychoanalyst whose range of interests, like those of Duras, Ernaux, and Hébert, has at times been obscured by the attention paid to her feminism. This concept is the 'semiotic,' which Kristeva characterizes as a 'feminine' element of language, even though it is by no means exclusive to the language of women (I will describe Kristeva's conception of the semiotic below). Applying the notion of the semiotic to Hébert's novel will help me to identify many of the novel's distinctive linguistic features and to pinpoint the manner in which they serve the novel's critique of both patriarchy and Puritanism. It will also lend support to my argument that the anxieties present in these two male narrators' narratives differ in at least one fundamental way from those evident in the narratives analysed in chapters 1 through 3 (I will name and discuss this difference below). While there are some notable differences, then, between the analysis in this chapter and those in the previous three, it is equally pertinent to this study, whose central object of exploration is not anxieties that belong exclusively to women but the innovative ways in which anxiety (no matter what kind and to whom it belongs) is textualized in contemporary women's writing in French. This reading of Hébert's novel will also contribute to another of this book's objectives, which is to identify the narrative techniques these women writers use to create what they feel is the most truthful portrait possible of the subject they treat.

The murders and most of the other events recounted in Hébert's story take place in a tiny, English-speaking village in Quebec during the summer of 1936. The title of the novel, *Les fous de Bassan*, refers to the marine birds, called 'boobies' or 'gannets' in English, that are omnipresent in this fictional coastal village, founded, the first narrator tells us, in 1782 by British loyalists fleeing Revolutionary America.[6] All five of the named narrators in the novel speak of these birds, some obsessively.[7] The gannets are noted especially for their cries, which several of the narrators characterize as 'perçants,' 'déchirants,' or 'assourdissants' (piercing, ear-splitting, deafening).[8] If taken literally, these adjectives describe sounds so loud that they pierce the eardrum and render deaf those who hear them. In the two narratives on which I focus – the 'livre' (book) of Nicolas Jones, pastor of Griffin Creek, and the second of two letters by Stevens Brown, Nicolas's ne'er-do-well nephew (and, as it turns out, the murderer of the two girls) – there is a marked obsession not only with the deafening cries of the gannets but with almost any and every kind of sound that reaches these two men's ears. *Les fous de Bassan* is not the only novel in

Hébert's œuvre in which sounds and characters' (both male and female) perceptions of them are foregrounded. For the guilt-ridden and anxious Élisabeth d'Aulnières in *Kamouraska*, for example, an overflowing gutter 'fait un bruit assourdissant' (makes a deafening noise) and when the doorbell rings during the night, she is 'épouvantée par tout ce fracas' (terrified by all this racket).[9] In *L'enfant chargé de songes*, the sensitive and introverted protagonist Julien, who has travelled from calm Quebec to feverish Paris, is bothered by 'le flot incessant des voitures sur le quai [qui], pareil à une armée aux rangs serrés, couvre tout de son vacarme assourdissant' (the endless wave of cars along the quay [which], like the serried ranks of an army, covers everything with its deafening racket).[10] And in *Le premier jardin*, the restless actress Flora Fontanges, who has travelled in the opposite direction from Julien, is abruptly awakened from a dream-laden sleep by '[un v]acarme d'aspirateur et de clefs remuées dans le corridor, [un] vrombissement de voitures, [des] voix confuses du côté de la rue' ([t]he din of a vacuum cleaner and of keys clattering in the hallway, the hum of cars, blurred voices from the street).[11] Still, while sounds and the human sense of hearing seem to hold a privileged place in Hébert's work, an attentive reading of *Les fous de Bassan* makes clear that this is by far the 'noisiest' of all the author's texts. Throughout the novel, but especially in the two narratives analysed here, several dozens of sounds of diverse qualities and volumes, emanating from human, animal, as well as inorganic sources, are evoked, and the variety of vocabulary used to transcribe them is striking, to say the least. The array of substantives signifying sound in the novel includes but is not limited to: *murmure* (murmuring), *rumeur* (hum), *clameur* (clamour), *vacarme* (uproar), *fracas* (din), *chahut* (racket), *battement* (beating), *vrombissement* (buzzing), *grondement* (growling), *jappement* (barking), *glapissement* (yelping), *pépiement* (chirping), *beuglement* (belowing), *raclement* (scraping), *ronflement* (snoring), *gémissement* (groaning), *cri* (cry), *clapotis* (lapping), *cliquetis* (rattling), and *tic-tac* (tick-tock). People, animals, and things in this fictional world never simply exist; rather, they *gueulent* (yell), *s'ésclaffent* (burst out laughing), *hurlent* (howl), *s'égosillent* (sing at the top of their voice), *geindent* (groan), *roucoulent* (coo), *chuchotent* (whisper), *sifflent* (whistle), *soufflent* (blow), *sonnent* (ring out), *s'entrechoquent* (bang against one another), *toquent* (knock), *cognent* (bang), *crépitent* (crackle), or *claquent* (bang).

Of particular interest in this chapter is that, in stark contrast to the young Clara in Hébert's *Aurélien, Clara, Mademoiselle et le lieutenant anglais* (1995) – a country girl who is enchanted by sounds of all kinds, especially those of nature, ('parfois Clara se laissait aller à des trilles d'oiseaux, connus d'elle seule, si limpides et purs qu'elle se taisait brusquement, suffoquée de bonheur' [sometimes Clara would abandon herself to the trill of birds, known by her alone, so limpid and pure that she would become speechless suddenly, breathless with happiness])[12] – Nicolas Jones and Stevens Brown invariably perceive sound, whether soft or loud, singular or recurrent, natural or man-made, as *violent.* They experience sound as an assault on both their bodies and their psyches, and indeed, in the epigraph to the version of the story told by another narrator, Stevens's 'idiot' brother Perceval, sound and violence are explicitly linked: 'It is a tale told by an idiot, full of sound and fury' (136). This line is spoken by Shakespeare's Macbeth, and the 'it' to which he refers is human life, which, while it runs its course, is filled with desire, turmoil, and tragedy (figured here as sound and fury), but which ends in silence and utter emptiness.[13] In what follows, I will suggest that the violence that sound exacts upon Stevens Brown and Nicolas Jones is a literal echo of the violence (of both their own and others' making) they have experienced in their past. Their association of certain sounds with violence renders Nicolas and Stevens hypersensitive to sound in general and leaves them in a perpetual state of anxiety that they believe only silence can assuage (which is an assumption I will throw into question). Although, as I have suggested, many kinds of sounds provoke anxiety in these two narrators, they are especially sensitive to the sound of certain voices, the 'voices' of the gannets included. I will therefore pay particular attention to the novel's presentation of voice.

In *Les fous de Bassan*, it is certainly in emptiness, if not in silence, that the lives of both Nicolas Jones and Stevens Brown, like Macbeth's, appear to be ending. In the second of his two narratives, dated autumn 1982, Stevens writes of having escaped from the veterans' hospital in Montreal where he had been living since the end of the Second World War in order to find the silence he needs to write an account of the summer of 1936. In his narrative, also dated autumn 1982, the elderly Nicolas is finishing his days in the nearly deserted Griffin Creek in a house being slowly destroyed by the salt, termites, and worms of the land he used to believe was 'promised' for his now nearly decimated flock (14; 23). It is with an analysis of this latter narrative, which opens the novel, that I will begin exploring the connection in Hébert's text between sound and violence, and the extreme anxiety – indeed, the madness in Stevens's case – that the narrators' apprehension of this connection provokes.

'Le livre de Nicolas Jones, automne 1982'

That sounds of all kinds disturb Nicolas deeply is evident from the very first lines of his narrative. At the beginning of this diary-like account, the pastor is gazing out at the grey sea that lies before Griffin Creek when he hears in the distance 'une rumeur de fête, du côté du nouveau village ... [La] fanfare se mêle au vent. M'atteint par rafales. Me perce le tympan' (from the new village, the hum of festivities ... The brass band is drowned by the wind. I hear spurts of music. Earsplitting).[14] The French-speaking Catholics who now inhabit a new section of Griffin Creek are celebrating the village's bicentennial, 'comme si,' the old man complains, 'c'étaient eux les fondateurs' (as if they were the ones who had founded it) (13; 9). The wind, described throughout the novel as having a voice of its own, here carries with it the voices and music of the barbarian invaders and tolls the proverbial bell (yet more racket) for the Griffin Creek of the pastor's younger days. Yet Nicolas acknowledges that this is not the first invasion the village has seen; when the cousins Nora and Olivia Atkins failed to arrive home the night of their murders in 1936, 'leur signalement [a été] donné par toutes les radios canadiennes et américaines' ([t]heir descriptions [were] broadcast on every Canadian and American radio station) (38; 26). Siren-like, the strident voice of the radio (a modern device utterly misplaced in this village, which is isolated not only in space but in time as well) beckoned to the Griffin Creek of 1936 a crowd of outsiders – policmen, investigators, and gapers – who cracked the hermetic village open like a bird's egg, then left its contents to rot. It was this first invasion, in Nicolas's eyes, that precipitated the village's agonizing demise. Childless, the pastor has since been condemned to watch the youth of Griffin Creek slip away as if upon the tide, like the bodies of the two murdered girls. On this sonorous night in 1982, he also hears, as if in accompaniment to the music and voices of the new village, 'des jappements lointains, toute une meute céleste qui s'éloigne dans la nuit' (distant barking, hounds of heaven moving away in the night) (24; 18). This is a signal, he concludes, that in their autumnal migration southward, even the gannets, natives of the land before any white man arrived there, are abandoning him to his memories.

Nicolas's attempt to take refuge from sound by going inside the house is thwarted by the domestic din made there by his twin nieces-turned-servants (Stevens's younger sisters): 'Des bruits de vaisselle sans fin, les verres qui s'entrechoquent. Le cliquetis des couverts sur l'évier. Il faudrait empêcher les jumelles de faire tant de vacarme' (The noise of dishes, endless. Glasses clink. Plates clatter against the sink. Must tell the twins not to make such a racket) (20; 14). He silences these sounds by sending the twins to bed, but with the interior of the house grown quiet, the external noises he had earlier fled now infiltrate the house: 'Dehors le crissement des insectes se déchaîne dans la nuit, enveloppe la maison d'une couverture bruissante' (Outside, the rustling of insects erupts in the night, wrapping the house in a murmuring blanket) (22; 15).

Nicolas retires to his study, but the sounds of the insects that have replaced those of the truant birds are quickly subsumed by yet more noises, these even more disturbing than any that had preceded them. It is the source rather than the character of these new noises that makes them so alarming to the pastor, for they come from neither the inside nor the outside of the house. They seem to originate, rather, within Nicolas's own body: 'Il se passe quelque chose d'étrange à l'intérieur de la pièce où je demeure rivé à mon fauteuil. On dirait que mon sang bat hors de moi, cogne dans les murs et les poutres du plafond. Rumeur sourde, martelée. Combien de temps vais-je pouvoir supporter cela?' (Something strange is going on inside the room where I am riveted to my chair. It's as if my blood is pounding outside of me, rapping against walls and beams. A muffled rumble, a throbbing. How long will I be able to bear it?) (22; 15). Imitating the drums heard earlier, Nicolas's own blood seems to beat a muted rhythm against the walls not only of his chest but of the very house. This sound is particularly anxiety-producing for the pastor because, as André Brochu maintains, this exteriorization of his beating heart seems to him to be 'la manifestation intempestive, scandaleuse des sources secrètes de l'affectivité' (the unwelcome and scandalous manifestation of the secret sources of emotion).[15] That is, this sonic exposure of Nicolas's flesh-and-blood heart is also the exposure of all that it symbolically contains – his deepest emotions and desires, which the stern pastor jealously guards.

This disturbingly audible heartbeat seems to echo that heard by the protagonist of another North American story of murder, Edgar Allan Poe's 'The Telltale Heart.' The heart whose beating Poe's anti-hero hears is that, he believes, of his murder victim, whose body he has cut up and hidden beneath the floorboards. Though he will presumably face the gallows if he is found sane, the murderer vehemently defends himself against the charge of madness: 'TRUE! nervous, very, very dreadfully nervous I had been and am; but why WILL you say that I am mad? The disease had sharpened my senses, not destroyed, not dulled them. Above all was the sense of hearing acute. I heard all things in the heaven and in the earth. I heard many things in hell. How then am I mad?'[16]

This 'disease' of which he enigmatically speaks is not madness but rather, he believes, a heightened state of perception that is a sign of superiority rather than infirmity.[17] If he has in fact gone mad, he suggests, it was the beating of the 'hideous' heart that made him mad, and not madness that made him hear the heart.[18] The reader must presume, however, that the heartbeat is a symptom rather than the source of the man's madness and that, like Hébert's disturbed pastor, Poe's narrator is projecting internal sounds (his own, anxious heartbeat) outward. The 'acuteness' of this latter's hearing proves to be a liability rather than an advantage, given that it is his inability to endure this sound that drives him to confess his crime. The fact that both he and Nicolas are tortured by the sound of their own heartbeat is a sign, moreover, not just of their madness (to which the title of Hébert's novel gestures), but of their *guilt*, a sentiment from which Nicolas, though not a murderer, has ample reason to suffer, as will become apparent below.[19]

Against the background of the beating heart, the tormented pastor then begins to experience what must be considered the paradigmatic sign of madness: he begins hearing *voices*. 'Des voix, rien que des voix, des sons, rien que des sons. Allumer une autre pipe, les oreilles pleines de la musique d'autrefois et de voix aigrelettes' (Voices, nothing but voices, sounds, nothing but sounds. I light another pipe, ears filled with the music of bygone days and shrill voices) (29; 20). These voices and sounds emanate not from the present, but from the past – specifically, the summer of 1936: 'Que se taise à jamais la voix de Felicity Jones qui gronde son fils, comme s'il avait cinq ans' (Let the voice of Felicity Jones be silent forever, scolding her son as if he were five years old) (41; 28).[20] Nicolas's mother Felicity (Stevens's maternal grandmother) had been an indifferent caretaker to her sons and grandsons, but she had loved and nurtured the two granddaughters, Nora and Olivia, her daughters had produced. Dominated and often abused by their despotic fathers and husbands, almost none of the several mothers in the novel is capable of mustering much warmth for her sons or, in many cases, for her daughters either.[21] Not permitted as a child to take part in his mother's pre-dawn swims on the beach of Griffin Creek (outings to which Felicity later invites Nora and Olivia), Nicolas carries into old age his unfulfilled desire for maternal love: 'Par quelle prière magique, quelle invention de l'amour fou pourrais-je délivrer le cœur de ma mère? J'en rêve comme d'une mission impossible' (What magic prayer, what invention of mad love would let me free my mother's heart? I dream of it as of some impossible mission) (25; 17). As Karen Gould writes, both Nicolas's and Stevens's 'experience of motherhood is fundamentally one of vulnerability and rejection,' and this experience serves as a foundation for both men's virulent misogyny. For the two of them, Gould continues, 'the search for the maternal is a hopeless venture inasmuch as the life-giving force and emotional sustenance embodied by the maternal figures are what they want, cannot secure for themselves, and consequently loathe.'[22]

As his reaction to the sudden resurgence of Felicity's voice suggests, for Nicolas, the mother's voice is not the 'sonorous envelope' it is supposed to be, a soothing sound that holds the child in a state of blissful unity with the mother.[23] Rather, Felicity's voice unnaturally resembles the prohibitive, castrating voice of the father – with the difference that it does not promise the boy a future share in the father's authority in exchange for the castration it augurs. The mother cannot give, after all, what she does not have. In the novel, in fact, the mother's voice in general is stripped of any real power in that the reader never 'hears' it directly. Felicity's voice, for example, is always presented second-hand, through Nicolas's or Stevens's memories of her (mostly scolding) words to them. Indeed, none of the mothers in the novel has a narrative of her own; these voices are silenced, as they must be if the children of these mothers are to be successfully initiated into the masculine symbolic order, an order that divides rather than unifies.[24]

It is evident in the novel that Nicolas's frustrated desire for a nurturing mother has been perverted into a generalized rage against women, who are for him agonizingly inaccessible when they are desirable and irritatingly and noisily omnipresent when they are not. Nicolas's vexation at his niece-servants' domestic din demonstrates that the sounds women make with both their voices and the movements of their bodies are the most insufferable of the multitude of noises that torment the pastor. Compounding the offensiveness of his nieces' femininity is the femininity of the objects (such as *la vaisselle*) they bang interminably together, as well as that of the base domestic tasks for which they are responsible: 'Les voici qui raclent le fond de l'évier avec de l'Old Dutch. N'en finissent plus de faire du train' (Now they are scouring the sink with Old Dutch. There's no end to their racket) (20; 14). Though the twins harbour a (feminine, it seems to Nicolas) desire to make and listen to noise of all kinds, as if it were music, his authority over them usually prompts them to stifle it: 'Si les jumelles s'enchantent du bruit rythmé de la pluie tambourinant dans la cuvette, ont envie de battre des mains et de danser tout autour elles n'en laissent rien voir' (If the twins rejoice at the rhythmical sound of the rain drumming into the basin, feel an urge to clap their hands and dance around it, they don't let it show) (53; 36). In their love of pure noise, the twins are the auditorily hypersensitive pastor's nemesis. Despite their predilection for sound, however, they are exasperatingly oblivious to the noise Nicolas makes to summon them. Though 'il agite la sonnette de toutes [s]es forces' (he ring[s] the bell as hard as [he] can), still the twins do not appear. Clear of conscience, unlike their uncle, '[elles] dorment à poings fermés' ([they] sleep like logs) (29; 20).

Though the twins rarely speak, and though they suppress their urge to dance and clap, they are apparently unable (or else they refuse) to contain their frequent laughter: 'Dès que j'ai le dos tourné,' Nicolas grumbles, 'les jumelles retrouvent leurs secrets de jumelles, des rires étouffés, des gloussements' (As soon as my back is turned, the twins return to their twins' secrets, to their muffled laughter, their chuckles, and furtive caresses) (19; 13). Whatever private joke they are sharing, the paranoid pastor is certain it is on him. The laughter of Felicity, Nora, and Olivia torments him as well, racked as he is with jealousy and desire as he furtively watches them swim together. (39; 26). Laughter is of course mythologically associated with the feminine, and therefore it is a particularly irritating sound to Nicolas, as it is to his nephew Stevens, who has so little tolerance for laughter that it is Nora's mocking 'rire hystérique' (hysterical laughter) on the beach late one night in 1936 that ignites his murderous rage (244; 180).[25]

The voices from the past that resound in Nicolas's head on the night he describes in 1982 are not all laughing, however, nor are they exclusively female. Surprisingly, even more painful than the memory of his mother's disapproving voice is the memory of his *own* voice as a young man, delivering sermons in the tiny church of Griffin Creek: 'Surtout ne pas entendre à nouveau le prêche du révérend Nicolas Jones qui roucoule et s'enchante à mesure de l'écho de sa propre voix' (Above all not to hear again the sermon of the Reverend Nicholas Jones, who coos and rejoices at the sound of his own voice) (29; 20). This aversion is especially surprising considering a claim he proudly makes a bit earlier in his narrative: 'Un jour j'ai été le Verbe de Griffin Creek, dépositaire du Verbe à Griffin Creek, moi-même Verbe au milieu des fidèles, muets par force, frustes par nature, assemblés dans la petite église de bois' (One day I was the Word of Griffin Creek, guardian of the Word at Griffin Creek, myself the Word amid the faithful, who were silent through strength, unpolished by nature and gathered together in the little wooden church) (19; 13). As a boy, Nicolas had trained his voice along the shore of Griffin Creek, practising the thundering sermons he would later make: 'Je m'adresse à l'eau, désirant parler plus fort qu'elle, la convaincre de ma force et de ma puissance' (I address the water, wanting to talk louder than it, to convince it of my power and strength) (25; 17). As a child he had already understood that the Word is power; in becoming pastor, he would ascend from the symbolic order of ordinary men into a more privileged symbolic order – that of the church. Within this order, the final signified is not the imaginary and lost mother, as Lacan would have it, but (a very masculine) Father. As 'maître des saintes Écritures' (master of the Holy Writ), it is 'au nom de Dieu' (in the name of God) that the adult Nicolas speaks to his flock (28; 19). But the boy's precocious use of the power of the Word to subjugate the vociferous and feminine sea serves as a prelude to the principal use he will make of that power later in life, which is to wield it especially over *women*. 'Sans jamais les toucher,' Nicolas says of his twin servants, 'rien qu'avec ma voix de basse caverneuse, je les retourne comme des feuilles légères dans le vent' (Never touching them, using only my cavernous bass voice, I turn them over like light leaves in the wind) (18; 12). Of the pastor's seemingly divine verbal authority over the women of Griffin Creek, fellow misogynist Stevens remarks, 'Il n'y a que mon oncle Nicolas pour les calmer et leur faire entendre raison. Au nom de Dieu et de la loi de l'Église qui sait remettre les femmes à leur place' (There's no one like my uncle Nicholas to calm them down, make them listen to reason, in the name of God and the law of the church. There's no one like him to know how to put women in their place) (88; 63).

During the summer of 1936, Nicolas exercises his power of the Word over two women, or near-women, in particular: his blossoming young nieces, Nora and Olivia Atkins. 'Depuis quelque temps je choisis avec encore plus de soin les psaumes et les hymnes du dimanche en pensant aux petites Atkins [...] Je les prépare comme de jeunes fiancées, attentives au chant de l'amour en marche vers elles, dans la lumière de l'été' (For some time now I have been choosing the Sunday psalms and hymns with special care, thinking of the Atkins girls ... I prepare them as if they were young women betrothed, attentive to the love song coming toward them in the summer light) (28; 19). But the old man knows very well that the kind of love his voice spoke in 1936 was less divine than profane, and it is for this reason in particular that the memory of the sound of his own voice is now so repulsive to him. Using the present tense to convey how immediate these images still are to him almost fifty years later, Nicolas notes that as the girls sit (sat) listening to him that summer, 'leurs yeux de violette et d'outremer se lèvent vers moi pour ma damnation' (their eyes, violet and ultramarine, are raised up to me, for my damnation) (28;

19). For the girls' benefit alone, 'je module. J'articule chaque son, chaque syllabe, je fais passer le souffle de la terre dans le Verbe de Dieu' (I modulate, enunciate each sound, each syllable, turning the breath of the earth into the word of God) (28; 19). In her rich analysis of especially Christian myth imagery in *Les fous de Bassan*, Ruth Mésavage writes that this 'souffle de la terre' (breath of the earth) that Nicolas infuses into the Word is his sexual desire for the girls (especially Nora), a desire which will cause his undoing. 'Trop tenté par la beauté toute naturelle, voire animale de la petite Nora' (Too tempted by the natural, even bestial, beauty of little Nora), the pastor contaminates the divine Word with human and indeed incestuous lust.[26]

Expanding on Mésavage's analysis, I want to suggest that the metaphorical 'souffle de la terre' that inflates Nicolas's sermon can be thought of, at a linguistic level, as a manifestation of what Kristeva calls the *semiotic*. For Kristeva, meaning is conveyed through language by two means. The usually dominant means of signification in language is the *symbolic*, which is the formalized structure of language, the codes and rules by which rational meaning is made and understood. Kristeva calls the second means the semiotic, which is the non-structured, material element of language. In speech, the semiotic manifests itself in the tone, pitch, and rhythm of the speaker's voice, for example, or in his or her gestures and facial expressions; in written language, it is signalled through such details as 'poetic' figures, rhyme, or the disposition of words on the page.[27] Whereas the symbolic elements of language originate in the speaker/writer's intellect and appeal to the listener/reader's intellect, the semiotic originates in and appeals to the *body*. It is through the semiotic that the body enters into signification, that it 'speaks.' Kristeva maintains that what the body 'says,' or rather betrays, through the semiotic are its innermost drives (*pulsions*).[28]

Though 'cassée et essoufflée' (broken and breathless) (54; 36) in 1982, in 1936 Nicolas's voice is 'belle' (beautiful), and in his sermon, he admits, 'je fais des effets de voix pour cette petite fille [Nora] [...] Je soigne mes gestes oratoires. Je les arrondis dans la lumière d'été' (I use my voice dramatically for that little girl [Nora] ... I pay attention to my oratorical gestures. Round them off in the summer light) (30; 20). In playing with his voice and his gestures during the sermon, Nicolas very deliberately makes the materiality of his language take precedence over its codified semantic meaning and thus permits the semiotic to dominate the symbolic. Indeed, this is not unusual in speech acts such as sermons, whose purpose, like poetry's, is more to make the auditor feel than think. In its palpable semiotic materiality – the timber of Nicolas's voice, the catch of his breath, the strength and warmth of his hands and arms as they execute their gestures – what the sermon makes felt is the very corporeality of its production. When listening to the sermon, Nicolas's auditors are exposed less to the spirit of God than to the flesh of man.

Mésavage argues that the divine is conspicuously absent from Nicolas's 1982 narrative as well. In the very first paragraph, which reads, in its entirety, 'La barre étale de la mer, blanche, à perte de vue, sur le ciel gris, la masse noire des arbres, en ligne parallèle derrière nous' (The slack line of the sea, white, as far as the eye can see; against the gray sky, in a parallel line behind us, the black bulk of trees) (13; 9), there are no verbs. For Mésavage, 'l'absence de verbes signifie l'absence du Verbe de Dieu auquel le révérend voudrait bien se substituer' (the absence of verbs signifies the absence of the Word [*Verbe*] of God, which the reverend would like to embody).[29] She characterizes this verbless paragraph as an example of ekphrastic writing, writing that represents visually what it says semantically. In ekphrastic writing, Mésavage clarifies, 'nous avons deux images qui se superposent: l'une pour l'intellect – dans le cas présent, absence de signifiant verbal, l'autre pour l'imagination – absence de signifié: l'Esprit de Dieu' (we have two images that are superimposed: one for the intellect – in this example, the absence of a verbal signifier; and the other for the imagination – the absence of a signified: the Spirit of God).[30] In other words, there is no *verbe* here because there is no *Verbe*. From the summer of 1936 on, then, the pastor's house will slowly become not only the worm-eaten tomb of a broken man, but 'le tombeau de la lettre réifiée, répétée, itérée et dépouvue de l'esprit qui anime, inspire et insuffle le sens' (the tomb of reified and trite language, deprived of the spirit that could animate, inspire, and breathe meaning into it).[31]

As an old man, Nicolas is aware that the divine was absent from his sermons that summer and presumes that this absence was 'heard' by his auditors as well (as Poe's narrator supposes that the detectives also hear the beating heart). Appropriating Nora's voice, he imagines in the following way the girl's impressions as she listened to him preach one day in 1936:

Mon oncle Nicolas parle de Dieu, pense Nora Atkins, mais depuis quelque temps je n'entends plus la parole de Dieu dans la voix de l'oncle Nicolas. C'est comme si Dieu se taisait dans la voix de l'oncle Nicolas. La voix sonore

de l'oncle Nicolas, sans rien de pieux dedans, la belle voix de l'oncle Nicolas comme une écale brillante, vide de tout contenu, basse et virile, fluide
comme de la fumée. J'aime le son de sa voix d'homme dans la petite église.

Uncle Nicholas is talking about God, thinks Nora Atkins, but for some time
now I haven't heard the word of God in my uncle's voice. It's as if God had
disappeared from my uncle's voice. My uncle's resonant voice has no piety
in it, my uncle's voice as beautiful as a gleaming shell, devoid of content, virile and bass, fluid as smoke. I like the sound of his male voice in the little
church.[32]

Appropriately enough, in his 1982 narrative Nicolas speaks only *about*
this 'empty' 1936 sermon; he does not reproduce the text itself. The signifiers he uses in his narrative to refer to the sermon thus have no signified within that narrative. In a *mise en abyme* of empty mirrors, this lack of
a signified (the text of the sermon itself) in the narrative reflects the spoken sermon's lack of its intended signified (God). However, although
the pastor's sermon may indeed be 'vidée de son signifié sacré' (emptied
of its sacred signified), as Mésavage has it,[33] in a Kristevan framework it is
by no means 'vide de tout contenu' (empty of all content) as Nicolas
himself (speaking through Nora) claims (30; 20); it is not made only of
'words, words, signifying nothing' (46; 31).[34] As I have already suggested,
Nicolas's sermon does indeed signify: what it reveals, through the dominance of the semiotic in it, is the pastor's earthly and incestuous desire
for his nieces. Although this desire must be vigilantly repressed under
the symbolic order (whose very foundation is the prohibition against
incest), Nicolas cannot stem, indeed, does not appear to want to stem –
'je fais des effets de voix pour cette petite fille' (I use my voice dramatically for that little girl), and so on – the semiotic discharge of desire in
his speech (30; 20).[35]
  The passage above in which the elderly Nicolas imagines Nora's reac-
tions to his 1936 sermon is further significant because it contains precisely the kind of language – predominantly semiotic – that I have
suggested the pastor used in this (now missing) sermon. The phrase 'la
voix de l'oncle Nicolas' (the voice of Uncle Nicolas), for example, is
repeated four times instead of being replaced in some instances by a
pronoun, as it would be in less 'poetic' (or semiotic) language. The rhetorical device of repetition draws at least as much attention to the *sound*
of the words repeated as to their meaning, and it is indeed the sound of
her uncle's voice, and not what it says, that Nora (supposedly) finds

appealing. In addition, there are three metaphors in this passage (or more precisely, three similes) that further reveal the semiotic at work. Metaphors, though certainly understandable to the intellect, are intended first and foremost to appeal to the five senses, for they evoke images (as in 'écale brillante' [gleaming shell]), smells and sensations (as in 'fluide comme de la fumée' [fluid as smoke]), and sounds (like the sound of the voice itself, which is transformed by these metaphors into smells, sensations, and images). Nicolas's 1982 narrative, then, simultaneously speaks of (in its reference to the sermon) and serves as an example of semiotic language.

In his narrative, the old pastor goes on to complain of hearing yet a third, and perhaps even more disturbing, voice from his past. On the rare occasions his twin servants do speak, he remarks with irritation that their mouths resemble 'la bouche baveuse de leur frère Perceval' (the drooling mouth of their brother Perceval), and it is out of this mouth that issues the final voice Nicolas hears: 'La voix de Perceval siffle à mes oreilles [...] D'où vient que sa voix perçante persiste encore dans ma tête, en dépit du temps qui passe ?' (Perceval's voice whistles in my ears ... Why does his piercing voice still persist in my head, in spite of the time that has passed?) (50; 34). Nicolas's question is disingenuous, however, because he knows perfectly well why Perceval's voice haunts him: one summer night in 1936, Perceval interrupted the pastor's attempt to seduce Nora – physically this time rather than just verbally – in the village boathouse. Although he has no, or else very little, command of speech, Perceval manages to communicate this knowledge to the pastor's bland and 'barren' wife Irène, who consequently commits suicide.[36] Resolutely accusatory despite its near-wordlessness, Perceval's voice returns from the past to remind the pastor of his sins.

This is perhaps not the only explanation for Nicolas's hatred of his nephew's voice; another is undoubtedly Perceval's 'femininity.' Along with feminine physical traits, such as a mouth that resembles that of his sisters, Perceval also possesses, as Annabelle Rea points out, feminine character traits, such as his sensitivity and his intuition.[37] Perceval's grandmother Felicity includes him in her feminine morning swims and thus treats him as one of her granddaughters (until, that is, he seizes Nora one day in his own fit of incestuous desire) (117; 84–5). Moreover, Perceval is also frequently characterized as child-like: Nicolas calls the strapping fifteen-year-old 'cet enfant' (that child) (50; 34), and Nora notes that 'sa figure est celle d'un petit enfant qu'on aurait soufflée comme un ballon pour la faire grandir de force' (his face is like that of a little child that's been blown up like a balloon to force it to grow) (116; 84). Patriarchy's tendency towards conflation of the mother with the child, the container with the contained, effectively makes such infantilization the equivalent of feminization.

Above and beyond Perceval's appearance and behaviours, what makes the pastor associate him with the feminine is his near exclusion from the (masculine) symbolic order. Although one of the six narratives in the novel is attributed in part to Perceval, he, like Faulkner's character Benji on whom he is based, '[n'a p]as de mots' ([doesn't have] words) (140; 102).[38] Symbolic elements of language such as syntax, grammar, and words themselves are beyond his grasp. He expresses himself through gesticulations and through cries (*des cris*) and weeping (*des pleurs*), vocal sounds traditionally associated with women. Kristeva herself characterizes such semiotic elements of signification – non-linguistic vocal sounds and gestures – as feminine in that they are the means through which the child communicates with the mother, before his submission to the *nom-du-père* (the name-of-the-father), in Lacan's terms, which permits his entrance into the symbolic order.[39] It is only when the developing child perceives his separateness from the mother – and indeed from everything around him (this is Lacan's mirror stage)[40] – that he needs language in order to symbolize all that he is now missing. Although the unconscious and chaotic drives that underlie the semiotic are supposed to be repressed under the symbolic order (for they essentially aim towards the restoration of a unity, albeit imagined, with the mother), Kristeva maintains that the semiotic 'transgresses' the name-of-the-father and is always present, to a greater or lesser degree, within signification – greater in artistic as well as psychotic discourse (for the psychotic has lost his sense of a unified self, required for the use of symbolic language), and lesser in more 'rational' discourse.[41]

In his final narrative, Stevens calls the voice of the 'idiot' 'la voix primaire' (the primal voice) (232; 171), thereby suggesting his own perception of the primitive, pre-societal, and thus pre-symbolic nature of Perceval's voice. In the narrative attributed to Perceval, presumably written for him by a sort of 'ghost' writer (as are the post mortem 'thoughts' of the murdered Olivia in her narrative), the wordless young man explains his need to cry out, 'de joie ou de peine. Une espèce de son incontrôlable. Commence dans mon ventre. Monte dans ma poitrine. Serre ma gorge. Gicle dans ma bouche. Éclate à l'air libre. Ne peux m'en empêcher. Un son qui file jusqu'au ciel après avoir creusé son trou noir dans mes os' (from joy or sorrow. An uncontrollable sound. It starts in my belly. Rises into my chest. Chokes me. Squirts into my mouth. Bursts into the open air. I can't stop it. A sound that digs a black hole in my bones, then flies up into the sky) (140–1; 102). In his description of the cry's passage through his belly, his chest, his throat, his very bones, Perceval emphatically identifies the body (rather than the psyche or the intellect) as the source of his cry. Perceval's tendency throughout his narrative to omit the grammatical subject 'je' (I) (demonstrated here in 'ne peux m'en empêcher' [can't stop it]) furthermore reflects (ekphrastically, to apply Mésavage's term here) his status as a pre-linguistic, pre-symbolic (non-)subject who lacks, precisely, the notion of subjectivity or self.[42] Whereas Kristeva valorizes the cry as a semiotic transgression of symbolic law, to the verbally punctilious Nicolas, former 'maître du Verbe' (master of God's Word) of Griffin Creek, such an involuntary and uncontrolled vocal emission is odious. Nicolas also abhors the cry because he presumes it to be inherently meaningless, devoid (like the sermon whose memory torments him) of a signified. But like any semiotic expression, as noted, the cry is far from meaningless. In Les fous de Bassan, Janet Paterson writes, 'le cri c'est ce qui permet l'expression de l'inexprimable, de l'irrépétable. C'est-à-dire que là où la vérité ne se laisse pas dire, le cri, qui se trouve en excès du langage, exprime le désir et surtout son impasse' (The cry is what permits the expression of the inexpressible, the unrepeatable. That is, there where truth cannot be spoken, the cry, which is in excess of language, expresses desire, and especially its impasse).[43] As an expression of the frustrated desire for Nora and Olivia that Perceval shares with his uncle, his cry is the semiotic equivalent of Nicolas's sermon. With its paradoxical double meaning – that of a lack of meaning and that of an excess of meaning that should be repressed at all cost – the cry is for Nicolas a distressing sound in the extreme.

Late during the night in 1982 that Nicolas describes in his narrative, the multiple voices that had been filling his head finally quiet, allowing him to fall asleep. But sleep offers no respite for those, like Élisabeth d'Aulnières of Kamouraska or Flora Fontanges of Le premier jardin, whose memories, repressed by day, quickly take advantage at night of the space left by dormant perception. The peace of the pastor's sleep is thus shattered when one of the earlier voices returns, this time in altered form: 'Vu Perceval en songe, ange d'apocalypse, debout sur la ligne d'horizon, corps d'homme, tête de chérubin, les joues gonflées à tant souffler dans la trompette du Jugement' (Saw in my dreams Perceval, angel of the apocalypse, standing on the horizon, a man's body, a cherub's head, his cheeks distended from blowing into the Last Trumpet) (51; 35). Having witnessed the pastor's attempted seduction of Nora, Perceval is figured in the dream as the boisterous bearer of the news of Nicolas's damnation. In the midst of this acoustic apocalypse heralded by Perceval's trumpet, Nicolas sees 'des petits personnages noirs qui s'agitent sur la grève, en proie à la désolation, [et qui] écoutent la voix de leur désespoir, tonitru-ante [...] Finiront par se boucher les oreilles avec leurs mains' (small black figures moving about on the beach, victims of desolation, listening to the thundering voice of their despair ... Finally cover their ears with their hands) (51; 35). In his dream, then, all the inhabitants of Griffin Creek appear to share in his guilt and anxiety, for like him they want nothing more than to become deaf to the sound of Judgment Day. Nico-las's attempt earlier that evening to simulate deafness by 'drowning' him-self in the silence of the night ('Lâcher la nuit visqueuse dans toute la maison. M'en remplir les yeux et les oreilles. Ne plus voir. Ne plus enten-dre' [Turn loose the viscous night, all through the house. Let it fill my eyes and ears. Let me no longer see. No longer hear] [49; 33]) had been misguided, however, because it is precisely in perfect silence that the sounds contained within his memories and dreams reverberate with the most force.

In her analysis of Hébert's first published novella, 'Le torrent' (1950), Constantina Mitchell argues similarly that even the real, physiological deafness of the protagonist François, provoked by a blow to the head by his puritanical mother, does not protect the boy from the voices that damn him.[44] His hope that he will be freed from these voices upon falling deaf, Mitchell writes, 'sera vite démenti,' because 'l'intériorisation des sons' – François's memory of them – 'prolonge, et exacerbe même, la con-flagration biblique prêchée par la mère.' Like the Pastor in his apocalyptic dream, François 'dit goûter, de son vivant, au jugement dernier.'[45] In 'Le torrent,' François does gain physical autonomy when his mother is killed by the horse Perceval, but the tenacity of memory forecloses any possibil-ity of psychological liberation. As Mitchell points out, the horse's name contains the words *percer* (to pierce) and *-céphale* (head), which evoke 'le geste violent par lequel le narrateur perd l'ouïe.'[46] In *Les fous de Bassan*, the voice of another Perceval, Nicolas's nephew, indeed inflicts on the pas-tor the violence that his name promises. Perceval's voice, like the voice of the dead mother in 'Le torrent' (and like the heart in Poe's story), effects its work from *the inside out*, and so like François, Nicolas quickly discovers that deafness, whether real or contrived, offers no defence against – indeed exacerbates – the 'sound and the fury' of memory.

As morning approaches and the aural memories and dreams of the night give way to noises emanating once again from the world outside, Nicolas Jones hears 'un coq, quelque part dans la campagne, [qui] s'égosille, en vain appelle le point du jour' (a rooster, somewhere in the countryside, crowing until it's hoarse, calling in vain for daybreak) (50; 34). This line is of interest because it is echoed later in some of the first lines of Nora Atkins's narrative. In Nora's jubilant text, however, it is as if the echo of the pastor's plaintive line has, like the reflection of an image, been inverted: 'Des chants de coq passent à travers le rideau de cretonne, se brisent sur mon lit en éclats fauves. Le jour commence' (The songs of a coq filter through the cretonne curtains, shatter on my bed in musky fragments. Day is beginning) (111; 81). Unlike the unappealing cock the pastor hears, who screeches until he is hoarse yet never manages to summon the sun ('en vain appelle le point du jour' [calling in vain for daybreak]), the cock outside Nora's window 'sings' as he awakens her to a sunny morning. Through her window Nora also hears birds, but the sounds they make for her are 'des pépiements' (chirping) (111; 81) rather than the aggressive 'jappements' (barking) (24; 16) or 'cris assourdissants' (deafening cries) (95; 68) that so repel the pastor and his nephew Stevens.[47] In her narrative, Nora demonstrates, like the pastor's twin nieces and like Clara in *Aurélien, Clara, Mademoiselle et le lieutenant anglais*, a 'feminine' love of sounds of all kinds, like 'le chant des oiseaux [et] la rumeur des insectes [qui] se mêlent au chant des hymes, au son de l'harmonium' (the singing of birds and the murmur of insects that blend with the hymns, with the sound of the harmonium) (117–18; 85).[48]

Significant to my discussion of Kristeva's notion of the semiotic is that Nora and Nicolas not only hear the same world differently, but also *see* it very differently; specifically, they see it in vastly different colours (I will outline the connection between colour and the semiotic below). Nora's descriptions of herself and her surroundings almost always include colour; on the morning on which her narrative opens, she notes the blue spruce and the black eyes of the blackbirds and thrushes outside her window (111; 81), the blue basin and white towels beside her bed (112; 81), and the pink reflections of the rising sun upon the grey sea (113; 82). Outside she observes the green stems and the silver and mauve heads of the ripe hay she helps harvest, and the white and green hydrangeas (which will turn a rosy brown in autumn) and the white and pink phlox in her cousin Maureen's garden (122; 88 and 134; 96). On the evening of her murder, she stops to gaze at the orange halo of the rising moon, which will soon turn to bright white (135; 97). Nora does not simply admire the hues of nature, she also envelopes her own, blossoming body in vivid colour: she receives a green dress for her birthday (111–12; 81) and is wearing a pink one when she is murdered (180; 133). And it is through the variously coloured items of clothing, all belonging to her, that wash up on the shore following the girls' disappearance that the inhabitants of Griffin Creek learn of the cousins' fate: first a blue bracelet (179; 132), then a pink belt (179; 133), and finally a brown coat (183; 135).

Not surprisingly, the vibrant Nora also has bright red hair (111; 81). While Nicolas had red hair as a young man, his head has since been 'envahie par des poils blancs' (overgrown with white strands) (15; 10), and his eyes have been as if covered with a grey film: as the opening lines of his bleak narrative attest ('La barre étale de la mer, blanche [...] sur le ciel gris, la masse noire des arbres' [The slack line of the sea, white [...] against the gray sky, the black bulk of trees] [13; 9]), the elderly pastor sees the world entirely in black, white, and grey. Colour, when it does impose itself on his line of sight, has as painful an effect on his eyes as sound does on his ears. He complains that the houses of the new villagers are 'peinturlées en rouge, vert, jaune, bleu, comme si c'était un plaisir de barbouiller des maisons et d'afficher des couleurs voyantes' (daubed with red, green, yellow, blue, as if they took pleasure in smearing houses with garish colors) (13; 9). When the colour-phobic pastor decides to create a 'galerie des ancêtres' (gallery of ancestors) in his home, he paints all of his male ancestors 'en habit noir et linge blanc [...] Identiques, interchangeables' (in black suits and white linen ... Identical, interchangeable) (15; 10). Having been given the task of painting the female family members, Nicolas's twin nieces, on the other hand,

> livrées aux couleurs et aux pinceaux [...] ont barbouillé sur les murs des flots de dentelle, des volants, des carreaux, des pois, des rayures multicolores, des fleurs, des feuilles, des oiseaux roux, des poissons bleus, des algues pourpres [...] Éclaboussées de couleurs de la tête aux pieds, elles s'extasient devant leurs œuvres.

> set loose with brushes and paint ... have slathered the walls with cascades of lace, with flounces, checks and dots and multicolored stripes, with flowers, leaves, red birds, blue fish, crimson seaweed ... Spattered with colors from head to toe, they go into raptures before their creations. (16; 11)

Their uncle is enraged ('Tout un mur gâché' [A whole wall spoiled] [18; 12]) by such an undisciplined exercise of imagination and, more specifically, by the vibrancy with which the twins have recreated the faces of the three women who died during the summer of 1936 (Nora, Olivia, and Nicolas's wife Irène). That the twins paint these women together and in a way – colourfully – that would certainly displease the pastor suggests, as several critics have noted, that they hold Nicolas responsible not only for Irène's death, but for Nora's and Olivia's as well (because of his sullying of Nora, because of the patriarchal and misogynist example he set for the men of Griffin Creek, or perhaps because they believe that is was he and not Stevens who committed the murders). The three deaths are indeed related in that first, they were all the result of errant and incestuous male desire, and second, they were all caused by asphyxiation (Irène hanged herself and Nora and Olivia were strangled) – an end that, significantly, robs the victim of her voice even before it extinguishes her life.

In regard to the relationship between colour and the semiotic, for Kristeva, colour is to painting what non-linguistic sounds are to speech: they are both elements of semiotic rather than symbolic expression. Unlike representational forms, colours do not have predetermined, codified signifieds: a colour does not in and of itself represent a particular object or entity in the world.[49] In a Kristevan analysis of Jackson Pollack's painting 'Blue Poles,' John Lechte maintains that 'to the extent that the color and the texture of the paint as such is perceptible and nothing is represented, incest is connoted. By this we mean that the symbolic as any form of limit, separation, or distancing is, if not entirely absent, at least radically diminished.'[50] That is, in Pollack's painting, there are no discernable representations of phenomena such that the viewer can distinguish one from the other and name; the 'landscape' the painting depicts, then, is the landscape of unity ('incest') that the young child sees before he becomes conscious of the difference (between his own body and everything around him) that irreparably divides him from his mother. Even in representational paintings such as Giotto's, colours, Kristeva herself argues, 'have a noncentered or decentering effect, lessening both object identification and phenomenal fixation.'[51] In other words, certain uses of colour in classical painting, she maintains, can 'distract' the eye from seeing fixed, representational forms (paint disposed on the canvas to look like objects in the world). Certain uses of colour in painting, like certain uses of rhythm or sound in speaking, are semiotic discharges of drives – drives towards reunification with the forbidden mother, drives towards escape from the constraints of the symbolic order, and drives, finally, towards the dissolution of the self (because for Kristeva, as for Freud, the human drive that supersedes all others is finally the death drive).[52] In *Les fous de Bassan*, Nicolas's aversion to colour, like his aversion to 'meaningless' sound, can thus be interpreted as a manifestation of his aversion to the semiotic, to the eruption into the symbolic realm of pre-symbolic, 'feminine' drives.

Although mastery of the symbolic element of language is always illusory, Nicolas, as noted, feels that he once possessed such mastery but that he lost it in the summer of 1936 when he allowed his bodily desires to contaminate his speech and finally his actions. He still believes that he holds an 'autorité absolue' (absolute authority) over at least his twin servants, but the women's half-concealed laughter and the explosion of their normally stifled creativity in the *galerie des ancêtres* belie this contention. Nicolas does admit that what he has left in Griffin Creek is 'un ministère dérisoire, de peu d'envergure' (a pathetic ministry, small in scale) (18; 12). In this last choice of words, 'envergure,' one of whose meanings is 'wingspan,' we can perhaps read an allusion to the ever-present gannets of the novel's title. Moreover, given that the root word of 'envergure' (wingspan) is 'vergue' or 'verge' (penis), if, as Paterson and Brochu both suggest, 'l'oiseau détient un sens phallique' (the bird is a phallic symbol),[53] we can deduce that the principal feeling the feminine semiotic evokes in the pastor is one of impotence. In 1982, the pastor's nephew Stevens, now old, broken, and alone, finds himself in a similar state of emasculation, and it is to his final narrative that I will now turn.

'Dernière lettre de Stevens Brown à Michael Hotchkiss, automne 1982' (Last letter of Stevens Brown to Michael Hotchkiss, Autumn 1982)

In this narrative Stevens Brown writes of being tormented, like his uncle, by sounds of all kinds, and he also writes of experiencing, like Poe's madman, a certain sharpening not just of his hearing but of all five of his senses. Since the war he has been living 'les nerfs à vif' (nerves frayed) in a perpetual state of anxiety, which, he maintains, 'vient sans doute de ce que mes yeux ont vu, de ce que mon nez a senti, de ce que mes oreilles ont entendu, de ce que mon palais a dégusté, de ce que mes mains ont fait avec et sans fusil. Un vrai régal pour tous les sens' (comes, most likely, from what my eyes have seen, what my nose has smelled, my ears have heard, my palate has tasted, my hands have done – with and without a gun. A real feast for the senses) (230; 169). In regard to his hearing, he is also like both Nicolas and Poe's narrator in that the 'sounds' to which he is most sensitive are those emanating from within his own mind. Some of these are aural memories of the cries of the gannets of Griffin Creek (to which he has not returned in more than forty years), which are still so literally piercing that he feels eviscerated by them: 'Leurs cris perçants, gravés dans ma mémoire, me réveillent chaque nuit, me changent en poissonnaille, étripée vivante, sur les tables de vidage' (Their piercing cries engraved in my memory awaken me every night, change me into a mound of fish, gutted alive on the cleaning tables) (247; 182). His aversion to the gannets undoubtedly stems from their metonymical relationship to the seashore at Griffin Creek, which served, Stevens reveals in this narrative, as the scene of Nora and Olivia's murders. More generally, Stevens attributes his hypersensitivity to sound to 'trop de bruit et de fureur depuis mon enfance' (too much sound and fury since childhood) (245; 180), a childhood overshadowed by an authoritarian father and an indifferent mother. As deprived of maternal love as Nicolas, Stevens claims that his mother 'dégage du froid comme d'autres de la chaleur. C'est encore étonnant qu'elle puisse mettre au monde des enfants vivants, sortis d'un ventre aussi polaire' (gives off cold the way other people give off heat. It's surprising she can even bring live infants into the world, with such a glacial belly) (86; 62). By running away from home at sixteen, Stevens disavows his unrequited desire for the mother more forcefully than does Nicolas, with the result that his misogyny is even more virulent than his uncle's – so virulent that he murders two young women so as to witness no longer 'leurs manières de filles mièvres, écœurantes, leur excitation à fleur de peau' (their mawkish, disgusting girls' manners, their ready excitement) (239; 176). Stevens also differs from his uncle in that he is handsome rather than ugly; if Nicolas once held power over the women of Griffin Creek, it was uniquely an oratorical power. Stevens's power (to which Nora and Olivia are fatefully not immune) is sexual. Contemptuous of the women around him despite, or rather because of, their desire for him, Stevens uses this weapon less often to satisfy his own sexual appetite than to frustrate theirs, and indeed to punish them for their immodesty.[54]

Stevens reveals in the last lines of his narrative (which are also the last lines of the novel) that he in fact confessed to the murders in 1936, but that during his trial this confession was deemed coerced, and he was therefore acquitted of the crimes. Earlier in his narrative, we also learn that Stevens served in the Second World War and has spent the years between the war's end and 1982 in a veterans' hospital in Montreal, nursing wounds '[qui] ne sont pas visibles à l'œil nu' (invisible to the naked eye) (230; 169). He suffers from haunting – indeed traumatic – memories that reproduce with precision the colours, sensations, smells, tastes, but especially the sounds of the original experiences they recorded. Many of these recurring acoustic memories date from the war: 'Tant de balles et d'éclats d'obus sifflent dans la salle [d'hôpital], tout autour des hommes endormis, dans le silence de la nuit' (So many bullets, so much shrapnel whistle through the hospital room, all around the sleeping men, in the silence of the night) (231; 170). These shells have left Stevens physically 'indemne de la tête au pied' (unscathed from head to toe), but mentally he has become 'détraqué [...] Complètement détraqué. Sujet aux crises de nerfs. Tremble et transpire sans raison' (unhinged ... Completely unhinged. Subject to attacks of nerves. Tremble and sweat for no reason) (231; 171). Although Stevens insists that such 'crises' are 'rien que les séquelles de la guerre' (only the aftermath of the war) and that 'Griffin Creek n'y est pour rien' (Griffin Creek has nothing to do with it) (132; 171), the memories that pursue him the most tenaciously are those of the beaches, not of Normandy, but as for Nicolas, of Griffin Creek: 'Je lève le bras, [les oiseaux] s'envolent et ils crient. Je laisse tomber mon bras sur le drap d'hôpital, et ils reviennent en masse et ils crient à nouveau, s'aiguisent le bec contre mon crâne. Crier avec eux pour couvrir leur vacarme n'est pas une solution, m'épuise et me déchire' (I lift my arm, the birds scatter, they cry. I drop my arm on the hospital sheet and flocks of them return and they cry once more, sharpening their beaks against my skull. Crying out with them to cover their din is no solution, it exhausts me and tears me to shreds) (230; 170). This is not surprising, for it was on the shore at Griffin Creek that Stevens's first and most grisly battle – that against the feminine 'rire hystérique' (hysterical laughter) and 'cris perçants' (piercing cries) of his two young cousins – took place long before the war had begun (244; 180 and 248; 183). Although Stevens thought he had succeeded in 1936 in stifling these feminine sounds by sealing indefinitely the throats that produced them, and though he thought he had escaped 'indemne de la tête au pied' from that battle as well, like François in 'Le torrent,' he discovers that such sounds as these live on, amplified one hundred-fold, in memory.

In 1982, Stevens flees the veterans' hospital to spend his last days in a dingy hotel room in Montreal, presumably before committing suicide with the several dozens of pills he has stolen from the hospital pharmacy (229; 169). This last narrative (like his first, written in 1936) is a letter to a friend he met during his wanderings in the United States before returning to Griffin Creek in the summer of 1936. In the hospital there is simply too much noise, 'trop de larmes et de jurons [qui] laissent des traces dans l'air épais' (too many tears and curses, which leave their traces in the thick air), for him to think and write in peace (233; 172). In his hotel room, however, Stevens is as little able to find the silence he seeks as is Nicolas in his study in Griffin Creek. Just as the sounds of the country infiltrate Nicolas's worm-eaten house, here in Montreal, 'la rumeur de la ville gronde sous [l]es fenêtres' (the sounds of the city rumble beneath the windows) (234; 173). But shutting such exterior noises out does Stevens no more good than it does Nicolas, as he also must then wage a losing battle against the noises from *within* the building: 'le murmure des déshabillages sans entrain [...] L'infâme bruit des lavabos et des chasses d'eau [...] Quelques toux et raclements [...] agaçants comme des moustiques dans l'obscurité' (the murmur of half-hearted undressing ... The loathsome noise of taps running and toilets flushing ... A few lingering coughs and throat-clearings ... irritating as mosquitoes in the dark) (237; 174). What Stevens wishes for and must patiently await, 'jusqu'au dernier glapissement de la télévision' (to the TV's last yap), is 'le silence absolu de la maison endormie' (the utter silence of the sleeping house) (234; 173).

Unlike Nicolas, Stevens does not wish for silence so that he may sleep in peace. His objective, he says, is 'me concentrer sur mes écritures [...] N'être que celui qui écrit dans une chambre étrangère ce que lui dicte sa mémoire' (to concentrate on my writing ... To be merely a man writing in a strange room what his memory dictates) (234–5; 175). Stevens's past does resurge in its fullest force in the silence of the present, as does his uncle's. But whereas the pastor seeks reprieve from all sounds, whether from the present or the past, from the outside or the inside of his mind, Stevens wants to silence those of the present/outside precisely in order to hear better those of the past/inside. Ultimately, he too wishes to squelch these acoustic memories, once and for all; however, the method by which he will do this is not by falling asleep or by becoming 'deaf,' but rather by becoming an author. That is, he will convert these insufferable sounds and voices into *written* – and therefore *silent* – words.

As Janet Paterson points out, unlike the other narrators in the novel, Stevens frequently draws attention to the fact that he is *writing* his narrative.[55] It is specifically in order to write that he left the crowded and noisy veterans' hospital: 'Faire le vide en soi et autour de soi. Habiter un espace nu. Une sorte de page blanche et que les mots viennent à mon appel pour dire la guerre et tout le reste. Je les attends, un par un, pleins d'encre et de sang, qu'ils s'alignent sur le papier, dans l'ordre et dans le désordre, mais que les mots se pointent et me délivrent de ma mémoire' (Create a vacuum inside yourself and all around you. Inhabit a naked space. A sort of blank page and let the words come when I beckon them, to recount the war and all the rest. I wait for them, one at a time, filled with ink and blood, lining up on the page, in order and disorder; just let the words appear and deliver me from my memory) (233; 172). Though the atmosphere Stevens wants to create is more lugubrious than the one in which the writer in *Entre la vie et la mort* writes (despite that novel's morbid title), the two men await much the same process: of fluid words flowing onto their paper (or dripping like blood, in Stevens's case), words that capture exactly the reality they are seeking.[56] At first, the process Stevens begins is an oral/aural one – he 'calls' out to the words, and they come to 'tell' him the story that his wordless acoustic memories cannot articulate ('Que les mots viennent à mon appel pour dire la guerre et tout le reste' [Let the words come when I beckon them, to recount the war and all the rest]). But once he writes these words down in his black notebook, they will be trapped – to use an appropriate metaphor – like birds in a cage. Adopting an Aristotelian attitude, Stevens believes that when the oral/aural is turned into the written, it loses its presence and therefore its power. Whereas Aristotle valorized the spoken word for its presumed capacity to render more present, more *real* what it expresses, Stevens prefers the written word precisely for its presumed impotence in the evocation of the real.

The passage above calls to mind *Entre la vie et la mort* in this respect also: in that novel, the source of one of the writer's (many) anxieties is his suspicion that putting pre-linguistic sensations into language, more specifically into writing, will 'kill' them (for his goal is to keep them alive). Likewise, writers of autobiography like Duras and Ernaux are usually anxious to find ways to communicate their memories – even painful ones – in such a way that the events and sensations they recount are as vivid and present to the reader as they were (and often still are) to them. Stevens, on the other hand, is a killer, and he carries his murderous intent into the domain of writing. Instead of young women, his victims this time will be memories – memories that remain stubbornly alive even after forty years – and his weapon of choice will be not his hands but his pen.

Significantly, Kristeva also uses a life–death lexicon when speaking of linguistic expression, and her use of it is less metaphoric than Sarraute's.

For Kristeva, the semiotic element of language is literally where the living body, with all its pulsating drives, makes its presence felt. Whether Stevens succeeds in his strange objective of producing 'dead' writing might be gauged by determining the relative absence or presence of the semiotic in it. In her analysis of the novel, Paterson maintains that Stevens's final narrative is not just about madness; it is also a vehicle through which madness itself writes (without the author's 'permission,' as it were), just as, as I have argued, Nicolas's sermon both speaks of desire and is a vehicle through which desire speaks.[57] Paterson argues that in Stevens's narrative, 'les cris du fou [de Bassan]' (the cries of the gannet) to which he obsessively refers become, through the slippage of homonymic signifiers, 'l'écrit du fou' (the writing of the madman).[58] That is, Stevens's repeated linguistic references to the sound that literally drives him mad announce in black and white, unequivocally, that this is the writing of a madman. For Paterson, *Les fous de Bassan* in its entirety contains all the characteristics of the kind of text Kristeva calls 'psychotique' (psychotic) or 'délirant' (delirious).[59] 'Que ce soit au niveau de la forme,' Paterson writes,

> c'est-à-dire: circularité, transition sournoise du réel à l'imaginaire, écroulement de la linéarité, répétition obsessive, représentation problématique du sujet, inscription dans le discours d'un interlocuteur; ou que ce soit au niveau du sens: émergence de l'interdit, désir de la mère, viol, meurtre, ce discours tout comme le discours psychotique exprime l'irrépétable en disant la signification du désir et de son impasse.

> Whether it be on the level of form, that is: circularity, sly transitions between the real and the imaginary, the breaking down of linearity, obsessive repetition, problematic representations of the subject, the inscription in the discourse of an interlocutor; or at the level of meaning: the emergence of the forbidden, desire for the mother, rape, murder; this discourse, just like psychotic discourse, expresses the unrepeatable by speaking the meaning of desire and its impass.[60]

Based on these multiple criteria, the 'maddest' narrative of the six in the novel is the final one, just as the maddest of the six narrators is surely he whose death drive has overcome its repression and exploded into the symbolic (social) order in the form of two murders and an imminent suicide. As Stevens himself affirms the integrity of his body, his text announces the dissolution of his psyche, as a passage I have already partially cited demonstrates:

Intact, puisque je te dis que je suis intact. Passé à travers la guerre comme à travers les mailles d'un filet. Indemne de la tête aux pieds. Pas la moindre petite cicatrice. Détraqué seulement. Complètement détraqué. Sujet aux crises de nerfs. Tremble et transpire sans raison. Les dents qui claquent. Les draps qui se mouillent de sueur sous mes épaules, au creux de mes reins [...] La racine du cri vrillé dans ma poitrine, vieil héritage de famille sans doute [...] Hurler comme mon frère Perceval.

I'm intact, I tell you, intact. Slipped through the war as if it were a net. Unscathed from head to foot. Not the slightest scar. Only unhinged. Completely unhinged. Subject to attacks of nerves. Tremble and sweat for no reason. Teeth chatter. Sheets wet with sweat under my shoulders, in the small of my back ... The root of a cry boring into my chest, an old family heritage no doubt ... Howl like my brother Perceval. (231–2; 171)

This passage reveals that since writing his first narrative, dated summer 1936 and narrated in a more conventional form, Stevens has adopted not only the cry of his brother but also his almost total rejection of the subject pronoun 'I' and the unified subjectivity it announces. No longer *maître de ses mots* (master of his words) like the uncle he once emulated, the older Stevens produces a narrative that seems to propel itself forward without his agency (and indeed he waits, as we have seen, for the words to 'line up on the paper,' as if of their own volition). The obsessive repetitions in this passage (*intact/intact/indemne*, *à travers/à travers*; *détraqué/détraqué*) and throughout Stevens's narrative can be read, moreover, as marks less of the intellect than of the body, with its endlessly repetitive and circular biorhythms. If the body's presence is not obvious in these repetitions, it is certainly so in Stevens's enumeration of no less than seven body parts in eight lines of text.

In one of the final passages of the novel, it becomes clear that it is not only as an old and broken man that Stevens has experienced the dissolution of the psyche and of the self to which his writing is witness. During the moments on the beach when the younger Stevens murders Nora and Olivia, the violent drives his body had until that point contained suddenly cross the borders of the self and metamorphose into the furious wind that Stevens alone experienced that night:

Tout le monde dans la région est d'accord pour assurer qu'il n'y avait pas de vent ce soir-là et que la mer n'avait jamais été aussi paisible. Et pourtant, moi, Stevens Brown [...] j'affirme que subitement quelque chose s'est rompu dans l'air tranquille, autour de nous. La bulle fragile dans laquelle nous étions encore à l'abri crève soudain et nous voilà précipités, tous les trois, dans la fureur du monde.

Everyone in the area agrees, maintains there was no wind that night, that the sea had never been so calm. Yet I, Stevens Brown ... declare that something suddenly broke in the quiet air around us. The fragile bubble still sheltering us suddenly bursts and all three of us are hurled into the furor of the world. (243–4; 179)

This 'bulle fragile' (fragile bubble) is Stevens's own tenuous notion of self, which bursts here, precipitating the psychotic delirium during which the boundaries separating Nora, Olivia, and himself are erased. The radical *in*difference Stevens experiences between himself and others becomes evident when, in the midst of his madness, he remarks of Nora, 'cette fille est folle' (this girl is mad), thereby projecting his psychosis, as the pastor does his guilt, upon those around him (244; 181). Yet not only does Stevens's interiority spill out into the world, the world also invades that interiority: 'L'abîme de la mer nous contient tous, nous possède tous et nous résorbe à mesure dans son grand mouvement sonore' (The sea's abyss contains us all, possesses us all, pulls us along in its great, sonorous swells) (247; 182). For Stevens at this moment, as Brochu writes, 'il n'y a ni dedans ni dehors' (there is neither inside nor outside); all is self and nothing is self.[61] Released into this world without borders, Stevens's liberated desires 'speak' nowhere more distinctly than in his account of Olivia's rape: '[Je m]'enferme avec elle, au centre d'elle. Mourir ainsi au cœur de ce linge froissé, déchiré. Pénétrer au plus profond d'elle' ([I] close myself in with her, in the center of her. And die this way at the heart of that torn and crumpled linen. Penetrate to her very depths) (248; 182). The boundaries of Olivia's body are demolished by the irrepressible and violent expansion of a 'self' that recognizes no limits.

Stevens's conflation of the womb and the tomb here also confirms that the drive for the unity and quiescence whose energies are expelled in his narrative is indeed the death drive. In fact, several times in his narrative Stevens explicitly expresses the wish to die. At the veterans' hospital, he says, 'ce n'[était] pas tant de mourir dont j'avais le plus peur, mais de me réveiller le matin. Retrouver l'horreur du matin' (it [wasn't] dying that scared me so much as waking up in the morning. To rediscover the horror of the morning) (235; 173). Thanks to the pills he has brought with him to the hotel and lined up in neat rows on his writing desk, he has 'la vie, la mort à portée de la main' (life and death within [his] reach) (236; 174). He wishes to end his life in this hotel room, 'vidé de toute mémoire, pareil à une poupée de son que l'on éventre' (emptied of all memory like a disemboweled doll) (236; 174). This imagery of evisceration appears several times in Stevens's narrative: as mentioned above, his memories of the gannets' cries leave him feeling 'étripé vivant' (gutted alive) (247; 182), and as he is taking the bodies of Nora and Olivia out to sea, 'l'étonnement,' he writes, 's'enfonce dans ma poitrine telle la lame d'un couteau. Me déchire lentement' (amazement ... sinks into my chest, like the blade of a knife. Slowly rends me) (249; 183). It is as if this prolonged cutting open is what has finally allowed the secret that Stevens has been hiding for more than forty years – that of the murders he committed in 1936 – to come out.[62]

Since the sensations and desires that Stevens's acoustic memories revive are, then, clearly present in his writing, it would seem that his plan of silencing these memories by converting them into written and, moreover, colourless signs – for they are now nothing but black marks on white paper – fails. Yet is it appropriate to call Stevens's text 'living' when the drives that vivify it are murderous? The evisceration that writing effects on him, moreover, leaves Stevens bleeding drive energy, whose depletion will lead as inevitably to his death as would that of his blood. The semiotic 'bleeding' perceptible in Stevens's text can only lead the reader to assume, then, that his efforts to create the most perfect silence of all – that of death – succeed. So while Stevens manages to animate his narrative to a degree undreamed of by Sarraute's ineffectual writer, he does so only by pouring every ounce of his own life blood into it. Whereas the texts that Sarraute's anguished writer seems to constantly re-begin could be said to be abortive (as could the 'conditional' narrative in Duras's 'Madame Dodin'), Stevens's text is murderous.[63] It brings about the death not only of its narrator, but of the greater narrative – Hébert's novel – in which it is imbedded.

If Stevens's final letter differs from the writer's text in *Entre la vie et la mort* and from the conscientious tenant's 'virtual' letter in 'Madame Dodin,' both his and his uncle's narratives do have more in common with the two other principal texts discussed in this book, Duras's 'Monsieur X.' and Ernaux's *La honte*. First, their narrators all struggle with (or against) distressing memories, and second, they try in one way or another to come to terms with these memories through writing. Furthermore, and perhaps more significantly, all of these narrators reveal certain secrets about themselves and their past, with the effect that their

...... itives could all be read as *confessions*. 'Ce que j'ai à faire, ce que je me suis juré de faire,' Stevens writes, '[c'est t]e dire la vérité, old Mic, toute la vérité, rien que la vérité' (What I have to do, what I've sworn to do [...] [is] to tell you the truth, old Mick, the whole truth and nothing but the truth), as if he were back on the witness stand in 1936, with his hand placed on the bible (237; 175). The confessions in these men's narratives are radically different in nature, however, from the revelations in Duras's and Ernaux's texts. In these latter texts, what is 'confessed' are emotions: fear, despair, shame, guilt, and certainly anxiety. Of note is that in each text it is principally the violent actions of a man – the Gestapo agent in 'Monsieur X.,' the father in *La honte* – that give rise to these emotions.[64] In the narratives of Nicolas and Stevens, on the other hand, anxiety and guilt are not so much confessed as *betrayed*. They are revealed, unintentionally, by the semiotic nature of the narrators' language. But what is really confessed in these narratives are not emotions, but *acts*: the violent acts of domination, seduction, molestation, rape, and murder.

Nicolas's and Stevens's confessional narratives have a precedent in another Hébertian tale of murder, *Kamouraska*. As Brochu notes in a comparison of the two texts, both *Les fous de Bassan* and *Kamouraska* are based on *faits divers* (news items) that Hébert had heard or read, both are structured in Brochu's terms around 'le dévoilement d'un secret' (the revelation of a secret), and in both, the murderer or murderers escape justice (but not the ravages of their own consciences).[65] One way in which *Kamouraska* differs from *Les fous*, however, is that in the former, the murder victim is a man, and the confession it presents is that of a woman, Élisabeth d'Aulnières. Although it is actually Élisabeth's lover, Doctor Nelson, who murders her husband, she is entirely complicit in the plans to carry out the act. The acute anxiety that the resurgence of memories eighteen years later produces in Élisabeth (and that leaves her as sensitive to sound as Stevens and Nicolas) is due then, in part, to a guilty conscience. Yet the novel makes clear, as Brochu points out, that if Élisabeth is guilty of her husband's death, her reasons for desiring that death are justified. Her motives are a need for liberation, or *délivrance*, from her husband, who terrorizes her in his drunken fits of rage and despair.[66] Élisabeth does agree to marry him, but she does so in a society that teaches her that it is only through marriage that a girl can leave behind childhood and the tutelage of her parents and become a woman (as the term 'vieille fille' attests). But what Élisabeth discovers, twice, is that marriage does not liberate but rather enslaves – in her case, to the violent caprices of a first husband and to incessant impregnation by a second.[67] She is indeed her first husband's assassin, but she is also his victim, as well as that of her hypocritical society. That society is hypocritical because, in the end, it censures Élisabeth more for flaunting an illicit love affair with one outsider than for murdering another (whom no one, after all, could tolerate).

Unlike Élisabeth, Stevens, who was already enjoying a freedom absolutely inaccessible to his female cousins (he had left Griffin Creek five years earlier to travel and work in the United States), cannot claim the desire for liberty as a motive for the murders he commits. His motive, as we have seen, is the despotic desire to silence the feminine voices and annihilate the feminine bodies that simultaneously attract and repulse him and that remind him of a maternal love that will always elude him. Stevens's act is a narcissistic assertion of masculine power that was never in jeopardy (despite Nora's peevish but fatal accusation that Stevens 'n['est] pas un homme' [is not a man]).[68] Élisabeth's act (or her complicity in Nelson's act) shares with Stevens's a certain narcissism, but it is also and more importantly a desperate revolt against a real and inexorable feminine impotence. Still, whatever their motives, Stevens and Élisabeth are both assassins, and consequently they are both haunted by their memories; despite their 'success' at murder, neither can manage to kill the 'longue racine sonore' (long, sonorous root) that carries into the present the damning voices of their pasts.[69]

The consequences of Élisabeth's self-confession remain unclear to the reader of *Kamouraska*. The concurrence of this inner release of repressed memories and the death of her insipid second husband could be read as signalling a kind of delayed *délivrance* for Élisabeth, despite her anxiety about what this unfamiliar liberty may bring.[70] In *Les fous de Bassan*, the results of Nicolas's confession are indeterminate as well; we do not know whether his *livre* (book) will have a readership other than himself or, if it does not, whether the act of having confronted (that is, listened to) his memories will change him. His apocalyptic dream perhaps does alter something inside him, for at the end of his narrative, he admits that while in name he may still be the 'pasteur légitime' of the last inhabitants of Griffin Creek, he is in reality only their 'frère,' and their 'frère indigne' (unworthy brother) at that (53; 36). He thus appears, through his very un-Protestant confession, to be acknowledging and assuming some of the guilt he had earlier insisted on projecting onto his flock.

The aftermath of Stevens's confession appears more certain. His semiotic narrative bears the traces of a total release of drive energy that brings about neither remorse, nor redemption, nor even, it would seem, relief. What it produces, rather, is death. Well in character, the hubristic Stevens ends his murderous narrative by expressing the hope of soon joining his blameless brother Perceval: 'Que cet enfant m'accueille en Paradis. Amen' (May that child greet me in Heaven. Amen) (249; 183). Functioning in a manner contrary to that of the bullets and shells he faced during the war, the pills lined in a row before him will destroy Stevens's body, but will, he believes, leave his spirit, and his ego, 'indemnes' (unscathed).

The acts of narration studied in the previous three chapters, although anxious and arduous, are certainly less grim than Stevens's. Those inscribed in 'Monsieur X.' and in *La honte* in particular are productive instead of destructive, in the sense that the narratives to which they give birth, rather than imposing silence, inspire yet more narrative, yet more 'noise.' The anxious energy that goes into their production is not exhausted by that production. Still, Dominique Denes's assertion that 'Marguerite Duras conçoit la mise en mots comme la mise à mort par excellence' (Marguerite Duras considers the act of 'putting into words' a 'putting to death' par excellence), suggests that Duras may have shared some of Stevens's notions about the fatal consequences of writing.[71] In an interview given in 1967, which Denes quotes, Duras states, 'J'écris pour me déplacer du moi au livre [...] Pour me massacrer, me gâcher, m'abîmer dans la parturition du livre [...] La libre disposition du moi, je l'éprouve dans ces deux cas : à l'idée du suicide et à idée d'écrire' (I write in order to step outside myself and to put myself into the book ... In order to massacre, ruin, destroy myself in the birthing of the book ... I feel a freedom of the self, a self-determination, in these two cases: in the idea of suicide and in the idea of writing.'[72] For Duras, then, as for Stevens, producing a 'living' text requires the annihilation of the self, as if there were not enough life for both, as if the text needed to take over the space, and the liberty, once held by the ego. But while Duras's state-ment must be understood as artistic hyperbole and as symptomatic of her penchant for making dramatic and quotable statements (for it was her liver rather than her books that killed her), in Hébert's novel, Stevens truly does appear to exchange his own life for his text's.

But if the endings of the three other, principal narratives examined in this book are more assuring than that of Hébert, still there are allusions in all of them to death. The situations that give rise to these narrators' anxiety and their desire to narrate seem to them to be matters of 'life and death,' and in each of their texts, the menace of murder, whether literal or figurative, is palpable. In 'Monsieur X.,' this menace is the unpredictability of a sadistic and perhaps even mad Gestapo agent; in *La honte*, it is the father's terrifying and unforeseen assault on the mother; in *Entre la vie et la mort*, it is the writer's own involuntary but irrepressible tendency to drive the life out of his own texts; and in *Les fous de Bassan*, it is the village men's misogyny and the repression of their corporeal desires, which constantly threaten to reemerge in destructive ways. Moreover, multiple references to real, historical murders make their way into the œuvres of Duras, Ernaux, and Hébert through the fictionalization or the mention of often grisly *faits divers* and, in the cases of Duras and Ernaux, through commentary on war and genocide.[73] Duras and Ernaux have also, while experiencing or recovering from serious illnesses, reflected in their writing on their own mortality.[74]

That there are such allusions to death in the works discussed here is not surprising, given that death, an imminent yet (usually) unpredictable and unfathomable event, is a paradigmatic source of human anxiety, and that writing is a paradigmatic means of trying to elude death by securing one's (at least literary) immortality. Perhaps even Stevens, while hoping to quiet once and for all the voices inside him, desires at the same time that his own voice continue to be heard *outre tombe*. The actual fate of his narrative – whether it reaches its addressee or some other audience – remains a mystery. The narratives of Duras, Sarraute, Hébert, and Ernaux have reached their audience, and the fate of these writers' œuvres seems more certain. Their texts, powerful enough to resist the forces of anxiety that threatened to suppress them at their very inception, will likely survive well into a future whose readers will not be indifferent to the realities and truths their narrators attempt to apprehend.

Conclusion

In 'Fathers, Daughters, Anxiety, and Fiction,' Sheryl Herr discusses the effects of the burden of thousands of years of literary 'fathering' on both male and female twentieth-century writers. In it she quotes the comments of Donald Barthelme, a postmodern American writer 'fathered' by James Joyce. Reminded by the interviewer to whom he is responding that he once suggested that collage was 'the central principle of all art in the twentieth century,' he supplies the following elaboration: 'The point of collage is that unlike things are stuck together to make, in the best case, a new reality. This new reality, in the best case, may be or imply a comment on the other reality from which it came, and may be also much else. It's an *itself,* if it's successful: Harold Rosenberg's "anxious object," which does not know whether it's a work of art or a pile of junk (Maybe I should have said that anxiety is the central principle of all art in the [twentieth century].'[1]

Although of a different nationality and of course gender than the writers discussed in this book (I will return to this last point shortly), and although his ludic prose could hardly be qualified as 'realist,' however widely that word might be used, in his response Barthelme nevertheless touches on the primary issues in question in this study.[2] He goes so far, perhaps half-jokingly, perhaps in all seriousness, as to place anxiety at the heart of all art in the last century. Evoking Harold Rosenberg's concept of the 'anxious object,'[3] Barthelme sees modern artistic creation as so profoundly impregnated with anxiety that a work of art in the twentieth (and presumably twenty-first) century manifests not only the anxiety of its creator but somehow its very own anxiety as well.[4] As the artist's offspring, the object seems to inherit, as if by genetic means, its progenitor's anxiety. It is plagued by uncertainty, the fundamental ingredient of anxiety, for it cannot decide whether, to borrow from Sarraute one final time, it is living (a 'work of art') or dead (a 'piece of junk'). Barthelme's work of art displays the same indecision as the narrator of Duras's 'Madame Dodin' (discussed briefly in chapter 1), who is so afraid of producing trash (in which Mme Dodin is already up to her eyeballs) instead of art that she abandons her literary ambitions altogether.[5] In addition, Barthelme's personification of the work of art calls to mind the multiple scenes in Sarraute's *Entre la vie et la mort* in which the writer's rather haggard Muse slips on his text like a half-finished dress in order to keep him, her *couturier*, on the right path; or it evokes those scenes in which the writer appears as a Gallic Dr Frankenstein, intent on infusing life into the moribund text that resists (re)animation.[6]

Commenting on Barthelme's remarks, Herr writes, 'Whether the anxiety is that of influence, of interpretation, or of personal trauma, Barthelme's equation of anxiety and art attests to the condition of postmodern writing, its interminable having-been-fathered and its inherited efforts to make from that derivative status something original.'[7] The several different kinds of anxiety Herr cites all surface in the narratives I have studied. The anxiety of influence is certainly most palpable in Sarraute's novel, but traces of it can be detected in all of the principal texts discussed in this study: Duras, Ernaux, and Sarraute make multiple references to probably the most imposing father of all twentieth-century French writers, Marcel Proust, while Hébert pays homage to Shakespeare, Faulkner, Gide, and Cixous, among others. Related to the anxiety of influence, the anxious desire for originality and brilliance is also present, most obviously in *Entre la vie et la mort*, but also in *La honte*, for example, when the narrator expresses disappointment upon perceiving the banality of what she has written.[8] In her preface to 'Monsieur X. dit ici Pierre Rabier,' Duras writes that she hesitated to publish the narrative not only because of the sensitive nature of its content, but also because she felt that it was 'en quelque sorte anecdotique' (somewhat anecdotal) – that is, not significant enough to capture the reader's interest or to merit his time ('ça ne s'agrandissait jamais, ça n'allait jamais vers le large de la littérature' [it never became anything greater, never took off into literature]).[9] And in 'Madame Dodin,' the narrator laments her inability to write a text about her concierge that would be different from (that is, more effective than) all the previous literary texts about concierges that had failed to change tenants' attitudes towards their real concierges.

The name Herr gives to the second anxiety she mentions, the 'anxiety of interpretation,' could itself be interpreted in several ways. Is this the writer's anxiety that, by choosing the wrong words, she will serve as a poor interpreter between the reality she perceives and the readers to whom she is trying to communicate that reality? Or rather is it the anxiety that her work, though indeed 'alive,' will be misinterpreted by her readers? This first kind of anxiety can be seen especially in 'Madame Dodin,' where the narrator feels the responsibility, as well as the presumptuousness, of attempting to interpret Mme Dodin's words and actions, her very being, for a bourgeois readership. It is also expressed by the narrator of 'Monsieur X.' when she states, well into her narration, that she 'n'[a] jamais trouvé comment le dire, comment raconter à ceux qui n'ont pas vécu cette époque-là, la sorte de peur que c'était' (never figured out how to express it, how to tell those who didn't live through it what sort of fear it was).[10] The second kind of 'anxiety of interpretation' seems to be expressed by Sarraute's writer, who in a moment of confidence tries to make his obtuse other see the beauty in one of his sentences. *La honte*'s narrator, in turn, fears that despite her careful work, her readers will interpret the scene as 'un événement banal' (a banal event) rather than as the utterly unique, and terrifying, experience that it was.[11]

Finally, the third kind of anxiety Herr cites, the anxiety of trauma (that is, the permanent and pervasive anxiety with which trauma leaves it victims), clearly manifests itself in 'Monsieur X.,' *La honte*, and *Les fous de Bassan*. So although the texts examined in this book have neither the same subject matter nor the same form, they are all infected with the same malady – anxiety – that according to Barthelme ensures, paradoxically, their success.

In the interview cited above, Barthelme also invokes another concept that has been central to my discussions of these four authors' texts: reality. He touches on the question that is raised most explicitly, but not exclusively, in the texts by Ernaux and Sarraute: Does the literary text always create its own reality, even when the writer's objective is to reflect or reveal an already existing reality? Put somewhat differently, can a text refer to a prior and exterior reality, or can it only ever refer to a reality of its own fabrication (its own 'fictional' or 'imaginary' world)? Barthelme's answer to these questions seems to be that, if the work of art is 'successful' (what pressure this anxious object is under!), it does both: it both 'comes from' an existing reality or realities and 'makes' a new reality. It effects this simultaneous transformation and creation, Barthelme suggests, through the technique of collage.

At the level of narrative structure, a literary text might then borrow, combine, modify, and/or subvert elements of established narrative forms in order to constitute itself as a new form. *Les fous de Bassan*, for example, borrows its plurivocal narration from Faulkner's *The Sound and the Fury*. Yet Hébert widens the range of voices to include that of a dead woman and thereby 'spiritualizes' Faulkner's psychological realism. Her novel also adopts devices from several different literary genres, such as the mystery or crime novel (several characters are presented as suspects and are interrogated by detectives; pieces of evidence turn up one by one; the identity of the killer is revealed only at the end; and so on) and the romance (the primary topic of Nora's and Olivia's narratives is their awakening desire for romantic and sexual love), but it cannot be categorized under any one of them. 'Monsieur X. dit ici Pierre Rabier' is a structural collage as well, a fusion of different tenses, moods, memories, and voices that creates a truthful representation of at least two realities: that of living in fear for one's life, and that of the difficulty of both remembering and narrating such a reality years later. *La douleur* as a whole, moreover, is a structural collage, a collection of several different stories, written in a variety of genres (diary, memoir, fiction, or a mixture of these), that offer the portrait of several different Durases (the distraught wife, the courageous resistant, the seductress, the torturer, and so on). *Entre la vie et la mort* is also a collage at the level of structure in that it is a collection of scenes arranged without apparent temporal or logical order.

The narration of *La honte* is more conventionally realist and less plurivocal than those of the other texts examined, but it is, like 'Monsieur X.,' an articulated collection of memories presented in no other order than that in which they surface in the narrator's mind. The list of objects from her past that the narrator gathers together – the two photos, the missal, the sheet music, and so forth – form, furthermore, a very literal collage, a scrapbook, around which she constructs a self. This self, in turn, is a composite of multiple selves loosely 'glued' together by the text. *La honte* also soundly adheres (to prolong the collage metaphor) to Barthelme's definition of 'successful' art in that its narration is laden with uncertainty and indecision: the scene retains its incomprehensibility even after its narration, and the narrator, like that of Sarraute's *Enfance*, is forever unsure of the veracity of what she has narrated.

At the level of content, an autobiographical text, for example, might begin as a 'transcription' or a verbal representation of memories of real events. Yet the text itself inevitably becomes its own event-to-be-remembered – the event of narrating for the narrator (or writing for the writer), and the event of reading for the reader. In both *La douleur* (in the prefaces to the texts) and *La honte*, the narrator speaks frequently about the act of writing. Writing therefore becomes a part of the texts' content; that is, it figures as one among many of the *events* recounted in the narratives. Each text then both reproduces (symbolically) and produces real events. It refers to events that are both independent of it and dependent on it and interweaves them to form its substance.[12] The 'unlike things' stuck together in the content of Sarraute's work are the proliferating metaphors, the often wildly disparate images that are continually juxtaposed and superimposed, layer upon layer, to allow the reader to conceive of realities that ordinary verbal constructions could never evoke. Moreover, the 'protagonist' of the novel, the writer, is himself a collage, a collage of many different writers.

Leaving Barthelme for a moment but continuing the discussion of both anxiety and reality (that *in* the work of art as well as that *of* the work of art), I want to return briefly to David Ellison's *Of Words and the World*, his study of 'referential anxiety' in contemporary French fiction, cited in the introduction. In that book, Ellison poses the following questions: 'Might there be a point at which the turn away from the referent reverses itself, where minimalism and textual self-referentiality reach their limits? And if so, can there be something like a *return to the referent* as exterior reality, a new embracing of the world in its extensiveness that is not a pale and naive reflection of past tradition but a textual praxis reinvigorated by the arduous passage through inwardness as such?'[13] (Ellison's emphasis).

Ellison's hypothesis of a return to the referent in literature is supported by the proliferation in the 1970s and 1980s of literary autobiographies, including those by writers, such as Sarraute, Robbe-Grillet, and Duras, associated more or less closely with the *nouveau roman* (the extent to which these texts are or are not departures from their authors' earlier work is in part the topic of one of Ellison's chapters). It seems to me that such a return to the referent has occurred in the domain of criticism as well. The relatively recent shift in emphasis in language and literature departments from highly abstract 'theory' to the more concrete 'cultural studies' is symptomatic of a swing in the referential pendulum. Many scholars are now more interested in talking about what and how *things* mean (whether material objects such as sport shoes or cell phones, or cultural phenomena such as the cult of celebrity or globalization) than about how language means. They also tend to use language less hyperself-consciously than during the height of poststructuralism in the 1980s. They nevertheless remain mindful of poststructuralism's lessons. The 'things' that are now the subject of much critical thought are most intriguing to scholars in their capacity not as referents of linguistic signifiers, but rather as signifiers themselves. Most often they signify something about the people who covet, possess, suffer from, love, or hate them: their political or sexual persuasion, their social class, their level of education, their particular anxieties and desires, and so on. Informed by structuralist and poststructuralist theories, cultural studies emphasizes these multiple points: that in human society, just about everything *means*; that things (including words and discourses) often mean something other than what they appear or claim to mean; and that the relationship between these things and their meaning(s) (between these signifiers and their signifieds) is not natural or essential but rather culturally determined.

This apparent return to the referent in literature, art, and criticism has also clearly spread to popular forms of entertainment. One of the 'things' that have caught the attention of scholars in cultural studies in the past several years is the phenomenon of 'reality television' (a subject search in the collective catalogue of college and university libraries in Ohio in 2007, for example, turns up fourteen critical books on the topic, most published since 2002). The enormous global popularity of 'reality' television shows six years after the premiere of the first of the newest generation of this genre, CBS's *Survivor*, suggests that the 'real,' or at least what is presented as real, is now much more intriguing to viewers than fiction. According to the Screen Actors Guild, in the United States in 2004, the number of hours of reality programming per week increased by 128 per cent over the previous year. This increase was accompanied by a reduction of 21 per cent in the number of hours per week of situation comedies.[14] The phenomenon has gripped almost the entire world, and France and Canada are no exceptions. Both countries import American-made shows, but they also produce their own, such as M6's *Loftstory* and *La Nouvelle Star* in France and TVA's *Occupation Double* and *Star Académie* in Quebec. The content of reality shows is 'real' in the sense that what is filmed (the love affairs, the rivalries, the cat fights, the crying) is actually happening and is, for the most part, not formally scripted, but how 'real' is it in the sense of 'truthful' or 'authentic'? This is one of the questions posed by the authors of studies on the phenomenon.

Many of these reality shows are based on drawn out and obviously very public competitions during which participants are under constant scrutiny and must continually ask themselves what the consequences of their every action, gesture, look, and word will be. Will the choices they make cause them to be rejected, kicked out, voted off, fired? Overpowered, out-sung, under-weighed? If so, how, when, and by whom? More stressful still are the elements of the competition that are beyond their control: Will they develop laryngitis? Will a judge take a dislike to them? Will their physical appearance disappoint? Will they be sabotaged? The uncertainty built into these shows with the objective of creating drama makes them a Petri dish for anxiety. Indeed, it would seem that this is what producers count on and what viewers want to see. Judging by these shows' ratings, the opportunity to observe others grow anxious to (or beyond) the point of mental breakdown is enormously appealing.

Perhaps by playing the role of peeping Tom into others' 'real' lives, viewers can potentially enjoy a vicarious cathexis of some of their own anxieties. Of these they are doubtless in no short supply, for the anxiety epidemic that according to Barthelme has overtaken art and literature in the twentieth century has spread not only to popular entertainment, but also, as discussed in my introduction, to society at large. Although it was the period immediately following the Second World War that Auden christened the 'Age of Anxiety,' our own, contemporary era, in which ever-proliferating types of anti-anxiety medications seem to be as widely available as cold remedies, could arguably be considered more rife with anxiety than his, despite (or perhaps because of) our medical efforts to quell it. Some of the sources of contemporary anxieties are variations of old ones, but others are perhaps new. In the West, for example, anxieties about the threat of a U.S.–Soviet nuclear war have been supplanted by anxieties about the threat of (more and more deadly) acts of terrorism. Terrorism is inherently more anxiety-provoking than declared war, as those threatened by it are excruciatingly uncertain about when, where, and how it will strike, and even who will be behind it. In the social sphere, anxieties about being trapped in predetermined familial roles, classes, occupations, and geographical spaces have been superseded, at least in the middle and upper classes, by anxieties about too many choices and too much freedom in the construction of one's life and very identity. And in an age in which an exponentially increasing pool of information is more and more available more and more quickly to those who know how to access it, the anxiety over being deemed uninformed, technologically inept, and obsolete in one's profession can become overwhelming.

Much of contemporary anxiety is undoubtedly a side effect of the extreme geographical, social, and cultural mobility of the contemporary era, and of the radical questioning of identity that has accompanied such mobility. As I demonstrated in my introduction, the lives of the four writers discussed in this book were affected by one or several of these kinds of mobility in profound and enduring ways. These writers all underwent displacements that had the potential, at the very least, to provoke in them feelings of instability and uncertainty, feelings on which anxiety feeds. Whether anxiety shows up in each of their texts in its content or its form (as a theme or as a force that shapes the narrative), or in both, these texts all have something to tell us about the kinds of anxiety from which both men and women suffer in contemporary society and about the varied and often enigmatic effects of anxiety on the human mind and body. By becoming writers, these women gained the means by which to verbalize and exteriorize (in their texts) their own anxieties and, in doing so, perhaps to alleviate them to some extent, either permanently or at least during the circumscribed period of writing. Yet at the same time, by becoming writers they also assumed the anxiety-inspiring responsibility of authorship, of being the herald (or the animator) of a previously unknown, misrecognized, or misunderstood reality. They have done so, moreover, in tenaciously patriarchal societies that still today find ways to challenge women who claim this burdensome authority. Anxiety does not belong exclusively to the twentieth century, or to writers, or to women; but there is reason to think, as I have demonstrated, that the share of it that befalls twentieth- (and twenty-first-) century women writers may be particularly onerous. Their readers are thankful, however, that the desires that compel these women to pick up their pens, or rather to turn on their computers (to provide a more 'realistic' image), prevail over the anxieties that threaten to make them turn them back off.

Notes

Introduction

1 Sublimation is the conversion of instinctual and usually sexual desire for an 'inappropriate' object (one's own mother, for example) into desire for a more socially acceptable one. For one of Freud's first mentions of sublimation, see his 'Three Essays on the Theory of Sexuality,' in *Standard Edition of the Complete Psychological Works of Sigmund Freud*, 7:135–243, ed. James Strachey (London: Hogarth, 1953–74). For a discussion of how the repression of desire can result in physical illness, see Freud and Josef Breuer's *Studies on Hysteria*, in *Standard Edition*, 2:1–306.

2 For a basic definition of anxiety, see, for example, 'Anxiety, Fear, and Depression,' in the *Encyclopedia of Psychiatry, Psychology and Psychoanalysis*, ed. Benjamin B. Wolman (New York: Aesculapius, 1996), 43–4.

3 See especially chapters 1 and 8 of Peter Brooks's *Reading for the Plot: Design and Intention in Narrative* (Cambridge, MA: Harvard University Press, 1992).

4 See Freud's 'Inhibitions, Symptoms, and Anxieties,' *Standard Edition*, 20:75–171, or his 'Anxiety and Instinctual Life,' *Standard Edition*, 22:81–111, especially 81–95. He conceived this theory of anxiety (that it is a fear of one's own desires) rather late in life, and it is significantly different from his original theory, which he sets forth in 'On the Ground for Detaching a Particular Syndrome from Neurasthenia under the Description "Anxiety Neurosis,"' *Standard Edition*, 3:85–117. In this original theory, anxiety is sexual energy that has not been given proper release. Anxiety is therefore the result of repression of sexual energy. In his later theory, Freud maintains that anxiety is the intuition that certain sexual desires, if acted upon, would be socially condemned and therefore must be repressed. In this second scenario, anxi-

ety causes, rather than is caused by, repression. Anxiety is then the anticipation, as noted above, of an undesirable consequence or situation, and as such it can compel the individual to act (which is, in Freud's formulation, to repress).

5 Marguerite Duras, 'Monsieur X. dit ici Pierre Rabier,' in *La douleur,* 89–135 (Paris: Gallimard, Folio, 1985), trans. by Barbara Bray as 'Monsieur X, Here Called Pierre Rabier,' in *The War: A Memoir,* 71–112 (New York: Pantheon, 1986); Annie Ernaux, *La honte* (Paris: Gallimard, NRF, 1997), trans. by Tanya Leslie as *Shame* (New York: Seven Stories, 1997); Nathalie Sarraute, *Entre la vie et la mort* (Paris: Gallimard, Folio, 1968), trans. by Maria Jolas as *Between Life and Death: A Novel* (New York: G. Braziller, 1969); Anne Hébert, *Les fous de Bassan* (Paris: Seuil, 1982), trans. by Sheila Fischman as *In the Shadow of the Wind* (Toronto: Stoddart, 1983). Throughout this book I will provide English translations of all quotes in French. I have based most of my translations on published translations when available, although in most cases I have modified mine in order to give the reader the best sense possible of the language of the original. When there exists a published English translation, I cite it once and then simply give page numbers for the English edition after those for the French edition in each additional reference.

6 Sandra M. Gilbert and Susan Gubar, *The Madwoman in the Attic: The Woman Writer and the Nineteenth-Century Literary Imagination* (New Haven: Yale University Press, 1979), 49.

7 Nathalie Sarraute, *Entre la vie et la mort,* 153; 161.

8 In chapter 3 I will reflect further on Sarraute's use of gender, and her claim that it is unimportant, in the construction of both her characters and her innumerable metaphors. It is interesting to note that Sarraute's Russian mother, a writer of novels and stories for both children and adults, published under a masculine pseudonym. See Mimika Cranaki and Yvon Belaval, *Nathalie Sarraute* (Paris: Gallimard, 1965), 14.

9 Samuel Beckett, *L'Innommable* (Paris: Minuit, 1953).

10 Gustave Flaubert, *Correspondance,* vol. 2 (1847–52), in *Œuvres complètes de Gustave Flaubert* (Paris: Conard, 1926), 2:162.

11 The most famous cases of such extreme authorly anxiety are those of Kafka and Mallarmé. Fortunately, whether because of their love for great literature or their desire for great profit, the faithful companions to whom these writers appeal rarely seem to respect their last wishes.

12 Gilbert and Gubar, *The Madwoman in the Attic,* 51.

13 Harold Bloom, *The Anxiety of Influence: A Theory of Poetry,* 2nd ed. (Oxford: Oxford University Press, 1997 [1973]). In my chapter on Sarraute's *Entre la vie et la mort* (chapter 3), I discuss Bloom's 'anxiety of influence' in more depth.

14 For examples of such a critique, see Toril Moi's *Sexual/Textual Politics: Feminist Literary Theory* (London: Routledge, 1985), 61–9; Frank Lentricchia's 'Patriarchy against Itself – The Young Manhood of Wallace Stevens,' *Critical Inquiry* 13 (1987): 742–86; and Chris Weedon's *Feminist Practice and Poststructuralist Theory* (Oxford: Blackwell, 1987), 152–8. This last critique focuses on Gilbert and Gubar's later work on twentieth-century women writers, *No Man's Land: The Place of the Woman Writer in the Twentieth Century*, 3 vols. (New Haven: Yale University Press, 1988–94). For defences of the value of *Madwoman*, on the other hand, see Øyunn Hestetun, *A Prison-House of Myth? Symptomal Readings in 'Virgin Land,' 'The Madwoman in the Attic,' and 'The Political Unconscious'* (Uppsala, Sweden: Uppsala University, 1993), 118–57, or Nancy K. Miller, '*Madwoman* Revisited,' in *Making Feminist History: The Literary Scholarship of Sandra M. Gilbert and Susan Gubar*, ed. William E. Cain, 87–104 (New York: Garland, 1994).

15 Nathalie Sarraute, 'Conversation et sous-conversation,' in *L'ère du soupçon*, 79–124 (Paris: Gallimard, 1956), 98; trans. by Maria Jolas as 'Conversation and Sub-Conversation,' in *Tropisms and the Age of Suspicion*, 97–120 (London: John Calder, 1963), 106.

16 All (white) Canadian women won the vote at the federal level in 1918; Quebec was the last province to grant women suffrage at the provincial level. If, however, we look at women's presence in national legislatures today, we find that the United States, Great Britain, and Canada actually join France in lagging far behind Northern European countries such as Norway, Finland, Sweden, and Denmark. In these latter nations in 2006, on average about 40 per cent of legislative seats were held by women (Interparliamentary Union, 'Women in National Parliaments: Situation as of November 2005,' 1996–2005, http://www.ipu.org/wmn-e/world.htm). In the United States, this figure is 15.7 per cent; in France, 14 per cent (despite France's 'loi sur la parité' of 2000, which stipulates that political parties must present an equal, or nearly equal, number of male and female candidates for elections); in the United Kingdom, 20 per cent, and in Canada, 21 per cent (United States Senate, 'Women in the United States Congress 1917–2006,' http://www.senate.gov/reference/resources/pdf/RL30261.pdf; Observatoire de la parité entre les femmes et les hommes, 'Les modes de scrutin et la parité entre les femmes et les hommes,' http://www.observatoire-parite.gouv.fr/portail/guide.htm; The United Kingdom Parliament, 'Statistics of Women in Parliament,' http://www.parliament.uk/commons/lib/research/notes/snsg-01250.pdf; Canadian Feminist Alliance for International Action, 'Canada Needs a Permanent Parliamentary Committee on Women's Equality,' http://www.fafia-afai.org/gvt/parliament.htm). In Quebec, on the other

hand, where the women's movement of the 1970s and 1980s seems to have been particularly successful, women hold 30 per cent of the seats in the provincial *assemblée* and continue to demand greater representation (Collectif féminisme et démocratie, 'Pour un mode de scrutin plus démocratique et égalitaire au Québec,' http://feminismeetdemocratie.typepad.com/ collectif/2004/09/volution_de_la_.html).

17 The *Révolution tranquille* (conceived in its broadest sense as spanning the years 1960 to 1980) refers to the mostly peaceful liberalization and modernization of Quebec, which up to that time had been culturally isolated from anglophone North America (while being economically colonized by it), and which had been allowed to stagnate socially and economically by its conservative Catholic clergy and politicians.

18 Until the late 1960s, Quebec had one of the highest birth rates among Western nations: 39.5 live births per 1,000 residents in 1900, and 30.3 in 1957. This particular form of resistance to cultural obsolescence was called 'la revanche des berceaux' (the revenge of the cradles). Today, with one of the lowest birth rates in the world (10 in 2005), Quebec is experiencing what might be called 'la revanche des femmes' (the revenge of the women). See Institut de la statistique, Québec, 'Naissances et taux de natalité, Québec, 1900–2004,' http://www.stat.gouv.qc.ca/donstat/societe/demographie/ naisn_deces/naissance/401.htm.

19 Susan Mann, *The Dream of Nation: A Social and Intellectual History of Quebec* (Montreal and Kingston: McGill-Queen's University Press, 1982), 279. For works that focus exclusively on French-Canadian women's history, see the groundbreaking study by Micheline Dumont et al., *L'histoire des femmes au Québec depuis quatre siècles* (Montreal: Quinze, 1982); or the more recent study by Andrée Lévesque, *Résistance et transgression: études en histoire des femmes au Québec* (Montreal: Remue-ménage, 1995).

20 In *Le Québec, un pays, une culture*, 2nd ed. (Monteal: Boréal, 2001), 150, Françoise Têtu de Labsade notes that Duplessis, premier of Quebec from 1936 to 1939 and again from 1944 to 1959, 'se méfie des artistes qui osent dire ce qu'ils pensent parce qu'ils éprouvent avec plus d'acuité ce que ressent la société qui les entoure. À cause de cette défiance, de tradition paysanne, pour tout ce qui est d'ordre intellectuel ou artistique, on appellera cette période "la grande noirceur"' (was wary of artists who dared say what they thought, because they felt with more acuity what the society around them felt. Because of this wariness – traditional among the peasantry – of all that is intellectual or artistic, this period was called 'The Great Darkness').

21 See Joan B. Landes, *Women and the Public Sphere in the Age of the French Revolution* (Ithaca, NY: Cornell University Press, 1988) and Candice E. Proctor,

Women, Equality, and the French Revolution (New York: Greenwood Press, 1990) for analyses of this division along gender lines of the public and private spheres in nineteenth-century France.

22 The Académie Goncourt, a literary society founded by the *frères* Goncourt in 1900, has conferred the most important literary prize in France each year since 1903. The women who have been members of the society are Colette, Judith Gautier, Françoise Mallet-Joris, Edmonde Charles-Roux (who became its first female president in 2002), and Françoise Chandernagor. Female recipients of the Prix Goncourt are Elsa Triolet (1944), Béatrix Beck (1952), Simone de Beauvoir (1954), Anna Langfus (1962), Edmonde Charles-Roux (1966), Antonine Maillet (1979), Marguerite Duras (1984), Pascale Roze (1996), and Paule Constant (1998). Visit the society's own website 'L'Académie Goncourt,' http://www.academie-goncourt.fr, for more information about the Académie and its prize.

23 Roland Barthes, 'The Death of the Author,' in *Image–Music–Text*, ed. and trans. Stephen Heath, 142–54 (New York: Hill and Wang, 1977); Michel Foucault, 'What Is an Author?,' trans. Josué V. Harari, in *Aesthetics, Method, and Epistemology*, ed. James D. Faubion, vol. 2 of *Essential Works of Foucault 1954– 1984*, 205–22 (New York: New Press, 1994). In his 1968 essay, Barthes argues against author-centred (and *for* reader-centred) criticism. Although his title is more of a rallying cry for a new kind of criticism ('Death *to* the author') than an obituary for a (not yet deceased) old kind, Barthes's idea caught on quickly. For Nancy K. Miller's analysis of the implications of the author's supposed demise for the feminist project of establishing a history of female authorship, see chapter 5, 'Changing the Subject: Authorship, Writing, and the Reader,' of her *Subject to Change: Reading Feminist Writing* (New York: Columbia University Press, 1988).

24 Susan Sniader Lanser, *Fictions of Authority: Women Writers and Narrative Voice* (Ithaca, NY: Cornell University Press, 1992), 7. Lanser discusses this notion of the fictionality of narrative authority, citing Edward Said's 'Molestation and Authority in Narrative Fiction,' in *Aspects of Narrative: Selected Papers from the English Institute*, ed. J. Hillis Miller, 47–68 (New York: Columbia University Press, 1971) as a denunciation of writers' assumption of such authority. She nevertheless argues that since the novel is 'a cultural enterprise that has historically claimed and received a truth value beyond the fictional,' the effect of this authority, if not its basis, is very real (*Fictions of Authority*, 7).

25 Michelle Craske, *Origins of Phobias and Anxiety Disorders: Why More Women Than Men?* (Oxford: Elsevier, 2003), 12–13.

26 Reuters Health, 'Anxiety Disorders,' December 2001, http://www

.reutershealth.com/wellconnected/doc28.html, under the subheading, 'Who Gets Anxiety Disorders?'

27 Jonathan Metzl, *Prozac on the Couch: Prescribing Gender in the Era of Wonder Drugs* (Durham, NC: Duke University Press, 2003), 152.

28 Craske, *Origins of Phobias and Anxiety Disorders*, 177.

29 Reuters Health, 'Anxiety Disorders.' The *Diagnostic and Statistical Manual of Mental Disorders*, 4th ed. (Washington, DC: American Psychiatric Association, 1994) lists several specific kinds of anxiety disorders but describes the principal criterion for the diagnosis of 'generalized anxiety disorder' as 'excessive anxiety and worry (apprehensive expectation), occuring more days than not for a period of at least 6 months, about a number of events or activities' (432). In reference to gender differences, the *DSM* states that 'in clinical settings, [generalized anxiety disorder] is diagnosed somewhat more frequently in women than in men (about 55%–60% of those presenting with the disorder are female). In epidemiological studies, the sex ratio is approximately two-thirds female.'

30 Michel Foucault, *Folie et déraison: histoire de la folie à l'âge classique* (Paris: Plon, 1961).

31 For a study on the notion of the 'medicalization of womanhood,' see Leslie Laurence and Beth Weinhouse, *Outrageous Practices: The Alarming Truth about How Medicine Mistreats Women* (New York: Fawcett Columbine, 1994).

32 Metzl, *Prozac on the Couch*, 126; cited in Sharon Kirkey, 'Prozac Pushers Target Women – Study,' 28 September 2003, CanWest News Service, http://www.ofcmhap.on.ca/addiction/prozac_pushers_target_women.htm. Building on feminist critiques of this 'medicalization of womanhood,' Metzl demonstrates how advertisements for prescription psychotropic medications 'translate existing passions about women into the promotion of specific products' (128). Advertisements in medical journals in particular, he argues, 'build on the correlation, begun in the 1950s, between specifically gendered notions of anxiety and the promise of pharmacochemical restoration. Reading against psychiatry's own claim to represent a more biologically "objectifiable," gender-neutral classification system, these ads offer an endless stream of enlarged, castrating mothers, colorfully frigid daughters, and shrunken, emasculated sons' (129).

33 B.K. Eakman, 'Anything That Ails You: Women on Tranqs in a Self-Serve Society,' *Chronicles: A Magazine of American Culture* 28 (August 2004), http://www.chroniclesmagazine.org/Chronicles/.html.

34 National Institute on Drug Abuse, 'Trends in Prescription Drug Abuse,' http://www.nida.nih.gov/ResearchReports/Prescription/prescription5.html#Gender; cited in Eakman, 'Anything That Ails You.'

35 Charles Fleming and Anne-Marie Morice, 'Europe Wants Citizens to Pop
    Fewer Pills,' *Wall Street Journal*, 25 February 2004, eastern ed., B1. Cited in
    Eakman, 'Anything That Ails You.'
36 Fleming and Morice, 'Europe Wants Citizens to Pop Fewer Pills,' B2.
37 Ibid., B1.
38 W.H. Auden, *The Age of Anxiety* (New York: Random House, 1947).
39 Alain Robbe-Grillet, 'Du réalisme à la réalité,' in *Pour un nouveau roman*
    (Paris: Minuit, 1963), 137.
40 David R. Ellison, *Of Words and the World: Referential Anxiety in Contemporary
    French Fiction* (Princeton, NJ: Princeton University Press, 1993), 9. In his dis-
    cussion, Ellison cites three critics in particular who theorized such a distinc-
    tion in the 1980s: Dina Sherzer, *Representation in Contemporary French Fiction*
    (Lincoln: University of Nebraska Press, 1986); Linda Hutcheon, 'Metafic-
    tional Implications for Novelistic Reference,' in *On Referring in Literature*, eds.
    Anna Whiteside and Michael Issacharof, 1–13 (Bloomington: Indiana Uni-
    versity Press, 1987); and Thomas Pavel, *Fictional Worlds* (Cambridge, MA:
    Harvard University Press, 1986).
41 Pavel, *Fictional Worlds*, 8, 6.
42 Ellison, *Of Words and the World*, 20.
43 It is true that Annie Ernaux's style can be characterized as 'realist,' but in
    'Annie Ernaux: un écrivain dans la tradition du réalisme,' *Revue de l'histoire
    littéraire française* 2 (1998): 247–66, Siobhán McIlvanney maintains that
    Ernaux does not simply imitate nineteenth-century realist style; she revital-
    izes it by adapting it to the principal subject she treats (the construction of
    social class) and to the 'age of suspicion' (suspicion of the supreme authority
    of the author, for one thing). In this regard, McIlvanney writes: 'Si la "vérité"
    des réalistes du XIXième siècle consistait à présenter au lecteur l'illusion
    d'objectivité en effaçant toute présence explicite de l'auteur, pour Annie
    Ernaux cette "vérité" consiste à dévoiler son propre rôle. L'écriture réaliste
    au XXe siècle consisterait donc à intérgrer l'acte d'écrire au récit et non de
    nier l'existence de l'auteur' (If the 'truth' of nineteenth-century realist
    authors consisted of giving the reader the illusion of objectivity by effacing
    any explicit reference to the author, for Annie Ernaux, this 'truth' consists of
    revealing her own role. Realist writing in the twentieth century consists
    therefore of integrating the act of writing into the narrative, and not of deny-
    ing the existence of the author) (260).
44 Gérard Genette, *Narrative Discourse: An Essay in Method*, trans. Jane E. Lewin
    (Ithaca, NY: Cornell University Press, 1980), 27.
45 In 'Un amour de Swann,' the first section of *À la recherche du temps perdu*, eds.
    Pierre Clarac and André Ferré (Paris: Gallimard, Pléiade, 1954), Proust

ignores, however, the normal limitations of a first-person narrator when he has his narrator authoritatively recount in minute detail the love affair of another man, a love affair that takes place, moreover, before the narrator's birth.

46 Jean-Paul Sartre, *La nausée* (Paris: Gallimard, 1938).

47 I will return to Robbe-Grillet's ideas concerning the relationship (or lack thereof, for him) between literature and reality in my discussion in chapter 3 of a fellow, but very different, *nouveau romancier,* Nathalie Sarraute.

48 Sarraute and at times Duras have been associated with the *nouveau roman,* and Duras with *l'écriture féminine.*

49 Sarraute's writing is not explicitly feminist, and the author would not have called herself a feminist. Yet because of her contention that male and female psyches function in exactly the same manner, and because of the example she set as a published and respected writer and critic, Ann Jefferson, in *Nathalie Sarraute, Fiction and Theory: Questions of Difference* (Cambridge: Cambridge University Press, 2000), 114, nevertheless does characterize her as a 'first-generation' feminist.

50 Jane Bradley Winston, *Postcolonial Duras: Cultural Memory in Postwar France* (New York: Palgrave, 2001), 1–8; Marguerite Duras, *Moderato cantabile* (Paris: Minuit, 1958); Duras, *L'amant* (Paris: Gallimard, 1984).

51 In her most recent texts, such as *L'événement* (Paris: Gallimard, 2000); *Se perdre* (Paris: Gallimard, 2001); *L'occupation* (Paris: Gallimard, 2002); and *L'usage de la photo,* with Marc Marie (Paris: Stock, 2003), Ernaux's writing appears to have become even more deeply personal and confessional, even – to some readers and reviewers – exhibitionist. Yet her preoccupation with both class and gender issues is still evident in these works, which I will discuss further in chapter 2.

52 See for example Nathalie Sarraute, 'Ce que je cherche à faire,' in *Nouveau roman: hier, aujourd'hui,* eds. Jean Ricardou and Françoise vos Rossum-Guyon (Paris: UGE, 1972), 45.

53 Nathalie Sarraute, 'Nouveau roman et réalité,' *Revue de l'Institut de Sociologie* [Brussels] 2 (1963): 432.

54 *Webster's Ninth New Collegiate Dictionary* (Springfield, MA: Merriam-Webster, 1986), 980.

55 Ibid., 1268.

56 This biographical information can be found in Frédérique Lebelley, *Duras, ou le poids d'une plume* (Paris: Grasset, 1994). Several of Duras's texts are also at least semi-autobiographical, such as *La douleur, Un barrage contre le Pacifique* (Paris: Gallimard, 1950), and *L'amant.*

57 Marguerite Duras, *Les impudents* (Paris: Plon, 1943); *Moderato cantabile* (Paris:

Minuit, 1958); and *Le ravissement de Lol V. Stein* (Paris: Gallimard, Folio, 1964).

58 Frédérique Lebelley, *Duras ou le poids d'une plume*, 305. 'Durasoir' is a play on the combination of the author's name and 'rasoir,' which literally means 'razor,' but which in its figurative sense means 'boring.'

59 This information can be found in Ernaux's œuvre itself, each text of which is autobiographical to a greater or lesser degree.

60 The *agrégration* is a highly competitive national examination one must pass in order to teach at the university level in France.

61 Annie Ernaux, *L'écriture comme un couteau*, interview by Frédéric-Yves Jeannet (Paris: Stock, 2003), 35.

62 This information can be found in the preface to Nathalie Sarraute's *Œuvres complètes*, ed. Jean-Yves Tadié (Paris: Gallimard, 1996), xxix–xlvi, as well as, in part, in Cranaki and Belaval, *Nathalie Sarraute*, 11–18.

63 Yet when asked in an interview in what ways her bilingualism had influenced her writing, Sarraute replied, 'Il n'y a pas eu de bilinguisme. C'est une erreur complète qu'on répète toujours' (There wasn't any bilingualism. It's a total error that everyone keeps repeating) ('Dialogue avec Nathalie Sarraute,' interview by Françoise Dupuy-Sullivan, *Romance Quarterly* 37 [1990]: 191). Since Sarraute actually did speak and read Russian, this is a curious remark. Perhaps she meant that French was the principal language in which she had been educated and the only language in which she wrote.

64 Since there is as yet no published biography of Hébert (aside from brief biographical sketches in a few critical volumes, such as Pierre Pagé's *Anne Hébert* [Ottawa: Fides, 1965], 9–28), I have taken this information from the Anne Hébert website, 'Biographie inédite,' http://pages.infinit.net/ahebert2/biograph.htm.

65 Anne Hébert, *Le torrent* (Montréal: Hurtubise HMH, 1976).

66 There is at least one instance, however, in which one of these authors clearly abandons this carefulness. I will discuss this instance in chapter 3.

67 Duras, 'Monsieur X.,' 90; 71.

68 Strictly speaking, the character on whom I focus in Sarraute's *Entre la vie et la mort* is not the novel's narrator (who is all but invisible); he is, however, a writer whose anxiety about writing/narrating is patent.

1: 'Truth' in Memory and Narrative

1 Marguerite Duras, *La douleur* (Paris: P.O.L., 1985); trans. Barbara Bray as *The War: A Memoir* (New York: Pantheon, 1986). More 'typical' of the Duras of the decades mentioned are, for example, the highly stylized and unrealistic

texts included in the so-called India cycle, or the downright abstruse *L'homme assis dans le couloir* (*The Man Seated in the Corridor*) (Paris: Minuit, 1980). The 'India cycle' includes three narratives and three films: Marguerite Duras, *Le ravissement de Lol V. Stein* (Paris: Gallimard, Folio, 1964); *Le vice-consul* (*The Vice-Consul*) (Paris: Gallimard, Imaginaire, 1965); *L'amour* (*Love*) (Paris: Gallimard, 1971); *La femme du Gange* (*The Woman of the Ganges*) (Paris: Benoît-Jacob, 1973); *India Song* (Paris: Films Armorial, 1975); and *Son nom de Venise dans Calcutta désert* (*Her Name of Venice in Deserted Calcutta*) (Paris: Benoît-Jacob, 1976). I will discuss the first two of these in more depth later in this chapter.

2 Marguerite Duras, *L'été 80* (Paris: Minuit, 1980); *L'amant* (Paris: Minuit, 1984).

3 Philippe Lejeune, *Le pacte autobiographique* (Paris: Seuil, 1975), 26. A translation of the chapter from which this quote is taken appears in Lejeune, *On Autobiography*, ed. Paul John Eakin and trans. Katherine Leary (Minneapolis: University of Minnesota Press, 1989), 13–14.

4 Duras, *Les impudents* (Paris: Plon, 1943); *Un barrage contre le Pacifique* (Paris: Gallimard, 1950).

5 Lejeune, *Le pacte autobiographique*, 36; 22.

6 Ibid., 37; 23.

7 *La douleur* does not actually conform to Lejeune's strict definition of 'autobiography' in that it does not emphasize the history of the author's personality, but rather covers only a very precise period in her life (*Le pacte autobiographique*, 14; 4–5). Yet because of the identity of the author, narrator, and protagonist in the first four narratives (despite the use of the fictional name 'Thérèse' in the third and fourth, which I will comment on later in the chapter), these narratives are nevertheless autobiographical texts, each of which Lejeune might label 'mémoires' or 'journal intime' (personal diary) – two genres related to autobiography that do fulfil its principal requirement ('identité') (14; 4–5).

8 For example, David R. Ellison, *Of Words and the World: Referential Anxiety in Contemporary French Fiction* (Princeton, NJ: Princeton University Press, 1993) (discussed in my introduction), and Raylene L. Ramsay, *The French New Autobiographies: Sarraute, Duras, and Robbe-Grillet* (Gainesville: University Press of Florida, 1996), analyse the autobiographies of Duras and the New Novelists published in the early 1980s and discuss the idea that they signalled a new interest among these authors in extra-textual reference. While this is partially true, Ellison and Ramsay also stress the ways in which these authors remain faithful in these postmodern autobiographies to their fundamental literary projects by self-reflexively questioning such reference and thus con-

tributing to a redefinition of the very genre. For a discussion of women writers' contribution to the evolution of autobiography and to its elevation within the French literary hierarchy in the 1980s, see Michael Sheringham, 'Changing the Script: Women Writers and the Rise of Autobiography,' in *A History of Women's Writing in France*, ed. Sonya Stephens, 185–203 (Cambridge: Cambridge University Press, 2000).

9 Marguerite Duras, 'Monsieur X. dit ici Pierre Rabier,' in *La douleur*, 89–135; trans. by Barbara Bray as 'Monsieur X, Here Called Pierre Rabier,' in *The War: A Memoir*, 71–112 (New York: Pantheon, 1986).

10 Pierre Péan, *Une jeunesse française: François Mitterrand, 1934–47* (Paris: Fayard, 1994).

11 Leslie Hill, *Marguerite Duras: Apocalyptic Desires* (London: Routledge, 1993), 125–6; Gabriel Jacobs, 'Spectres of Remorse: Duras's War-Time Autobiography,' *Romance Studies* 30 (1997): 49.

12 Marguerite Duras, 'Avril 45: nuit et Duras,' *Libération* [Paris], 17 April 1985, 37.

13 Gérard Genette, *Narrative Discourse: An Essay in Method*, trans. Jane E. Lewin (Ithaca, NY: Cornell University Press, 1980), 27.

14 In *Fiction et diction* (Paris: Seuil, 1991), 69–73, Gérard Genette affirms, against the arguments of Barbara Herrnstein Smith in 'Narrative Versions, Narrative Theories,' *Critical Inquiry* (1980): 213–36, that one can almost always speak of a story (*histoire*) in relation to a fictional narrative (*récit*), despite that story's lack of truth value or reality. Herrnstein Smith also argues that the lack of strict chronological order is most narratives makes it difficult to speak of 'story' (227); but Genette insists that however 'disordered' a narrative may be, enough information is usually offered for the reader or listener to be able to reconstruct – or construct in the case of fiction – the order of the story. Alain Robbe-Grillet's *La jalousie* (Paris: Minuit, 1957) is one notable exception to Genette's rule, however.

15 Marguerite Duras, 'Madame Dodin,' in *Des journées entières dans les arbres*, 119–84 (Paris: Gallimard, 1954), trans. by Anita Barrows as 'Madame Dodin,' in *Whole Days in the Trees*, 83–126 (London: John Calder, 1984); *Le ravissement de Lol V. Stein* (Paris: Gallimard, Folio, 1964), trans. by Richard Seaver as *The Ravishing of Lol V. Stein* (New York: Pantheon, 1966); *Le vice-consul* (Paris: Gallimard, L'Imaginaire, 1966), trans. by Eileen Ellenbogen as *The Vice-Consul* (London: Hamish Hamilton, 1968).

16 When I am speaking of 'Monsieur X.' the narrative, I will use the term 'narrator' to designate the 'I' inscribed there. On the other hand, when I am referring to the historical events the narrative is purported to represent, I will generally call the 'I' 'Duras.'

17 For a discussion of the role of women in the Resistance, see Paula Schwartz's 'Redefining Resistance: Women's Activism in Wartime France,' in *Behind the Lines: Gender and the Two World Wars*, ed. Margaret Higonnet et al. (New Haven: Yale University Press, 1987), especially 151.

18 The terms 'character-I' and 'narrator-I' are Gerald Prince's. See Prince, *Narratology* (Berlin, Germany: Mouton, 1982), 13–14.

19 A prolepsis, according to Genette, *Narrative Discourse*, 40, is 'any narrative maneuver that consists of narrating or evoking in advance an event that will take place later.'

20 According to Genette, ibid., 199–200, Proust, on the contrary, made every effort in his autobiographical fiction to restrict the focalization of the narrative to the hero's (the character-I's) thoughts and perceptions. In other words, he wanted to give away only as much as his character-I knew at any given moment in the narrative, thus concealing, unlike Duras in 'Monsieur X.,' the narrator-I's superior knowledge and understanding until the 'final revelation.'

21 The S.T.O. was the *Service du travail obligatoire*, created by the Vichy government in February 1943. Through it, young Frenchmen could be sent to work in German war factories. The only significant effect of the S.T.O., however, was to swell the ranks of the Resistance with those who refused to leave.

22 I count thirteen of these episodes, but the narrative could be divided slightly differently.

23 In his *Dictionary of Narratology* (Lincoln: University of Nebraska Press, 1987), 47, Gerard Prince describes an iterative narrative as '[a] narrative or part thereof with a frequency whereby what happens n times is recounted once.'

24 Prince, ibid., 57, defines the narrating instance as 'the act of recounting a series of situations and events and, by extension, the spatio-temporal context ... of that act.'

25 Duras, 'J'ai vécu le réel comme un mythe' (I lived the real like a myth), interview by Aliette Armel, *Magazine Littéraire*, June 1990, 20.

26 Duras, *Écrire* (Paris: Gallimard, NRF, 1993), 41; trans. by Mark Polizzotti as *Writing* (Cambridge, MA: Lumen, 1998), 18.

27 Duras, 'J'ai vécu le réel comme un mythe,' 20.

28 I say 'primarily,' because all writers of literature undoubtedly draw upon both imagination and memory, to varying degrees, to produce their texts, whether fictional, autobiographical, or something in between. As Armel notes in 'Duras: Repères biographiques,' 25, Duras's childhood memory of a wealthy and seductive colonial woman, Elizabeth Striedter, served as the seed of the fictional 'India cycle' (see note 1 of this chapter for the texts and films included in this cycle).

29 Lawrence Langer, *Holocaust Testimonies: The Ruins of Memory* (New Haven: Yale University Press, 1991), 3–9.
30 Charlotte Delbo, *La mémoire et les jours* (Paris: Berg, 1985), 14, cited in Langer, *Holocaust Testimonies*, 7.
31 Roberta Culbertson, 'Embodied Memory, Transcendence, and Telling: Recounting Trauma, Reestablishing Self,' *New Literary History* 26 (1995): 170.
32 Delbo, *La mémoire et les jours*, 14.
33 It is unfortunate that in English one cannot make the lexical distinction, as one can in French, between the concepts of *mémoire*, the storeroom of things learned and retained, and *souvenirs*, the individual impressions that *mémoire* contains.
34 Culbertson, 'Embodied Memory, Transcendence, and Telling,' 170.
35 Yet in Sartre's *La nausée* (Paris: Gallimard, 1938) and Sarraute's *Entre la vie et la mort* (Paris: Gallimard, 1968), for example, characters struggle to shake this linguistic grid and seem able, at least at fleeting moments, to catch glimpses of a pre-linguistic reality in all its chaos. Of course, in these novels such glimpses are represented, both paradoxically and necessarily, in language. For Sartre's protagonist, this is a nausea-inducing experience, whereas for Sarraute's – as I will show in chapter 3 – it is a joyous, almost ecstatic one.
36 Culbertson, 'Embodied Memory, Transcendence, and Telling,' 170.
37 Duras, *La douleur*, 90; 71–2.
38 Langer, *Holocaust Testimonies*, 7.
39 Marguerite Duras, 'Entretien Marguerite Duras – François Mitterrand: Le Bureau de la poste de la rue Dupin,' *L'Autre Journal*, 26 February – 4 March 1986, 37.
40 Suffering from a terrible sense of isolation as she waits for her husband, the narrator of the first text in the volume writes, using another metaphor, that she feels as if she has been 'coupée du reste du monde avec un rasoir' (cut off from the rest of the world by a razor) (*La douleur*, 59; 45).
41 Jacobs, 'Spectres of Remorse,' 50–1.
42 Duras, *La douleur*, 80; 63–4.
43 Langer, *Holocaust Testimonies*, 6.
44 Ibid., 19.
45 Both Gabriel Jacobs, 'Spectres of Remorse,' and Laurence D. Kritzman, 'Duras' War,' *Esprit Créateur* 33, no. 1 (1993): 63–73, discuss *La douleur*'s lack of – or rather refusal of – a clear ethical message. Jacobs notes that *La douleur* is 'full of grey areas between right and wrong action' (54); and Kritzman concludes his insightful essay with the following comments: 'The constant deflection of the nature of the just [in *La douleur*] suggests that the lesson

inscribed in Duras' sacred texts is one that is devoid of cognitive assumptions for it leaves us without criteria with which to judge. Perhaps the inability to establish a singular ethical perspective from which the idea of justice can be played out translates the pain resulting from the inconsistencies produced by the unspeakable horrors of war' (73).

46 Duras, 'Monsieur X.,' 134; 111. According to Péan, *Une jeunesse française*, 472, court transcripts that he consulted for his chapter on these events confirm that this is indeed what the real Duras did at Rabier's trial.

47 'D.' is Dionys Mascolo, for whom Duras divorced Antelme after the war and who, upon meeting this latter through Duras herself, became close friends with him, despite this love triangle.

48 The authenticity of this name is questioned by both Duras in 'Monsieur X.,' 108, and Mitterrand in 'Entretien Marguerite Duras – François Mitterrand,' 34, making the plot of this real-life tale resemble even more closely that of a spy novel. As I will discuss below, however, there are some who believe that this report of Delval's double identity is nothing more than the product of an overactive imagination, namely Duras's.

49 Péan, *Une jeunesse française*, 452.

50 There are five short prefaces in the volume, one introducing two narratives, and one introducing each of the other four. Each preface, including the first – which Péan mistakenly cites as the preface to the entire volume – appears only *after* the title of the particular narrative or narratives to which it refers.

51 In one episode in 'Monsieur X.,' Rabier tries to induce the narrator to reveal what she knows about Mitterrand, who was wanted by the Gestapo because of his Resistance activities.

52 Pierre Péan, 'Duras et la douleur,' e-mail to the author, 1 September 2004.

53 *L'espèce humaine* (Paris: Gallimard, 1957) is Antelme's account of the year he spent first in a French prison and then in several Nazi camps. It is in a sense a 'companion' text to *La douleur* in that it tells the part of the story that is 'missing' from this latter – the part of which *La douleur*'s narrator is so painfully ignorant. In his *Autour d'un effort de mémoire: sur une lettre de Robert Antelme* (Paris: Nadeau, 1987), Dionys Mascolo reproduces and comments on a letter Antelme sent him shortly after his return from the camps. The three interviews I will draw from in this section of the chapter are Duras, 'J'ai vécu le réel comme un mythe,' 'Entretien Marguerite Duras – François Mitterrand,' and 'Avril 45.'

54 Duras, 'Monsieur X.,' 96; 77.

55 Péan, *Une jeunesse française*, 451.

56 Duras, 'Monsieur X.,' 135; 112.

57 Ibid., 138; 115.

58 Jacobs, 'Spectres of Remorse,' 47.

59 Duras, 'Entretien Marguerite Duras – François Mitterrand,' 32.

60 Duras, 'Monsieur X.,' 93, 94, 106; 74, 75, 86.

61 For an account of Duras's alcoholism and final treatment for it, see Frédérique Lebelley, *Duras ou le poids d'une plume* (Paris: Grasset, 1994), 207–14 and 286–92.

62 In 'Avril 45,' 37, Duras states, 'A mon avis, j'ai dû commencer à écrire la *Douleur* quand on est allé dans des maisons de repos pour déportés. Je ne vois pas quand autrement' (I think I must have begun writing *La douleur* when we went to stay in some rest homes for deportees. I don't see when else).

63 Ibid., 37.

64 Duras, 'Monsieur X.,' 101; 82.

65 Ibid., 90; 72.

66 Jacobs, 'Spectres of Remorse,' 50.

67 Duras, 'Monsieur X.,' 104; 85.

68 Péan, *Une jeunesse française*, 461.

69 Duras, 'Entretien Marguerite Duras – François Mitterrand,' 39.

70 Duras, 'Monsieur X.,' 103; 83.

71 Péan, *Une jeunesse française*, 458.

72 Duras, *La douleur*, 138; 115.

73 Péan, *Une jeunesse française*, 467.

74 Then again, perhaps the romantic tangle presented in *Le ravissement de Lol V. Stein* (among Lol, Michael Richardson, Anne-Marie Stretter, Jacques Hold, and Tatiana Karl) rivals this real-life one.

75 For Mascolo's perspective on this triangular relationship, see his *Autour d'un effort de mémoire*, especially 40–3.

76 Lebelley, *Duras ou le poids d'une plume*, 114. In 'Spectres of Remorse,' 52, Jacobs also cites some of Lebelley's comments concerning Antelme's feelings.

77 Péan, *Une jeunesse française*, 467.

78 Duras, 'Monsieur X.,' 80.

79 Duras, 'Entretien Marguerite Duras – François Mitterrand,' 36.

80 Péan, *Une jeunesse française*, 475.

81 Jacobs, 'Spectres of Remorse,' 47–9.

82 Duras, *Écrire*, 41; 17.

83 Culbertson, 'Embodied Memory, Transcendence, and Telling,' 170.

84 Delbo, *La mémoire et les jours*, 14.

85 Jeanine Parisier Plottel, 'Memory, Fiction and History,' *Esprit Créateur* 30, no. 1 (1990): 48.

86 Duras, 'Monsieur X.,' 108; 88.

87 Duras, 'Monsieur X.,' 90; 71.

88 Some of my comments on 'Madame Dodin' here are derived from a more
    detailed analysis I make of the story in Willging, 'Narrative Urge, Narrative
    Anxiety: Taking Out the Trash in Marguerite Duras's "Madame Dodin,"'
    French Review 73 (2000): 699–709.

89 I say 'nearly sexless' because the narrator's gender is only revealed, in
    French, by two past participles (Duras, 'Madame Dodin,' 126 and 159).

90 I follow Maurice Grévisse in *Le bon usage*, 12th ed. (Paris: Duculot, 1986),
    1299, note 9, in calling the conditional a 'tense': 'Le conditionnel a
    longtemps été considéré comme un mode (du moins pour certains de ses
    emplois, car on distinguait souvent un conditionnel-temps [de l'indic.] et un
    conditionnel-mode). Les linguistes s'accordent aujourd'hui pour le ranger
    parmi les temps de l'indicatif, comme un futur particulier, futur dans le
    passé ou futur hypothétique' (The conditional has for a long time been con-
    sidered a mood [at least for certain of its uses, because one would often dis-
    tinguish between a conditional tense (of the indicative) and a conditional
    mood]. Linguists today agree that it should be categorized among the indic-
    ative tenses, like a particular kind of future, a future in the past or a hypo-
    thetical future) (Grévisse's brackets).

91 Saint-Germain-des-Prés, like the fictional *quartier* Sainte-Eulalie, which
    resembles it, was indeed a hotbed of literary activity from the 1890s through
    the 1950s. During the 1930s and 1940s especially, Beauvoir and Sartre wrote
    regularly at the Café de Flore and Les Deux Magots, which are only steps
    away from Duras's apartment on the rue Saint-Benoît. Duras's apartment
    itself was a de facto headquarters for the so-called groupe de la rue Saint-
    Benoît, a cohort of writers, intellectuals, and political activists that included
    Robert Antelme, Dionys Mascolo, Edgar Morin, and Claude Roy.

92 Jacques Lacan, *Encore*, ed. Jacques-Alain Miller, vol. 20 of *Le séminaire* (Paris:
    Seuil, 1975), 29.

93 Although Mme Dodin shares many of the character traits of the faithful but
    cantankerous Françoise in Proust's *À la recherche du temps perdu*, eds. Pierre
    Clarai and André Ferré (Paris: Pléiade, 1954), in their insensibility to real as
    opposed to literary injustice, it is Mme Dodin's tenants who resemble the
    maidservant here, of whom Proust's narrator wryly remarks, 'Les torrents de
    larmes qu'elle versait en lisant le journal sur les infortunes des inconnus, se
    tarissaient vite si elle pouvait se représenter la personne qui en était l'objet
    d'une façon un peu précise' (I came to recognise that, apart from her own
    kinsfolk, the sufferings of humanity inspired in her a pity which increased
    in direct ratio to the distance separating the sufferers from herself. The
    tears that flowed from her in torrents when she read in a newspaper of the

misfortunes of persons unknown to her were quickly stemmed once she had been able to form a more precise mental picture of the victims) (1:122; 1:171).

94 In *Le vice-consul,* the narrative of the homodiegetic narrator to whom I refer (Peter Morgan) is framed within the heterodiegetically narrated main narrative.

95 It has been argued, however, that the women being 'narrated' in *Le ravissement* and *Le vice-consul* do resist, indirectly, through their very silence. See for example Susan Cohen, 'From Omniscience to Ignorance: Voice and Narration in the Work of Marguerite Duras,' in *Remains to Be Seen: Essays on Marguerite Duras,* ed. Sanford Ames (New York: Peter Lang, 1988), 57–8.

96 Duras, *Le ravissement,* 14, 37, 44, 45, 56, 71, etc.

97 Duras, *Le vice-consul,* 73; 54.

98 Susan Suleiman, 'Nadja, Dora, Lol V. Stein: Women, Madness and Narrative,' in *Discourse in Psychoanalysis and Literature,* ed. Shlomith Rimmon-Kenan (London: Methuen, 1987), 144.

99 Martha Noel Evans, *Masks of Tradition: Women and the Politics of Writing in Twentieth-Century France* (Ithaca, NY: Cornell University Press, 1987), 130–1.

100 See Marcelle Marini, *Territoires du féminin avec Marguerite Duras* (Paris: Minuit, 1977), 31; Susan Cohen, *Women and Discourse,* 34; Laurie Edson, 'Knowing Lol: Duras, Epistemology and Gendered Mediation,' *SubStance* 68 (1992), 19; and Dina Sherzer, 'How Discourse Means: A View from Marguerite Duras's *Le vice-consul,*' *Neophilologus* 76 (1992), 370. In 'Nadja, Dora, Lol V. Stein,' 148, note 10, Suleiman does state that her reading 'situates [her] at a critical distance from the influential "anti-Lacanian" feminist reading proposed by Marcelle Marini,' a reading in which, Suleiman says, 'Duras's authorial attitude would have to be seen as ironic toward the male narrator.' Suleiman's reading, on the other hand, 'assumes a significant merging between Duras's authorial voice (and vision) and the voice of Jacques Hold – as if the subversive quality of the novel resided precisely in the "feminization" of the male narrator, who is "contaminated" by femininity both on the diegetic or story level (his involvement with Lol) and on the discursive level (Jacques's narration is hesitant, uncertain, full of silences, corresponding to Duras's notion of what a "feminine writing" might be' (148–9, note 10).

101 As we have seen, Morgan 'voudrait ... substituer à la mémoire abolie de la mendiante le bric-à brac de la sienne' (Duras, *Le vice-consul,* 73; 54), and Hold, 'connaissant cette femme' (knowing that women) as he claims he does, maintains that it is in fact Lol's wish 'qu['il] remédie ... à la pénurie

des faits de sa vie' (that he compensate ... for the lack of facts about her life) (Duras, *Le ravissement*, 37; 27).

102 Duras, *Le vice-consul*, 136; 106. Presumably Anne-Marie Stretter knows he is incapable of writing anything of value.

103 Ibid., 74; 56.

104 Versions of the mother's story are recounted in such texts as *Un barrage contre le Pacifique*, *L'Eden cinéma* (Paris: Mercure de France, 1977), *L'Amant*, and *L'amant de la Chine du Nord* (Paris: Gallimard, 1991), and elements of her personality can be discerned in characters in several other texts.

105 Lebelley, *Duras ou le poids d'une plume*, 320–3. In her account, Lebelley condemns as unconscionable Duras's public treatment of Christine Villemin.

106 Duras, 'Sublime, forcément sublime Christine V,' *Libération*, 17 July 1985, 4–6.

107 Ibid., 4.

108 Lebelley, *Duras ou le poids d'une plume*, 323.

109 Ibid., 322.

110 Dominique Denes, *Marguerite Duras: Écriture et politique* (Paris: L'Harmattan, 2005), 31. Denes's quotation marks indicate a quote from an interview Duras gave in *Libération*, 11 July 1980.

111 Marguerite Duras, *Emily L.* (Paris: Minuit, 1987).

112 Duras, *Les viaducs de la Seine-et-Oise* (Paris: Gallimard, 1959) and *L'amante anglaise* (Paris: Gallimard, 1967).

113 Duras, 'Sublime, forcément sublime Christine V.,' 4.

114 Evans, *Masks of Tradition*, 130–1.

115 Lebelley, *Duras ou le poids d'une plume*, 322–3.

116 Ibid., 323. 'L'affaire Villemin, c'est net, la discrédite' (The Villemin affaire, it's clear, discredits her), Lebelley asserts.

117 Duras, 'Madame Dodin,' 130; 92.

118 Annie Ernaux, *La honte* (Paris: Gallimard, NRF, 1997), 37; 32.

2: Shame in Memory and Narrative

1 Annie Ernaux, *La honte* (Paris: Gallimard, NRF, 1997); trans. by Tanya Leslie as *Shame* (New York: Four Walls Eight Windows, 1992). These earlier texts are Annie Ernaux, *Les armoires vides* (Paris: Gallimard, Folio, 1974), trans. by Carol Sanders as *Cleaned Out* (Lisle, IL: Dalkey Archives Press, 1990); *Ce qu'ils disent ou rien* (Paris: Gallimard, Folio, 1977); *La place* (Paris: Gallimard, Folio, 1984), trans. by Tanya Leslie as *A Man's Place* (New York: Four Walls Eight Windows, 1992); and *Une femme* (Paris: Gallimard, Folio, 1988), trans. by Tanya Leslie as *A Woman's Story* (New York: Four Walls Eight

Windows, 1991). These first two texts are designated as novels and are somewhat fictionalized versions of Ernaux's childhood and adolescence (the
female protagonists in them bear fictional names). The second two are
labelled *récits* (narratives) and are, the author has said, attempts at describing as objectively and accurately as possible, with no fictionalization or even
romanticization, the 'reality' of her experiences. In *L'écriture comme un couteau,* interview by Frédéric-Yves Jeannet (Paris: Stock, 2003), 21, Ernaux
states that in all her texts from *La place* on, 'le "je" du texte et le nom inscrit
sur la couverture du livre renvoient à la même personne' (the 'I' in the text
and the name printed on the cover of the book refer to the same person).
She thereby explicitly concludes with the readers of these texts Philippe
Lejeune's 'autobiographical pact,' which I discussed in chapter 1. Lejeune,
Le pacte autobiographique (Paris: Seuil, 1975), 26–7. A translation of the first
chapter of *Le pacte autobiographique,* in which Lejeune describes the 'rules' of
this pact, appears in Lejeune, *On Autobiography,* ed. Paul John Eakin and
trans. Katherine Leary (Minneapolis: University of Minnesota Press, 1989),
4–5.

2 Ernaux, *La place,* 24; 13.

3 Ernaux, *La honte,* 13; 13.

4 In *Annie Ernaux: An Introduction to the Writer and Her Audience* (Oxford: Berg,
1999), 21, Lyn Thomas qualifies this 'missing' event as 'perhaps the most significant absence of Ernaux's work' until the publication of *La honte.* She also
describes it as 'a murderous version of the primal scene: the twelve-year-old
Ernaux sees her father, not making love to her mother, but trying to kill her'
(74), thereby emphasizing, as I will here, the powerful psychological impact
this scene had on the girl.

5 Marguerite Duras, 'Monsieur X. dit ici Pierre Rabier,' in *La douleur* (Paris:
P.O.L., 1985), 90; trans. by Barbara Bray as 'Monsieur X, Here Called Pierre
Rabier,' in *The War: A Memoir* (New York: Pantheon, 1986), 71–2.

6 Ernaux, *La place* (Paris: Gallimard, Folio, 1984); Ernaux, *L'écriture comme un
couteau,* 21. This latter text is a year-long interview conducted entirely
through e-mail and subsequently published in book form.

7 These are the first three narratives in *La douleur.*

8 Annie Ernaux, *Les armoires vides* (Paris: Gallimard, Folio, 1974); *L'événement*
(Paris: Gallimard, Folio, 2000); *Passion simple* (Paris: Gallimard, Folio, 1991);
Se perdre (Paris: Gallimard, NRF, 2001).

9 Ernaux, *La honte,* 14–15; 14–15.

10 Ernaux, *La place,* 71; 59–60.

11 Gérard Genette, *Narrative Discourse: An Essay in Method,* trans. Jane E. Lewin
(Ithaca, NY: Cornell University Press, 1980), 52.

12 As noted in chapter 1, in *Narrative Discourse*, 27, Genette defines 'story' as the 'signified or narrative contents' and 'narrative' as the 'signifier, statement, discourse or narrative text itself.'

13 Ernaux, *La place*, 78; 66.

14 Ernaux, *La honte*, 20; 18.

15 Ernaux, *La place*, 108–10; 94–96.

16 Ernaux, *Une femme*, 35; 24.

17 Ernaux, *Passion simple*, 68–70; trans. by Tanya Leslie as *Simple Passion* (New York: Four Walls Eight Windows, 1993), 57–8.

18 Annie Ernaux, *Journal du dehors* (Paris: Gallimard, Folio, 1993), 19; trans. by Tanya Leslie as *Exteriors* (New York: Seven Stories, 1993), 17.

19 As Roland Barthes writes in 'The Death of the Author,' *Image–Music–Text*, ed. and trans. Stephen Heath (New York: Hill and Wang, 1977), 145, 'linguistically, the author is never more than the instance writing, just as *I* is nothing other than the instance saying *I*: language knows a "subject," not a "person," and this subject, empty outside of the very enunciation which defines it, suffices to make language "hold together," suffices, that is to say, to exhaust it.'

20 Ernaux, *La honte*, 132; 109.

21 Annie Ernaux, 'Annie Ernaux ou l'autobiographie en question,' interview by Philippe Vilain, *Romans 50/90* 24 (1997): 146.

22 Ernaux, *La honte*, 20; 19.

23 Cathy Caruth, 'Trauma and Experience: Introduction,' in *Trauma: Explorations in Memory*, ed. Cathy Caruth (Baltimore: Johns Hopkins University Press, 1995), 4.

24 Ernaux, *La honte*, 31; 27.

25 Caruth, 'Recapturing the Past: Introduction,' in *Trauma: Explorations in Memory*, 152–3.

26 Ernaux, *La honte*, 15; 15.

27 United States Surgeon General website, 'Anxiety Disorders,' in *Mental Health: A Report of the Surgeon General*, http://www.surgeongeneral.gov/library/mentalhealth/chapter 4/sec2.html.

28 Bessel A. van der Kolk and Onno van der Hart, 'The Intrusive Past: The Flexibility of Memory and the Engraving of Trauma,' in *Trauma: Explorations in Memory*, 172.

29 Pierre Janet, *L'évolution de la mémoire et la notion du temps* (Paris: Cahine, 1928).

30 Van der Kolk and van der Hart, 'The Intrusive Past,' 160.

31 *Diagnostic and Statistical Manual of Mental Disorders*, 3rd ed. (Washington, DC: American Psychiatric Association, 1987), 477.

32 Sigmund Freud and Josef Breuer, *Studies on Hysteria* (New York: Basic Books,

1957), 152, quoted in van der Kolk and van der Hart, 'The Intrusive Past,' 165.

33 Ernaux, *La honte*, 25; 22.

34 In *The Logic of Practice* (Cambridge, MA: Polity Press, 1990), 53, French sociologist Pierre Bourdieu defines the habitus as a 'system of durable, transposable dispositions, structuring structures, that is, as principles which generate and organize practices and representations that can be objectively adapted to their outcomes without presupposing a conscious aiming at ends or an express mastery of the operations necessary in order to attain them. Objectively "regulated" and "regular" without being in any way the product of obedience to rules, they can be collectively orchestrated without being the product of the organizing action of a conductor.' This quote is reproduced in Randal Johnson, 'Pierre Bourdieu on Art, Literature and Culture,' introduction to Pierre Bourdieu, *The Fields of Cultural Production: Essay on Art and Literature*, ed. Randal Johnson (New York: Columbia University Press, 1995), 5. More simply if less precisely put, an individual's habitus is the set of (culturally instilled) dispositions that generate his or her behaviours, perceptions, and tastes. In 'Bourdieu: le chagrin,' an article Ernaux published in *Le Monde* upon the sociologist's death (February 6, 2002, http://www.homme-moderne.org/societe/socio/bourdieu/mort/aernau.html), she writes of the 'prise de conscience sans retour' (irreversible epiphany) she experienced while discovering Bourdieu's theories of social structure and domination.

35 Ernaux, *La honte*, 37; 32.

36 Van der Kolk and van der Hart, 'The Intrusive Past,' 159.

37 Ibid., 163.

38 Marcel Proust, *À la recherche du temps perdu*, eds. Pierre Clarac and André Ferré, 3 vols. (Paris: Gallimard, Pléiade, 1954). Many of Ernaux's narrators in fact make several references to Proust throughout each of their texts. I will discuss some of these references further below.

39 Proust, *À la recherche du temps perdu*, 3:870; trans. by Andreas Mayor and Terence Kilmartin as *In Search of Lost Time*, 6:260 (New York: Modern Library, 1993). Cited in Leo Bersani, *Marcel Proust: The Fictions of Life and Art* (New York: Oxford University Press, 1965), 49.

40 Bersani, *Marcel Proust*, 6–7.

41 Ernaux, *La honte*, 27–9; 24–6.

42 Thomas, *Annie Ernaux*, 23.

43 Proust, *À la recherche du temps perdu*, 3: 696.

44 The title of this song, released in 1987, is actually 'Voyage, voyage.'

45 Ernaux, *Journal du dehors*, 62; 54–5.

46   'I'm Just Another Dancing Partner' is a 1955 song by the Platters. *Bel été* is
· the French translation of Italian author Cesar Pavese's *Bella estate* (Turin:
Einaudi, 1958).

47   In *L'écriture comme un couteau*, 42, Ernaux writes that certain songs for her are
'des "madeleines" à la fois personnelles et collectives' ([Proustian]
'madeleines' that are both personal and collective): 'Il y a peu de textes où je
n'évoque pas des chansons, parce qu'elles jalonnent toute ma vie et que cha-
cune ramène des images, des sensations, une chaîne proliférante de souvenirs, et le contexte d'une année' (There are few texts of mine in which I
don't mention songs, because they demarcate my life, and because each one
evokes images, sensations, a proliferating chain of memories, and the context of a year).

48   See chapter 1 of the present study for a discussion of Charlotte Delbo's
notion of sense memory, which she describes in *La mémoire et les jours* (Paris:
Berg, 1985), 14.

49   Ernaux, *La place*, 29; 17–18.

50   Marguerite Duras, 'Madame Dodin,' in *Des journées entières dans les arbres*,
119–84 (Paris: Gallimard, 1954); trans. by Anita Barrows as 'Madame Dodin,'
in *Whole Days in the Trees*, 83–126 (London: John Calder, 1984).

51   Ernaux, *La place*, 62; 50.

52   Although Ernaux's narrators often wryly point out the yawning gap between
Proust's style and esthetics and theirs, in *L'écriture comme un couteau*, Ernaux
writes an uncharacteristically lyrical and metaphorical passage whose form as
well as content attest, without any direct reference to him, to her affinity for
the author of *La recherche*: 'Ne peut-on voir la vie derrière soi comme une
série de chambres en abîme jusqu'à celle, définitivement opaque, neigeuse
tel un film mal enregistré sur magnétoscope, de la naissance' (Cannot we
see behind us something like a series of rooms *en abîme*, right down to the
one – forever opaque, blurry like a poorly recorded video – in which we were
born) (129–30).

53   Ernaux, *La honte*, 19; 18.

54   Ernaux, *Passion simple*, 66; 54.

55   Ernaux, *Une femme*, 104; 90.

56   Ernaux, *La honte*, 78; 67.

57   Lawrence L. Langer, *Holocaust Testimonies: The Ruins of Memory* (New Haven:
Yale University Press, 1991), 174–5, quoted in van der Kolk and van der Hart,
'The Intrusive Past,' 177.

58   Ernaux, *La honte*, 30; 26.

59   Van der Kolk and van der Hart, 'The Intrusive Past,' 178.

60   Ernaux, *La honte*, 20; 18.

61 Van der Kolk and van der Hart, 'The Intrusive Past,' 163.
62 Ibid., 163.
63 Ernaux, *Une femme*, 89; 76.
64 Ernaux, *Passion simple*, 31 and 58; 21 and 46.
65 Annie Ernaux, *Je ne suis pas sortie de ma nuit* (Paris: Gallimard, Folio, 1997); trans. by Tanya Leslie as '*I Remain in Darkness*' (New York: Seven Stories, 1999).
66 In *L'écriture comme un couteau*, 39, Ernaux indeed writes that one of her objectives in publishing *Je ne suis pas sortie de ma nuit*, which she says is the diary she kept during her mother's illness, was 'démystifier la clôture' (to demystify the closure) of *Une femme*, in which she had written the seemingly definitive line, 'Maintenant, tout est lié' (Now, everything is linked/tied together) (103; 89). '[L]a publication du journal,' she adds in *L'écriture*, 'me permet de faire "jouer" le premier texte, de lui donner un autre éclairage' (The publication of the diary allows me to make the first text appear less definitive, to throw a different light on it), just as I have argued *La honte* does for all of Ernaux's earlier texts about her adolescence (39).
67 Ernaux, *Une femme*, 106; 92.
68 Ibid., 106; 91.
69 Ernaux, *Passion simple*, 36, 40; 26, 28–9.
70 Ibid., 24; 14. Ernaux, *La honte*, 16; 15.
71 Ernaux, *Passion simple*, 65; 53.
72 Ibid., 76; 63–4.
73 Ernaux, *La honte*, 71–2; 61. Although the text has no chapters or other formal divisions, it appears to be informally organized into four sections, each of which begins at the top of a new page. The first part (13–39; 13–33) centres around the scene, the second (40–70; 35–59) around the narrator's childhood town, the third (71–107; 61–90) around her private school, and the last (108–33; 91–111) predominantly around a trip the narrator took to Lourdes with her father in the summer of 1952.
74 Jean Royer, 'Pour que s'abolisse la barrière entre la littérature et la vie,' *Le Devoir*, 26 March 1988, D1.
75 Ernaux, *La honte*, 86; 73.
76 In 'Stylistic Aspects of Women's Writing: The Case of Annie Ernaux,' *French Cultural Studies* 4 (1993): 22, Carol Sanders speaks of Ernaux's later texts as examples of ethnobiography or autoethnography, which Sanders describes as a 'new form which combines social history with authorial reflexion.' In her discussion she cites Françoise Lionnet's study of women's autobiographies, *Autobiographical Voices: Race, Gender and Self-Portraiture* (Ithaca, NY: Cornell University Press, 1989), in which Lionnet uses the term to characterize the works of many contemporary francophone women writers.

77 Laurence Mall, '"Moins seule et factice": La part autobiographique dans *Une femme* d'Annie Ernaux,' *French Review* 69 (1995): 47.

78 Ernaux, *La honte*, 38; 33.

79 'Six bicyclettes à Saïgon ...' refers to the war France unsuccessfully waged between 1946 and 1954 to retain Indochina as a colony. Jacques Duclos was a Communist deputy in the French National Assembly in 1952. On 28 May of that year, the PCF held a demonstration against the arrival of the American General Matthew Ridgeway, the new Supreme Allied Commander of NATO. That evening, French police arrested Duclos because they had found two (dead) pigeons in his car and suspected him of attempting to use them as messengers in a plot against the government that had welcomed Ridgeway and his cold warriors. Duclos claimed that the only plan he had for the pigeons was to roast them for dinner. The charges were subsequently dropped ('Chronologie sociale 1948–52,' Département de Sciences Sociales, Ecole Normale Supérieure, http://www.sciencessociales.ens.fr/hss2001/travail/chronologiechrono48_58.html). I am grateful to Nicolas Médevielle for his research into this last reference.

80 *Le Petit Robert 1* (1999), 1627.

81 Annie Ernaux, 'Entretien avec Annie Ernaux,' interview by Claire-Lise Tondeur, *French Review* 69, no. 1 (1995): 38.

82 Royer, 'Pour que s'abolisse la barrière entre la littérature et la vie,' D1.

83 Paul Auster, *The Invention of Solitude* (New York: Penguin, 1988), 161.

84 Ernaux, *La honte*, 26; 23.

85 Two (related) examples in *La honte* of objects that serve as signifiers of social class are, first, the chamber pot that sits at the top of the staircase between the family's *café* and *épicerie* and whose presence signals that they cannot afford to have a toilet installed in the house (50; 43); and second, the urine-stained nightgown in which the narrator's mother appears before her daughter's bourgeois teacher and classmates and which tells the tale of the family's 'dubious' (that is, lower-class) hygiene: 'on s'essuyait avec, après avoir uriné' (we wiped ourselves with it after urinating), the narrator states flatly (109–10; 92–3). In 'Memory Stains: Annie Ernaux's *Shame*,' *A/b: Auto/Biography Studies* 4 (1999): 43, Nancy K. Miller argues that this scene (which 'brought [her] up short' as a reader) is more fundamentally traumatic and shameful than the scene between the mother and father, because unlike this latter, it was *public*.

86 Thomas, *Annie Ernaux*, 35.

87 Royer, 'Pour que s'abolisse la barrière entre la littérature et la vie,' D1.

88 *Le petit écho de la mode*, a fashion magazine, is now defunct. *La veillée des chaumières*, still in existence, publishes excerpts from 'women's' literature.

89 Ernaux, *La honte*, 37–8; 32,

90 Siobhán McIlvanney, 'Annie Ernaux: un écrivain dans la tradition du réalisme,' *Revue de l'histoire littéraire française* 2 (1998): 254.

91 In *L'écriture comme un couteau*, 29, in response to a question about her use of the 'je,' Ernaux writes, 'dans *Journal du dehors* et *La vie extérieure*, où le "je" est très souvent absent, il n'y a pas moins de "vérité" et de "réalité" que dans les autres textes : c'est l'écriture, globalement, qui détermine le degré de vérité et de réalité, pas seulement l'emploi du "je" fictionnel ou autobiographique' (in *Journal du dehors* and *La vie extérieure*, in which the 'I' is often absent, there is no less 'truth' or 'reality' than in the other texts: it's the writing, overall, that determines the degree of truth and reality, not just the use of the fictional or autobiographical 'I'). By 'écriture,' Ernaux undoubtedly means, at least in part, the narrative structure and style chosen to investigate the subject at hand.

92 Ibid., 30.

93 Ernaux, *La honte*, 38; 33.

94 These narrators are not always successful in thus controlling the reception of their narratives. For just two examples of reviews that charge Ernaux with narcissism, exhibitionism, obscenity, or a combination of the three, see, in the case of *Passion simple*, Jean-François Josselin, 'Un gros chagrin,' *Nouvel Observateur* 1418 (9–15 January 1992): 69; and Pierre-Marc de Biasi, 'Les Petites Emma 1992,' *Magazine Littéraire* 301 (July–August 1992): 59–62. For Ernaux's thoughts on such reviews, which she attributes in part to just the kind of misogyny and social snobbery her texts denounce, see *L'écriture comme un couteau*, 107–10.

95 Mall, '"Moins seule et factice,"' 47.

96 Ernaux, *La place*, 45; 34.

97 Ernaux, *La honte*, 48–9; 41–2.

98 Lacan, *Encore*, vol. 20 of *Le séminaire* (Paris: Seuil, 1975), 29.

99 Ernaux, *Passion simple*, 42; 31. See also note 94 in the present chapter.

100 Ernaux, *La honte*, 31; 27.

101 Ernaux, 'Annie Ernaux ou l'autobiographie en question,' 146–7.

102 Annie Ernaux, 'Le silence ou la trahison?' interview by Jean-Jacques Gibert, *Révolution* 260, 22 February 1985, 53.

103 Claire-Lise Tondeur, 'Écrire la honte (Annie Ernaux),' *French Prose in 2000*, ed. Michael Bishop and Christopher Elson (Amsterdam: Rodopi, 2002), 134.

104 Annie Ernaux, *L'occupation* (Paris: Gallimard, NRF, 2002). Ernaux dedicated *La honte* to 'Philippe V.,' Philippe Vilain. While still a student, Vilain wrote to Ernaux, with whose work he had become fascinated, to ask if he could meet her. The two maintained a sexual relationship for six years, during which

time Vilain began publishing novels with Ernaux's publishing house, Gallimard. One of these, *L'étreinte* (Paris: Gallimard, 1998), describes in more sexually explicit detail than *L'occupation* the relationship between him and Ernaux. This affair echoes uncannily the one between Marguerite Duras and another young man, Yann Andréa, who, like Vilain, had been captivated by the work of an older writer and sought a meeting with her, which the latter granted. Both relationships were consummated within twenty-four hours of the first encounter, but according to Frédérique Lebelley, *Duras ou le poids d'une plume* (Paris: Grasset, 1994), 276, the one between Duras and Andréa did not remain sexual because of the latter's homosexuality. Andréa and Duras nevertheless maintained an intimate relationship until Duras's death in 1995. Like Vilain, Andréa wrote a book about the writer, whose work, and person, so fascinated him: *M.D.* (Paris: Minuit, 1983).

105 Annie Ernaux and Marc Marie, *L'usage de la photo* (Paris: Stock, 2005).

106 Ernaux, *Se perdre*, 12.

107 Ernaux, *L'écriture comme un couteau*, 93–4: 'Entre nous, est-ce que, à votre insu, vous n'obéirez pas à cette tendance inconsciente, généralisée, qui fait qu'on compare spontanément, en premier lieu, une femme écrivain à d'autres femmes écrivains?' (Between us, aren't you, without realizing it, succumbing to the unconscious, and common, tendency to compare immediately a woman writer to other women writers?). To his credit, Jeannet leaves this reproach in the published version of the interview, despite the permission to omit it that Ernaux's 'entre nous' seems to offer him.

108 Marguerite Duras, *Les impudents* (Paris: Plon, 1943); *Un barrage contre le Pacifique* (Paris: Gallimard, Folio, 1950); and *L'amant* (Paris: Gallimard, Folio, 1984).

109 For Ernaux's assessment of the burdens that go along with such recognition, see Nathalie Heinich's interview of Ernaux in her study of the sociological and psychological effects on writers of winning a literary prize, *L'épreuve de la grandeur: prix littéraires et reconnaissance* (*The Test of Grandeur: Literary Prizes and Recognition*) (Paris: Découverte, 1999).

110 Ernaux, 'Fragments autour de Philippe V.' ('Fragments Concerning Philippe V.'), *L'infini* 56 (1996), 26, cited in Nancy K. Miller, 'Memory Stains,' 47. Thomas has translated this text and reproduces it in its entirety in *Annie Ernaux*, 177–9.

3: The Anxiety of Influence and the Urge to Originate

1 Nathalie Sarraute, *Entre la vie et la mort* (Paris: Gallimard, Folio, 1968); trans. by Maria Jolas as *Between Life and Death: A Novel* (New York: G. Braziller, 1969).

2 Sarraute uses suspension points regularly in her work. Here and throughout this chapter, when these points appear in quotes without spaces between them, they are Sarraute's own. As Bernard Alazet notes in 'Le tragique en éclats,' *Revue des Sciences Humaines* 217 (1990): 45, Sarraute is partially quoting here a line from Mallarmé's poem 'Brise marine,' in *Œuvres complètes,* ed. Henri Mondor and G. Jean-Aubry (Paris: Gallimard, Pléiade, 1945), 38: 'le vide papier que sa blancheur défend' (the empty paper whose whiteness defends it). Later in this chapter I will discuss the importance of Mallarmé's and other angst-ridden poets' shadowy but pervasive presence in *Entre la vie et la mort.*

3 Gerald Prince, in *Dictionary of Narratology* (Lincoln: University of Nebraska Press, 1987), 73, defines perspective (also called 'point of view,' 'focalization,' or 'viewpoint') as 'the perceptual or conceptual position in terms of which the narrated situations and events are presented.'

4 A few proper names do appear in the novel, but all except one belong to real, historical figures – writers, in particular. The exception is a fictional writer named Régier, but he is only briefly mentioned and is not himself a 'character' in the novel (77; 76).

5 Valerie Minogue, *Nathalie Sarraute and the War of the Words* (Edinburgh: Edinburgh University Press, 1981), 139.

6 Sarraute, *Entre la vie et la mort,* 7; 1.

7 Minogue, *Nathalie Sarraute,* 139–40.

8 Sarraute, *Entre la vie et la mort,* 7, 20, 144; 1, 14, 150.

9 Nathalie Sarraute, *Portrait d'un inconnu* (Paris: Gallimard, Folio, 1948); *Martereau* (Paris: Gallimard, Folio, 1953); *Le planétarium* (Paris: Gallimard, Folio, 1959). All three of these novels predate Sarraute's almost total elimination from her texts of both proper names and an embodied, identifiable narrator.

10 Nathalie Sarraute, *Les fruits d'or* (Paris: Gallimard, Folio, 1963).

11 For example, early in the novel, the writer envisions a group of threatening women as having fingernails like scorpion tails (*Entre la vie et le mort,* 37; 32). Later, an *elle* who has apparently read a book the writer has written makes reference to his use in it of the image of fingernails like scorpion tails (104; 105), as if the book to which this *elle* refers is the book before Sarraute's reader's eyes – *Entre la vie et la mort.* Similarly, as mentioned, the title of the book that is the topic of discussion throughout *Les fruits d'or* is *Les fruits d'or.*

12 Nathalie Sarraute, 'Ce que je cherche à faire,' in *Nouveau roman: hier, aujourd'hui,* eds. Jean Ricardou and Françoise vos Rossum-Guyon (Paris: UGE, 1972), 35.

13 Nathalie Sarraute, *Tu ne t'aimes pas* (Paris: Gallimard, Folio, 1989). Valerie

Minogue, 'Le cheval de Troie. À propos de *Tu ne t'aimes pas*,' *Revue des Sciences Humaines* 217 (1990): 155–7.

14 In the interest of verbal economy, I will henceforth refer to the anonymous entities in Sarraute's novels simply as characters (without the qualifying quotation marks).

15 Nathalie Sarraute, *Tropismes* (Paris: Denoël, 1939).

16 Nathalie Sarraute, *Ouvrez* (Paris: Gallimard, Folio, 1997).

17 See Celia Britton's insightful essay on Sarraute's *sous-conversation*, 'Reported Speech and "sous-conversation": Forms of Intersubjectivity in Nathalie Sarraute's Novels,' *Romance Studies* 2 (1983): 69–79, for a more thorough examination of the concept, as well as Sarraute's own explanation of it in 'Sous-conversation,' in *L'ère du soupçon*, 79–124 (Paris: Gallimard, 1956).

18 Britton, 'Reported Speech and "sous-conversation,"' 77.

19 Sarraute, 'Ce que je cherche à faire,' 45.

20 Ibid., 45.

21 Sarraute, *Entre la vie et la mort*, 95; 96.

22 I speak of a 'tropismic tide' here, because in both her critical writings and her fiction, Sarraute most often metaphorically represents tropisms as liquids (or as being carried upon liquids) of different sorts. I have examined this metaphor in depth in Jennifer Willging, 'Partners in Slime: The Liquid and the Viscous in Sartre and Sarraute,' *Romanic Review* 92 (2001): 277–96, and I will refer to it further later in this chapter.

23 Sarraute, *Entre la vie et la mort*, 150; 157.

24 For example, in one scene in Henri Michaux's bizarre and darkly humorous prose poem 'Plume,' in *Plume, précédé de Lointain intérieur* (Paris: Gallimard, 1963), Plume and some fellow soldiers fire upon and kill 'un tas de Bulgares' (a bunch of Bulgarians) on a train one evening simply because, he says, 'on ne se fiait pas à eux' (we didn't trust them) (152). In another violent vignette, the normally meek Plume runs around town with a friend removing the heads from unsuspecting men, women, and dogs in order to offer them to an imposing but taciturn figure of authority (162–7). In a third narrative, he shrugs and falls back asleep upon learning that during the night, a train has run over his nagging wife, leaving her bloody limbs scattered about what is left of their bedroom (139–40).

25 Sarraute, *Entre la vie et la mort*, 105; 106.

26 Nathalie Sarraute, 'Nouveau roman et réalité,' *Revue de l'Institut de Sociologie* [Brussels] 2 (1963): 431–41.

27 *L'ère du soupçon* is the title of Sarraute's influential collection of essays on the contemporary novel (Paris: Gallimard, 1956).

28 Nathalie Sarraute, 'Ce que voient les oiseaux,' in *L'ère du soupçon* (Paris: Gal-

limard, Folio, 1956), 141; trans. by Maria Jolas as 'What Birds See,' in *Tropisms and the Age of Suspicion* (London: John Calder, 1963), 128.

29 *Nouveau roman: hier, aujourd'hui*, eds. Jean Ricardou and Françoise vos Rossum-Guyon (Paris: UGE, 1972), 50. See this volume, which is a transcription of the lectures and discussions at the 1971 Cerisy colloquium, for a fuller understanding of the ideological differences between Sarraute and other theorists and practitioners of the *nouveau roman*, such as Robbe-Grillet and Jean Ricardou.

30 Sarraute, 'Ce que je cherche à faire,' 50.

31 Sarraute, 'Nouveau roman et réalité,' 432.

32 Sartre privileged 'être' over 'exister,' for while all objects and creatures in the world exist, only human beings can *be*; that is, only they can choose their being or their essence through their actions. While Sartre praised Sarraute's work in a preface to her second published text, *Portrait d'un inconnu*, intellectual differences soon soured the two writers' relationship. See Willging, 'Partners in Slime,' for my discussion of some of these differences.

33 Sarraute, 'Nouveau roman et réalité,' 432.

34 Sheila M. Bell, 'Orchestrated Voices: Selves and Others in Nathalie Sarraute's *Tu ne t'aimes pas*,' in *Narrative Voices in Modern French Fiction*, eds. Michael Cardy, George Evans and Gabriel Jacobs (Cardiff: University of Wales Press, 1997), 22.

35 Sarraute, *Entre la vie et la mort*, 36; 31.

36 Maria Jolas, the translator of *Entre la vie et la mort* and many of Sarraute's other novels, has in fact translated the 'elle' in this passage as 'it,' a choice I find unfortunate for the reasons stated above.

37 Nathalie Sarraute, *Enfance* (Paris: Gallimard, Folio, 1983).

38 Sarraute, *Entre la vie et la mort*, 70; 68.

39 Harold Bloom, *The Anxiety of Influence: A Theory of Poetry*, 2nd ed. (Oxford: Oxford University Press, 1997).

40 Ibid., 7, 12.

41 Sarraute, *Entre la vie et la mort*, 83.

42 Minogue recognizes Mallarmé in the following passage: 'Un poète,' an *il* reminds the writer, 'c'est celui qui sait fabriquer un poème avec des mots' (A poet is someone who knows how to make a poem out of words) (31; 26, cited in Minogue, *Nathalie Sarraute*, 141). For another reference to Mallarmé, see note 2 of this chapter.

43 The Brontës are the only real-life female writers mentioned in *Entre la vie et la mort*.

44 When the writer proudly confides in an *elle* that while still a toddler he used to 'play' with words in his head, the *elle* coolly responds, 'Ah oui. Je vois ...

vous *faisiez* vraiment enfant prédestiné' (Ah, yes. I see ... you *played* the pre-destined child) (18; 13 emphasis mine). Her verb choice effectively denies him the status he claims.

45 Bloom, *The Anxiety of Influence*, 14–16.
46 Sarraute, *Entre la vie et la mort*, 61; 59. This 'buisson d'aubépine' (hawthorn bush) is another reference to Proust.
47 Bloom, *The Anxiety of Influence*, 60.
48 Both the English verb 'to divine' and the English adjective 'divine' are derived from the Latin noun 'divinitas' (f), which is defined in *Cassell's Latin Dictionary*, ed. D. Press Simpson (New York: Macmillan, 1959), 199, as both 'divine nature, divinity' and 'the power of prophecy or divination.'
49 Sarraute, *Entre la vie et la mort*, 75; 74.
50 Bloom, *The Anxiety of Influence*, 14.
51 Sarraute, 'Ce que voient les oiseaux,' 141; 128.
52 Sarraute, 'Nouveau roman et réalité,' 432.
53 Sarraute, 'L'ère du soupçon,' in *L'ère du soupçon*, 77; trans. by Maria Jolas as 'The Age of Suspicion,' in *Tropisms and the Age of Suspicion*, 95.
54 Sarraute, 'Ce que je cherche à faire,' 26.
55 Nathalie Sarraute, 'Flaubert le précurseur?' in *Paul Valéry et l'enfant d'éléphant. Flaubert le précurseur*, 61–89 (Paris: Gallimard, 1986), 61.
56 Gustave Flaubert, *Correspondance*, vol. 2 of *Œuvres complètes de Gustave Flaubert*, 1847–52 (Paris: Conard, 1926), 141.
57 Most critics today argue that these novelists did not achieve this goal and indeed that such a goal is unattainable. While the referential function of language can be diminished, it can never be completely suppressed. In his *Of Words and the World: Referential Anxiety in the Contemporary French Novel* (Princeton, NJ: Princeton University Press, 1993), discussed in my introduction, David R. Ellison suggests, for example, that in *Topologie d'une cité fantôme* (Paris: Minuit, 1976), 19, 'Robbe-Grillet begins with a theoretical model of textual self-reflexivity that yields to referential reality when man is reinserted into the text as decipherer of signs, as decryptor of his world.'
58 Sarraute, 'Flaubert le précurseur?' 64.
59 Sarraute, 'Ce que je cherche à faire,' 44; Jean-Paul Sartre, *La nausée* (Paris: Gallimard, Folio, 1938); Alain Robbe-Grillet, *La jalousie* (Paris: Minuit, 1957).
60 Sarraute, 'Flaubert le précurseur?,' 72–3.
61 Bloom, *The Anxiety of Influence*, 14.
62 See, for example, Sarraute's 'Nouveau roman et réalité,' 440, or 'La littérature, aujourd'hui – II,' *Tel Quel* 9 (1962): 51.
63 Sarraute, 'Conversation et sous-conversation,' 118.

64 Sarraute lived, and continued to write, until she was ninety-nine.

65 Minogue, *Nathalie Sarraute*, 168–9.

66 This letter was originally published in the *Times Literary Supplement* (13 March 1959) and is reproduced in Minogue, *Nathalie Sarraute*, 193–5.

67 Sarraute, 'Conversation et sous-conversation,' 98; 106.

68 Willging, 'Partners in Slime,' 277–9, 293–5.

69 Nathalie Sarraute, 'Dialogue avec Nathalie Sarraute,' interview by Françoise Dupuy-Sullivan, *Romance Quarterly* 37 (1990): 189. Sartre was five years Sarraute's junior, but he enjoyed literary success earlier than she did. He took an interest in *Tropismes* upon its publication in 1939 and wrote a laudatory preface for Sarraute's second text, *Portrait d'un inconnu*. This preface is reproduced in Sarraute, *Œuvres complètes*, ed. Jean-Yves Tadié (Paris: Gallimard, 1996), 35–9.

70 Nathalie Sarraute, 'Interview: Nathalie Sarraute,' by Pierre Boncenne, *Lire*, June 1983, 92.

71 Ann Jefferson, *Nathalie Sarraute, Fiction and Theory: Questions of Difference* (Cambridge: Cambridge University Press, 2000), 114.

72 Sandra M. Gilbert and Susan Gubar, '"Forward into the Past": The Complex Female Affiliation Complex,' in *Historical Studies and Literary Criticism*, ed. Gerome McGann (Madison: University of Wisconsin Press, 1979), 241–2. In this article, Gilbert and Gubar rework Bloom's theory of the anxiety of influence to fit the situation of women writers (thus performing their own revisionary ratio on the work of this theoretical father). They maintain that the twentieth-century woman writer must wrestle with an 'affiliation complex,' which means in part that she must choose between a literary patrilineage and a literary matrilineage and attempt to avoid the pitfalls of whichever path she chooses. For example, while opting to identify with male precursors might allow a female writer to share in their greater authority and glory, Gilbert and Gubar argue, it would also entail, as for Freud's Electra, a kind of 'murder' of the mother (242–3). As I have suggested, Sarraute seems to have identified with neither her male nor her female precursors, but rather, through her critical demonstrations of their limitations, to have refused both of their influences. Interestingly, Sarraute's mother, of whom she saw very little throughout her later childhood and adolescence and with whom she had a troubled relationship, was an author of children's books. Perhaps this very literal literary matrilineage prepared her early in life to deal with – and to throw off – the burden of poetic posteriority.

73 Frank Lentricchia, *After the New Criticism* (London: Athlone, 1980), 328.

74 Sarraute, *Entre la vie et la mort*, 61; 58.

75 For convenience, I am once again naming (and therefore killing) a reality that Sarraute only expresses through metaphors.

76 Willging, 'Partners in Slime,' 280–1.

77 Sarraute, *Entre la vie et la mort*, 39; 34.

78 Sarraute, 'Ce que je cherche à faire,' 35; 32.

79 Luce Irigaray, 'La "mécanique" des fluides,' in *Ce sexe qui n'en est pas un*, 103–16 (Paris: Minuit, 1977); trans. by Catherine Porter as 'The "Mechanics" of Fluids' in *This Sex Which Is Not One*, 23–33 (Ithaca, NY: Cornell University Press, 1985).

80 Ibid., 115; 117.

81 For Irigaray, she becomes then *l'afemme* instead of *la femme*, which is woman not as herself but rather as 'other' ('*autre*'), the object or imperfect double of man ('La "méchanique" des fluides,' 112; 113–14).

82 Sarraute, 'Ce que je cherche à faire,' 32–3.

83 Sarraute, *Entre la vie et la mort*, 174.

84 Minogue, *Nathalie Sarraute*, 91.

85 Roger Shattuck, who knew Sarraute and was clearly fond of her, describes her in 'The Voice of Nathalie Sarraute,' *French Review* 68 (1995): 955, as 'modest yet resolute.' In a yet stronger confirmation of Sarraute's intriguing if at times exasperating duality, Stanley Karnow, who was married for a time to Sarraute's daughter Claude, writes in *Paris in the Fifties* (New York: Random House, 1997), 26, that his mother-in-law could be 'uptight and relaxed, petulant and amiable, dour and jolly. Even so,' he adds, 'I adored her.'

4: The Sound of the Semiotic

1 Anne Hébert, *Les fous de Bassan* (Paris: Seuil, 1982), trans. by Sheila Fischman as *In the Shadow of the Wind* (Toronto: Stoddart, 1983).

2 At least one critic, however, calls into question the 'truth' of this revelation. See Marilyn Randall, 'Les énigmes des *Fous de Bassan*: féminisme, narration et clôture,' *Voix et Images* 43 (1989): 81–2.

3 Marguerite Duras, 'Monsieur X. dit ici Pierre Rabier,' in *La douleur*, 89–135 (Paris: Gallimard, Folio, 1985), 105–6; trans. by Barbara Bray as 'Monsieur X, Here Called Rabier,' in *The War: A Memoir*, 71–112 (New York: Pantheon, 1986), 86–7.

4 Annie Ernaux, *La honte* (Paris: Gallimard, NRF, 1997).

5 Anne Hébert, 'Le torrent,' in *Le torrent*, 19–56 (Montreal: Hurtubise HMH, 1976 [1950]); *Kamouraska* (Paris: Seuil, 1970); *Le premier jardin* (Paris: Seuil, 1988); and *L'enfant chargé de songes* (Paris: Seuil, 1992). For an analysis of the

theme of memory and its intrusion into the present in three of Hébert's later texts, namely *Le premier jardin* and *La cage, suivi de L'île de la demoiselle* (Montreal: Boréal, 1990), see Yvette Francoli, 'Anne Hébert: entre la mémoire et l'oubli,' *Francographies* 2 (1993): 333–41. Francoli argues that each of the three female protagonists in these texts wages a 'combat spirituel contre le refoulement [...] pour échapper au sort funeste prescrit par les augures et se libérer des chaînes du passé' (spiritual combat against repression ... in order to avoid the disastrous lot prescribed by the augurs and to free herself from the chains of the past) (334). As I will argue in this chapter, the two male characters on whom I focus are not nearly as successful at this kind of combat as are the female ones Francoli discusses.

6 Hébert, *Les fous de Bassan*, 14; 10.

7 I specify 'named' narrators, because in one of the six narratives in the novel, 'Le livre de Perceval Brown et de quelques autres' (The Book of Perceval Brown and a Few Others), several anonymous voices contribute to the narration.

8 Hébert, *Les fous de Bassan*, 39, 95, 166, 230, 247, et al.

9 Hébert, *Kamouraska*, 12, 20; trans. by Norman Shapiro as *Kamouraska* (New York: Crown, 1973), 6, 14–15.

10 Hébert, *L'enfant chargé de songes*, 11; trans. by Sheila Fischman as *Burden of Dreams* (Concord, ON: Anansi, 1994), 14.

11 Hébert, *Le premier jardin*, 133; trans. by Sheila Fischman as *The First Garden* (Toronto: Anansi, 1990), 109.

12 Hébert, *Aurélien, Clara, Mademoiselle et le Lieutenant anglais* (Paris: Seuil, 1995), 13.

13 William Shakespeare, *Macbeth* (New York: Dover, 1993), 77. Hébert uses a part of this same line in the text mentioned above, *Aurélien, Clara, Mademoiselle et le Lieutenant anglais*, 57–8, when the shell-shocked lieutenant's caretakers remark, 'Nous l'enverrons se refaire une santé, out of this world of sound and fury' (We'll send him off to restore his health, out of this world of sound and fury). In *Les fous de Bassan*, this quote also gestures towards William Faulkner's *The Sound and the Fury* (New York: Modern Library, 1992), whose structure – that of multiple narratives attributed to different homodiegetic narrators – inspired that of *Les fous de Bassan*. Certain themes, characters, and events in Hébert's novel echo those in Faulkner's as well. For comparative studies of the two novels, see Gregory Reid, 'Wind in August: *Les fous de Bassan*'s Reply to Faulkner,' *Studies in Canadian Literature* 16:2 (1991–2): 112–27; and Ronald Ewing, 'Griffin Creek: The English World of Anne Hébert,' *Canadian Literature* 105 (1985): 100–10.

14 Hébert, *Les fous de Bassan*, 13; 9.

15 André Brochu, *Anne Hébert: Le secret de vie et de mort* (The Secret of Life and Death) (Ottawa: Presses de l'Université d'Ottawa, 2000), 189.

16 Edgar Allan Poe, 'The Telltale Heart,' in *Collected Works of Edgar Allan Poe*, ed. Thomas Ollive Mabbott, 3:789–99 (Cambridge, MA: Harvard University Press, 1978), 792.

17 I am grateful to Susan Williams of the Department of English at Ohio State University for her explanation of this mysterious 'disease,' which the narrator explicates no further. According to Williams, 'the general consensus is that [Poe] isn't referring to any particular disease but rather to a general (and largely metaphorical) heightened state of consciousness – a technique he uses in many of his stories' (e-mail to the author, 17 May 2004).

18 Poe, 'The Telltale Heart,' 797.

19 In a passage in *Aurélien, Clara, Mademoiselle et le Lieutenant anglais*, 63, Clara's heartbeat is also exteriorized. But for the innocent Clara, who has just fallen in love with the English lieutenant, the beating, or rather fluttering, of her heart symbiotically echoes the familiar and comforting sounds of nature: 'Habituée depuis l'enfance à ce roulement d'eau devant sa porte, jour après jour [...] Clara en était venue à confondre le propre battement de sa vie avec la pulsation de la rivière. Et voici qu'elle s'étonne de sa confusion et de son tumulte intérieurs, reflétés en tourbillons dans la rivière en crue' (Used to hearing this lapping of water before her door, day after day, since childhood, Clara could no longer distinguish the beating of her own heart from the pulse of the river. But now she was stunned by the confusion and turmoil she felt and which were reflected in the swirling eddies of the swollen river).

20 For discussions of madness in *Les fous de Bassan*, see for example Annabelle M. Rea, 'The Climate of Viol/Violence and Madness in Anne Hébert's *Les fous de Bassan*,' *Quebec Studies* 4 (1986): 170–83; and Janet M. Paterson, 'L'envolée de l'écriture: *les Fous de Bassan* d'Anne Hébert,' *Voix et Images* 9 (1984): 143–51, which I will discuss later in the chapter.

21 There are several mothers mentioned by the various narrators in the novel. Olivia's mother, who is thoroughly subjugated (and probably beaten) by her husband as well as overwhelmed by domestic responsibilities, dies before the summer of 1936, thereby passing these responsibilities on to her only daughter (208–9; 155). Stevens's mother is also worn out by the care of her four children and is cold and harsh with both her daughters and her sons (it is with relief that she delivers her twin daughters over to their tyrannical uncle when they turn thirteen) (19; 13). Nora's mother, on the other hand, seems to maintain at least a tolerable relationship with her daughter, for Nora receives a kiss from her on her birthday (although this is apparently one of two kisses she receives in a year; the other is bestowed

on New Year's Day) (111; 81). There is only one truly 'motherly' mother in the novel, the mother of Bob Allen, a minor character who serves as one of the suspects in the case and who is not, significantly, from Griffin Creek. This mother has a soft and ample bosom and derriere and a rosy complexion, and she dresses in floral print (167; 123). In the scene in which she appears, moreover, she is in the kitchen baking a cake. To her son, she is, like her cake, 'énorme, comestible et nourrissante' (enormous, edible, and nourishing) and is thus the antithesis of the devouring mother of myth (168; 124).

22 Karen Gould, 'Absence and Meaning in Anne Hébert's *Les fous de Bassan*,' *French Review* 59 (1986): 927. For other analyses of Stevens's and Nicolas's relationships with their mothers, see especially Marie-Dominique Boyce, 'Création de la mère/mer: symbole du paradis perdu dans *Les Fous de Bassan*,' *French Review* 68 (1994): 294–302; Rea, 'The Climate of Viol/Violence in Anne Hébert's *Les fous de Bassan*'; Paterson, 'L'envolée de l'écriture: *les Fous de Bassan* d'Anne Hébert'; and Kathryn Slott, 'Submersion and Resurgence of the Female Other in Anne Hébert's *Les fous de Bassan*,' *Quebec Studies* 4 (1986): 158–69.

23 In *The Acoustic Mirror: The Female Voice in Psychoanalysis and Cinema* (Bloomington: Indiana University Press, 1988), 72, Kaja Silverman writes that 'it has become something of a theoretical commonplace to characterize the maternal voice as a blanket of sound, extending on all sides of the newborn infant.' She credits Guy Rosolato, 'La voix: entre corps et language,' *Revue française de psychanalyse* 38, no. 1 (1974): 81, and Mary Ann Doane, 'The Voice in the Cinema: The Articulation of Body and Space,' *Yale French Studies* 60 (1980): 33–50, for the term 'sonorous envelope.'

24 As Silverman eloquently puts it in *The Acoustic Mirror*, 73, 'the fantasy [of the mother/child unity] functions as a bridge between two radically disjunctive moments – an infantile moment, which occurs prior to the inception of subjectivity, and which is consequently "too early" with respect to meaning and desire, and a subsequent moment, firmly rooted within both meaning and desire, but consequently "too late" for fulfillment. The first of those moments, which can be imagined but never actually experienced, turns upon the imaginary fusion of mother and infant, and hence upon unity and plenitude. The second moment marks the point at which the subject introjects a preexisting structure, a structure which gives order, shape, and significance to the original ineffable experience.'

25 See, for example, Hélène Cixous's 'Le rire de la Méduse,' *L'Arc* (1975): 39–54. As Paterson notes in 'L'envolée de l'écriture,' 149, Hébert is most likely making indirect references to Cixous's essay when she has Stevens describe

Nora's laughter as 'hystérique' and Nicolas imagine his swimming mother as 'une méduse géante' (*Les fous de Bassan*, 35).

26 Ruth M. Mésavage, 'L'Herméneutique de l'écriture: *Les fous de Bassan* d'Anne Hébert,' *Quebec Studies* 5 (1987): 114.

27 Julia Kristeva, *La révolution du langage poétique* (Paris: Seuil, 1974), trans. by Margaret Waller as *Revolution in Poetic Language* (New York: Columbia University Press, 1984). For Kristeva's description of the symbolic and the semiotic, see especially the first section, 'Sémiotique et symbolique,' 17–100; 'The Semiotic and the Symbolic,' 19–106.

28 Kristeva, *Révolution*, 23; 25.

29 Mésavage, 'L'Herméneutique de l'écriture,' 112.

30 Ibid., 112.

31 Ibid., 115.

32 Hébert, *Les fous de Bassan*, 30; 20.

33 Mésavage, 'L'Herméneutique de l'écriture,' 117.

34 Here Nicolas makes reference to the same quote from *Macbeth*, 77, that serves as an epigraph to Perceval's text: 'It is a tale / Told by an idiot, full of sound and fury, / Signifying nothing.'

35 In his 1982 text, Nicolas does in fact reproduce one line from his 1936 sermon, but it is a line he did not author: 'Les fils d'Israël fructifièrent et foisonnèrent, ils se multiplièrent beaucoup, si bien que le pays en fut rempli' (Exodus 1:7; *Les fous de Bassan*, 31). While these words are the words of God, their subject matter is the very human act which Nicolas, in contemplating his enticing nieces, cannot rid from his mind.

36 Not surprisingly, Nicolas assumes it is his wife who is infertile (23).

37 Rea, 'The Climate of Viol/Violence and Madness in Anne Hébert's *Les fous de Bassan*,' 178.

38 See note 13 in reference to the influence of Faulkner's *The Sound and the Fury* on both the form and content of *Les fous de Bassan*.

39 Lacan writes in *Écrits* (Paris: Seuil, 1966), 278, that 'C'est dans le *nom du père* qu'il nous faut reconnaître le support de la fonction symbolique qui, depuis l'orée des temps historiques, identifie sa personne à la figure de la loi' (It's in the *name-of-the-father* that we must recognize the foundation of the symbolic function which, from the beginning of history, has identified the father with the figure of the law). According to Kristeva in *Révolution*, 26; 27, in the infant's pre-linguistic communication with the mother, 'il s'agit [...] de fonctions sémiotiques pré-œdipiennes, de décharges d'énergie qui lient et orientent le corps par rapport à la mère' (pre-Oedipal semiotic functions and energy discharges connect and orient the body to the mother).

40 Lacan, 'Le stade du miroir comme formateur de la fonction du Je,' in *Écrits* (Paris: Seuil, 1966), 93–100.

41 Kristeva, *Révolution,* 67–8; 69–70 (for a discussion of the transgressive nature of the semiotic) and 46–9; 47–50 (for a discussion of the predominance of the semiotic in artistic and neurotic or psychotic discourse).

42 Although references to the self are not entirely absent from Perceval's narrative, the 'I' is missing from the majority of sentences of which it is the implied subject, as in the following passage: 'Soulève le rideau. La lune est là. Dans la fenêtre. Moi. Enfermé tous les soirs dans la maison. Obligé de dormir à huit heures [...] Enfermé dans ma chambre pour la nuit. Pas envie de dormir. Envie de crier' (Lift the curtain. The moon is there. In the window. Me. Shut inside the house every night. Have to go to sleep by eight ... Locked up in my room for the night. Don't feel like sleeping. Feel like yelling) (139; 101). If Perceval did at one time have some notion of a self, it has been, he says, 'brisé en mille éclats' (shattered into a thousand fragments) precisely by the cry that digs its path through his body (141; 102).

43 Paterson, 'L'envolée de l'écriture,' 146.

44 Constantina Mitchell, 'La symbolique de la surdité dans le *Torrent* d'Anne Hébert,' *Quebec Studies* 8 (1989): 65–72.

45 Ibid., 69.

46 Ibid., 67.

47 Although Stevens's abhorrence of the gannets' cries (which I will discuss further later in the chapter) is more marked than Nicolas's, the language the pastor uses to describe the birds reveals his aversion to them: 'De grands oiseaux migrateurs, en formations serrées, passent au-dessus de Griffin Creek, projettent leur ombre noire sur le presbytère. J'entends des jappements lointains, toute une meute céleste qui s'éloigne dans la nuit' (Great migratory birds in close formation pass over Griffin Creek, casting their black shadow over the rectory. I hear a sort of barking in the distance, a celestial pack moving away in the night) (24; 16). These birds are for him sinister creatures, for they cast a black shadow over the presbytery as they fly over it. They also resemble a pack of barking dogs, animals whose mythological image is generally more infernal than celestial (one thinks most notably of Cerberus, the three-headed dog who guards the gates of hell).

48 As mentioned above, in *Aurélien, Clara, Mademoiselle et le Lieutenant anglais,* Clara, like Nora, is enchanted by sound. Her mother having died in childbirth, for Clara the sonorous envelope that the mother's voice normally creates has been appropriated by mother nature, with whom the girl learns to communicate semiotically. 'Clara grandissait dans le silence du père et les voix de la campagne. Bien avant toute parole humaine, la petite fille sut gazouiller, caqueter, ronronner, roucouler, meugler, aboyer et glapir' (Clara grew up enveloped in the father's silence and the voices of the countryside. Well before she could speak, the little girl knew how to chirp, cackle, purr,

coo, moo, bark and yap) (13). But when Mademoiselle, a red-headed school-teacher, arrives in Clara's village, a human voice suddenly captivates all the girl's attention, just as the voice of the red-headed pastor does Nora's: 'À mesure que l'institutrice parlait, chacun de ses mots inconnus et mystérieux se chargeait du même éclat rouge doré, superbe à mourir [...] Clara se plaisait à la forme sonore des mots nouveaux, dans la bouche de son institutrice, comme si elle découvrait une musique inconnue qui l'enchantait' (As the teacher spoke, each of her words, unknown and mysterious to the girl, took on the same gorgeous, golden-red shine [...] Clara reveled in the sound of new words in her teacher's mouth, as if she were discovering an unfamiliar music that enchanted her) (17–18). Unlike Nicolas's, the voice of the school-teacher, with the knowledge it imparts, empowers rather than subjugates its young listener. In this text, interestingly, it is a powerful surrogate mother rather than the girl's taciturn father who grants Clara access to the symbolic order. He hesitates before allowing her to attend school, 'se demand[ant] s'il était bon pour sa fille de quitter brusquement la vie profonde et noire où les choses ne sont jamais dites et nommées' – the semiotic – 'pour aller se perdre dans un monde bavard et prétentieux' (17). Yet the vibrant colours and the music contained within Mademoiselle's voice suggest that the symbolic order into which she introduces Clara is permeable to, indeed welcoming of, the feminine semiotic.

49 Julia Kristeva, *Desire in Language: A Semiotic Approach to Literature and Art*, ed. Leon S. Roudiez and trans. Thomas Gora, Alice Jardine, and Leon S. Roudiez (New York: Columbia University Press, 1980), 216.

50 John Lechte, *Julia Kristeva* (London: Routledge, 1990), 131. Lechte notes that Kristeva herself has characterized Pollack's Abstract Expressionism as semiotic in Kristeva, 'La voie lactée de Jackson Pollack, 1912–1959,' *Art Press* 55 (1982): 6.

51 Kristeva, *Desire in Language*, 225.

52 Kristeva, *Révolution*, 26; 27–8; Sigmund Freud, *Beyond the Pleasure Principle*, ed. and trans. by James Strachey (New York: Norton, 1961), 46–9 and 76–8. For Freud, the more obvious pleasure principle 'seems actually to serve the death instinct,' which is, in the end, the desire simply 'to return to the quiescence of the inorganic world' (77, 76). I will return to the concept of the death drive in my analysis of Stevens's final narrative.

53 Paterson, 'L'envolée de l'écriture,' 145. In the scene in which the frustrated Nicolas watches his mother and two nieces swim, he uses the following images to describe the flight of the gannets: 'En bandes neigeuses les fous de Bassan quittent leur nid, au sommet de la falaise, plongent dans la mer, à la verticale, pointus de bec et de queue, pareils à des couteaux, font jaillir des gerbes

d'écume' (In snowy bands the gannets leave their nest on the summit of the cliff, plunge vertically into the sea, pointed at beak and tails like knives, send up sprays of foam) (*Les fous de Bassan*, 39; 26). Paterson reads in this passage a 'conjonction entre les notions de vol et de désir' (a connection between the notions of flight and desire) (145). Brochu concurs that this passage 'comporte un schème de pénétration' (contains an image of penetration) and that 'le giclement d'écume qui s'ensuit a des connotations sexuelles évidentes' (the spray of foam that follows has obvious sexual connotations) (*Anne Hébert*, 193). I would add that Nicolas's comparison of the birds to knives is also one of many evocations of the violence that permeates the novel.

54 After having sexual relations with her at the beginning of the summer, Stevens announces to his cousin Maureen that he is leaving her because she is 'trop vieille' (too old) (175; 130). Yet more than her age it is undoubtedly her willingness, indeed her evident desire, to sleep with him that repulses him (69; 50). Stevens also 'punishes' Nora, much more brutally, for openly displaying her sexuality and for attempting to entice him into kissing or even deflowering her (90–2; 64–6). But it is upon the truly modest Olivia that Stevens exacts the ultimate male punishment of rape: 'La démasquer, elle, la fille trop belle et trop sage [...] Lui faire avouer qu'elle est velue, sous sa culotte, comme une bête' (Unmask her, the girl who is too beautiful and proper ... Make her admit that she's hairy under her panties, like an animal) (248; 182).

55 Paterson, 'L'envolée de l'écriture,' 148–9. Although the narratives of Nicolas, Nora, and Perceval are entitled 'livres' (books), their narrators themselves never refer to them as such; indeed they never refer to their own texts, or to writing them, at all. Perceval, moreover, as noted, is illiterate and therefore incapable of writing his own narrative. The reader is not encouraged, then, to think of these three narrators as the *writers* of these narratives, despite their autodiegetic narration.

56 In Sarraute's *Entre la vie et la mort* (Paris: Gallimard, Folio, 1968), 65; 63, the writer watches as 'les gouttelettes des mots s'élèvent en un fin jet, se poussant les unes les autres, et retombent. D'autres montent et encore d'autres... Maintenant le dernier jet est retombé...' (the little drops of words mount in a thin jet, they shove one another, then fall down again. Others mount, and others still...) (Sarraute's ellipses).

57 Desire is evoked in the content of Nicolas's sermon in the biblical passages he quotes. See note 35.

58 Paterson, 'L'envolée de l'écriture,' 147.

59 See Kristeva, *Folle vérité: vérité et vraisemblance du texte psychotique*, ed. Jean-Michel Ribettes (Paris: Seuil, 1979).

60 Paterson, 'L'envolée de l'écriture,' 148.

61 Brochu, *Anne Hébert*, 192.

62 Although he confessed to the murders orally in 1936, the text of that confession is 'missing' from the novel, just as is Nicolas's incriminating sermon. In his narrative, Perceval describes the moment when Stevens confesses but not the confession itself. Perceval hides outside the door of Stevens's bedroom as the detective interrogates him and bursts in just moments, apparently, after Stevens has broken down. Perceval finds him sitting silent in a chair, 'son cou cassé. Sa tête penchée sur sa poitrine' (His neck broken. His head drooping onto his chest) (192; 144). This imagery evokes both sexual impotence and the hanging, the execution, which is also missing, from both the narrative and the story.

63 Marguerite Duras, 'Madame Dodin,' in *Des journées entières dans les arbres*, 119–84 (Paris: Gallimard, 1954). I discuss this short story, whose narrator only speaks of writing a text about Madame Dodin in the conditional tense, near the end of chapter 1.

64 As noted in chapter 2, however, the behaviour of the mother and the daughter's reaction to it (as in the scene of the urine-stained nightgown, *La honte*, 109–10) are also at the origin of the shame, as well as the guilt, to which *La honte*'s narrator confesses.

65 Brochu, *Anne Hébert*, 164–5 (see also 109–10 and 163 for brief discussions of the *faits divers* on which the two texts are based).

66 Brochu, *Anne Hébert*, 112.

67 Élisabeth has eight children with Jérôme Rolland (Hébert, *Kamouraska*, 15; 14).

68 Hébert, *Les fous de Bassan*, 244; 189.

69 Hébert, *Kamouraska*, 34; 30.

70 'Si tu savais, Jérôme, comme j'ai peur' (If you only knew, Jérôme, how frightened I am), Élisabeth tells her still agonizing husband in one of the last lines of the novel (Hébert, *Kamouraska*, 250; 250). Interestingly, Hébert deprives her readers of a death scene, thus leaving open the possibility of a recovery (however miraculous) for Jérôme. Yet such a recuperation is hardly plausible, as it would constitute a crueller twist of fate than even a murderess deserves.

71 Dominique Denes, *Marguerite Duras: Écriture et politique* (Paris: Harmattan, 2005), 137.

72 Duras, interview by Jean Schuster, *Archibras*, no. 2 (1967): 179, quoted in Denes, *Marguerite Duras*, 138.

73 As noted here and in chapter 1, *faits divers* serve as the seeds of several of Hébert's and Duras's texts. In newspaper articles, Duras wrote about the

Villemin affair and also about several other real-life murders (these articles have been collected in *Outside* [Paris: Gallimard, 1984] and *Le monde extérieur* [Paris: P.O.L, 1993]). As for Ernaux, *La honte*'s narrator, for example, notes the more gruesome *faits divers* reported in the old newspapers she studies in order to understand better the period (summer 1952) in which the scene took place: 'Il y avait des faits divers atroces tous les jours, un enfant de deux ans mort subitement en mangeant un croissant, un fermier fauchant les jambes de son fils caché par jeu dans les tiges de blé, un obus de la guerre qui avait tué trois enfants à Creil. C'était,' she admits, 'ce que j'avais le plus envie de lire' (There were horrific news items every day: a two-year-old had died eating a croissant; a farmer had sliced off the legs of his son, playing hide-and-seek in the wheat fields; a bombshell had killed three children in Creil. This was what I wanted to read about most of all) (Ernaux, *La honte*, 34; 29). She also mentions the 'crime de Lurs,' which was the sensational and seemingly gratuitous murder of Sir Jack Drummond, his wife, and their ten-year-old daughter by a French peasant in August 1952 (118; 99). The narrators of Ernaux's *Journal du dehors* (Paris: Gallimard, Folio, 1993) and *La vie extérieure* (Paris: Gallimard, Folio, 2001) also make several references to various *faits divers* and to contemporary wars and genocides.

74 Ernaux has written about her battle with breast cancer in *L'usage de la photo* with Marc Marie (Paris: Stock, 2005), and Duras spoke about her nearly fatal treatment for alcoholism in 1982 and a five-month coma she experienced in 1988–9 in several texts and interviews, such as *La vie matérielle*, interview by Jérôme Beaujour (Paris: P.O.L., 1987).

Conclusion

1 Donald Barthelme, interview by Jerome Klinkowitz, in *The New Fiction: Interviews with Innovative American Writers*, ed. Joe David Bellamy (Urbana: University of Illinois Press, 1974), 51–2; quoted in Sheryl Herr, 'Fathers, Daughters, Anxiety, and Fiction,' in *Discontented Discourses: Feminism / Textual Intervention / Psychoanalysis*, ed. Marleen S. Barr and Richard Feldstein (Urbana: University of Illinois Press, 1989), 181–2.

2 Barthelme is considered to be a 'postmodern' writer for his own use of collage in the construction of his unconventional, often bizarre narratives: 'In his short stories and novels, Barthelme describes a world so unreal that traditional modes of fiction can no longer encompass it. His stories employ advertising jargon, counterfeit footnotes, recondite allusions, and various typographical and narrative extravagances to fit his own private vision of an

absurd reality' ('Donald Barthelme,' Encyclopedia.com, http://www.
encyclopedia.com/html/B/Barthelm.asp).

3   In *The Anxious Object: Art Today and Its Audience* (New York: Collier, 1973), 17,
    Harold Rosenberg speaks of a sort of identity crisis in which postwar art
    found itself. This anxiety of art 'relates to the awareness that art today sur-
    vives in the intersections between the popular media, handicraft and the
    applied sciences; and that the term "art" has become useless as a means for
    setting apart a certain category of fabrications.' This anxiety has connections
    with Bloom's anxiety of influence, for Rosenberg argues that the burden of
    the past forces artists to seek out such non-traditional forms that they no
    longer know if what they have created is still 'art.'

4   In a novel entitled *The Dead Father* (New York: Pocket Books, 1975), which
    Herr discusses in 'Fathers, Daughters, Anxiety, and Fiction,' Barthelme
    humorously explores the filial anxiety and resentment provoked by a con-
    trolling father whose crushing influence extends even beyond the grave.

5   Marguerite Duras, 'Madame Dodin,' in *Des journées entières dans les arbres*,
    119–84 (Paris: Gallimard, 1954).

6   Nathalie Sarraute, *Entre la vie et la mort* (Paris: Gallimard, 1968).

7   Herr, 'Fathers, Daughters, Anxiety, and Fiction,' 182.

8   Annie Ernaux, *La honte* (Paris: Gallimard, NRF, 1997), 16–17; translated as
    Shame, trans. Tanya Leslie (New York: Seven Stories, 1998), 16–17.

9   Marguerite Duras, 'Monsieur X. dit ici Pierre Rabier,' in *La douleur*, 89–135
    (Paris: Gallimard, Folio, 1985), 90; translated as 'Monsieur X, Here Called
    Pierre Rabier,' in *The War: A Memoir*, trans. Barbara Bray, 71–112 (New York:
    Pantheon, 1986), 72.

10 Ibid., 108; 88.

11 Ernaux, *La honte*, 16; 16.

12 While it may appear more logical to say that the writing produces the text
    rather than the other way around, it is, after all, the idea of or the desire for
    a text with one's name on it that often prompts the writing.

13 David R. Ellison, *Of Words and the World: Referential Anxiety in Contemporary
    French Fiction* (Princeton, NJ: Princeton University Press, 1993), 6.

14 Peter Shaughnessy, 'Reality TV on the Rise,' Backstage.com, August 26,
    2004, http://www.backstage.com/backstage/news/article_display.jsp?vnu_
    content_id=1000619793.

Bibliography

L'Académie Goncourt. http://www.academie-goncourt.fr.

Adams, Hazard, ed. *Critical Theory Since Plato*. New York: Harcourt, 1971.

Alazet, Bernard. 'Le tragique en éclats.' *Revue des Sciences Humaines* 217 (1990): 39–48.

Andrea, Yann. *M.D.* Paris: Minuit, 1983.

Antelme, Robert. *L'espèce humaine*. Paris: Gallimard, 1957.

Armel, Aliette. 'Duras: Repères biographiques.' *Magazine Littéraire*, June 1990, 25–7.

Auden, W.H. *The Age of Anxiety*. New York: Random House, 1947.

Auster, Paul. *The Invention of Solitude*. New York: Penguin, 1988 [1982].

Barthelme, Donald. Interview by Jerome Klinkowitz. In *The New Fiction: Interviews with Innovative American Writers*, edited by Joe David Bellamy, 45–54. Urbana: University of Illinois Press, 1974.

Barthes, Roland. 'The Death of the Author.' In *Image–Music–Text*, edited and translated by Stephen Heath, 142–54. New York: Hill and Wang, 1977.

– *Roland Barthes par Roland Barthes*. In *Œuvres complètes*, edited by Éric Marty, 1:79–250. Paris: Seuil, 1995 [1975].

Beckett, Samuel. *L'innommable*. Paris: Minuit, 1953.

Bell, Sheila M. 'Orchestrated Voices: Selves and Others in Nathalie Sarraute's *Tu ne t'aimes pas*.' In *Narrative Voices in Modern French Fiction*, edited by Michael Cardy, George Evans, and Gabriel Jacobs, 13–36. Cardiff: University of Wales Press, 1997.

Bersani, Leo. *Marcel Proust: The Fictions of Life and Art*. New York: Oxford University Press, 1965.

de Biasi, Pierre-Marc. 'Les Petites Emma 1992.' *Magazine Littéraire*, July–August 1992, 59–62.

'Biographie inédite.' *Anne Hébert*. http://pages.infinit.net/ahebert2/biograph.htm.

Bloom, Harold. *The Anxiety of Influence: A Theory of Poetry.* 2nd ed. Oxford: Oxford University Press, 1997 [1973].

Booth, Wayne C. *The Rhetoric of Fiction.* Chicago: University of Chicago Press, 1983.

Bourdieu, Pierre. *The Logic of Practice.* Cambridge: Polity Press, 1990.

Boyce, Marie-Dominique. 'Création de la mère/mer: symbole du paradis perdu dans *Les Fous de Bassan.*' *French Review* 68 (1994): 294–302.

Brett, E.A., and R. Ostroff. 'Imagery and Post-Traumatic Stress Disorder: An Overview.' *American Journal of Psychiatry* 142 (1985): 417–24.

Britton, Celia. 'Reported Speech and "sous-conversation": Forms of Intersubjectivity in Nathalie Sarraute's Novels.' *Romance Studies* 2 (1983): 69–79.

Brochu, André. *Anne Hébert: Le secret de vie et de mort.* Ottawa: Presses de l'Université d'Ottawa, 2000.

Brooks, Peter. *Reading for the Plot: Design and Intention in Narrative.* Cambridge, MA: Harvard University Press, 1992 [1984].

Canadian Feminist Alliance for International Action. 'Canada Needs a Permanent Parliamentary Committee on Women's Equality.' http://www.fafia-afai. org/gvt/parliament.htm.

Caruth, Cathy. 'Recapturing the Past: Introduction.' In *Trauma: Explorations in Memory,* edited by Cathy Caruth, 151–7. Baltimore: Johns Hopkins University Press, 1995.

– 'Trauma and Experience: Introduction.' In *Trauma: Explorations in Memory,* edited by Cathy Caruth, 3–12. Baltimore: Johns Hopkins University Press, 1995.

Chion, Michel. *La voix au cinéma.* Paris: Etoile, 1982. Edited and translated by Claudia Gorbman as *The Voice in Cinema* (New York: Columbia University Press, 1999).

Cixous, Hélène. 'Le rire de la Méduse.' *L'Arc* (1975): 39–54.

Cohen, Susan. 'From Omniscience to Ignorance: Voice and Narration in the Work of Marguerite Duras.' In *Remains to Be Seen: Essays on Marguerite Duras,* edited by Sanford Ames, 51–77. New York: Peter Lang, 1988.

– *Women and Discourse in the Fiction of Marguerite Duras: Love, Legends, Language.* Amherst: University of Massachusetts Press, 1993.

Collectif féminisme et démocratie. 'Pour un mode de scrutin plus démocratique et égalitaire au Québec.' http://feminismeetdemocratie.typepad.com/ collectif/2004/09/volution_de_la_ .html.

Cranaki, Mimika, and Yvon Belaval. *Nathalie Sarraute.* Paris: Gallimard, 1965.

Craske, Michelle G. *Origins of Phobias and Anxiety Disorders: Why More Women Than Men?* Oxford: Elsevier, 2003.

Culbertson, Roberta. 'Embodied Memory, Transcendence, and Telling:

Recounting Trauma, Reestablishing the Self.' *New Literary History* 26 (1995): 169–95.

Davis, Colin. 'Duras, Antelme and the Ethics of Writing.' *Comparative Literature Studies* 34 (1997): 170–83.

Delbo, Charlotte. *La mémoire et les jours*. Paris: Berg, 1985.

Denes, Dominique. *Marguerite Duras: Écriture et politique*. Paris: Harmattan, 2005.

Diagnostic and Statistical Manual of Mental Disorders. 3rd ed., rev. Washington, DC: American Psychiatric Association, 1987.

Doane, Mary Ann. 'The Voice in the Cinema: The Articulation of Body and Space.' *Yale French Studies* 60 (1980): 33–50.

Dumont, Micheline, Michèle Jean, Marie Lavigne, and Jennifer Stoddart (Le collectif Clio). *L'histoire des femmes au Québec depuis quatre siècles*. Montreal: Quinze, 1982.

Duras, Marguerite. *L'amant*. Paris: Gallimard, Folio, 1984.

– *L'amante anglaise*. Paris: Gallimard, 1967.

– *L'amant de la Chine du Nord*. Paris: Gallimard, 1991.

– *L'amour*. Paris: Gallimard, 1971.

– 'Assassins de Budapeste.' In *Outside: Papiers d'un jour*, 88–91. Paris: Albin Michel, 1981 [1958].

– 'Avril 45: nuit et Duras.' *Libération* [Paris] 17 April 1985: 37.

– *Un barrage contre le Pacifique*. Paris: Gallimard, 1950.

– *La douleur*. Paris: P.O.L., 1985. Translated by Barbara Bray as *The War: A Memoir* (New York: Pantheon, 1986).

– *Écrire*. Paris: Gallimard, NRF, 1993. Translated by Mark Polizzotti as *Writing* (Cambridge, MA: Lumen, 1998).

– *L'Éden cinéma*. Paris: Mercure de France, 1977.

– *Emily L.* Paris: Minuit, 1987.

– 'Entretien Marguerite Duras – François Mitterrand: Le Bureau de la poste de la rue Dupin.' *L'Autre Journal*, 26 February – 4 March 1986, 31–40.

– *L'été 80*. Paris: Minuit, 1980.

– *La femme du Gange*. Paris: Benoît-Jacob, 1973.

– *L'homme assis dans le couloir*. Paris: Minuit, 1980.

– *Les impudents*. Paris: Plon, 1943.

– *India song*. Paris: Films Armorial, 1975.

– 'J'ai vécu le réel comme un mythe.' Interview by Aliette Armel. *Magazine Littéraire*, June 1990, 18–24.

– 'Madame Dodin.' In *Des journées entières dans les arbres*, 119–84. Paris: Gallimard, 1954. Translated by Anita Barrows as 'Madame Dodin,' in *Whole Days in the Trees*, 83–126 (London: John Calder, 1984).

– *Moderato cantabile*. Paris: Minuit, 1958.

– *Le monde extérieur: Outside 2.* Paris: P.O.L., 1993.
– 'Monsieur X. dit ici Pierre Rabier.' In *La douleur,* 89–135. Paris: P.O.L., 1985. Translated by Barbara Bray as 'Monsieur X, Here Called Pierre Rabier,' in *The War: A Memoir,* 71–112 (New York: Pantheon, 1986).
– *Outside.* Paris: Gallimard, 1984.
– *Le ravissement de Lol V. Stein.* Paris: Gallimard, Folio, 1964. Translated by Richard Seaver as *The Ravishing of Lol V. Stein* (New York: Pantheon, 1966).
– *Son nom de Venise dans Calcutta désert.* Paris: Benoît-Jacob, 1976.
– *Les viaducs de la Seine-et-Oise.* Paris: Gallimard, 1959.
– *Le vice-consul.* Paris: Gallimard, Imaginaire, 1966. Translated by Eileen Ellenbogen as *The Vice-Consul* (London: Hamish Hamilton, 1968).
– *La vie matérielle.* Interview by Jérôme Beaujour. Paris: P.O.L., 1987.
Eakman, B.K. 'Anything That Ails You: Women on Tranqs in a Self-Serve Society.' *Chronicles: A Magazine of American Culture* 28 (August 2004). http://www.chroniclesmagazine.org/Chronicles/.html.
École Normale Supérieure, Département de Sciences Sociales. 'Chronologie sociale 1948–52.' http://www.sciencessociales.ens.fr/hss2001/travail/chronologiechrono48_58.html.
Edson, Laurie. 'Knowing Lol: Duras, Epistemology and Gendered Mediation.' *SubStance* 68 (1992): 17–31.
Ellison, David R. *Of Words and the World: Referential Anxiety in Contemporary French Fiction.* Princeton, NJ: Princeton University Press, 1993.
Ernaux, Annie. 'Annie Ernaux ou l'autobiographie en question.' Interview by Philippe Vilain. *Romans 50/90* 24 (1997): 141–7.
– *Les armoires vides.* Paris: Gallimard, Folio, 1974. Translated by Tanya Leslie as *Cleaned Out* (New York: Four Walls Eight Windows, 1992).
– 'Bourdieu : le chagrin.' *Le Monde* 6 Feb. 2002 <http://homme-moderne.org/societe/socio/bourdieu/mort/aernau.html>.
– *Ce qu'ils disent ou rien.* Paris: Gallimard, Folio, 1977.
– *L'écriture comme un couteau.* Interview by Frédéric-Yves Jeannet. Paris: Stock, 2003.
– 'Entretien avec Annie Ernaux.' Interview by Claire-Lise Tondeur. *French Review* 69, no. 1 (1995): 37–44.
– *L'événement.* Paris: Gallimard, Folio, 2000.
– *Une femme.* Paris: Gallimard, Folio, 1987. Translated by Tanya Leslie as *A Woman's Story* (New York: Four Walls Eight Windows, 1991).
– *La femme gelée.* Paris: Gallimard, Folio, 1981.
– 'Fragments autour de Philippe V.' *L'infini* 56 (1996): 25–6.
– *La honte.* Paris: Gallimard, NRF, 1997. Translated by Tanya Leslie as *Shame* (New York: Seven Stories, 1998).

– *Je ne suis pas sortie de ma nuit.* Paris: Gallimard, Folio, 1997. Translated by Tanya Leslie as *'I Remain in Darkness'* (New York: Seven Stories, 1999).
– *Journal du dehors.* Paris: Gallimard, Folio, 1993. Translated by Tanya Leslie as *Exteriors* (New York: Seven Stories, 1996).
– *L'occupation.* Paris: Gallimard, NRF, 2002.
– *Passion simple.* Paris: Gallimard, Folio, 1991. Translated by Tanya Leslie as *Simple Passion* (New York: Four Walls Eight Windows, 1993).
– *La place.* Paris: Gallimard, Folio, 1984. Translated by Tanya Leslie as *A Man's Place* (New York: Four Walls Eight Windows, 1992).
– *Se perdre.* Paris: Gallimard, NRF, 2001.
– 'Le silence ou la trahison?' Interview by Jean-Jacques Gibert. *Révolution* 260 (22 February 1985): 52–3.
– *La vie matérielle.* Interview by Jérôme Beaujour. Paris: P.O.L., 1987.
Ernaux, Annie, and Marc Marie. *L'usage de la photo.* Paris: Stock, 2005.
Evans, Martha Noel. *Masks of Tradition: Women and the Politics of Writing in Twentieth-Century France.* Ithaca, NY: Cornell University Press, 1987.
Ewing, Ronald. 'Griffin Creek: The English World of Anne Hébert.' *Canadian Literature* 105 (1985): 100–10.
Faulkner, William. *The Sound and the Fury.* New York: Modern Library, 1992.
Finch, Alison. *Women's Writing in Nineteenth-Century France.* Cambridge: Cambridge University Press, 2000.
Flaubert, Gustave. *Correspondance.* Vol. 2 of *Œuvres complètes de Gustave Flaubert* (1847–52). Paris: Conard, 1926.
Foucault, Michel. *Folie et déraison: histoire de la folie à l'âge classique.* Paris: Plon, 1961.
– 'What Is an Author?' Translated by Josué V. Harari. In *Aesthetics, Method, and Epistemology,* edited by James D. Faubion. Vol. 2 of *Essential Works of Foucault 1954–1984.* New York: New Press, 1994.
Francoli, Yvette. 'Anne Hébert: entre la mémoire et l'oubli.' *Francographies* 2 (1993): 333–41.
Freud, Sigmund. *Beyond the Pleasure Principle.* Edited and translated by James Strachey. New York: Norton, 1961.
– *Standard Edition of the Complete Psychological Works of Sigmund Freud.* Edited and translated by James Strachey. 20 vols. London: Hogarth, 1953–74.
Freud, Sigmund, and Josef Breuer. *Studies on Hysteria.* In *Standard Edition of the Complete Psychological Works of Sigmund Freud,* edited and translated by James Strachey, 2:1–306. London: Hogarth, 1953–74.
Genette, Gérard. *Fiction et diction.* Paris: Seuil, 1991.
– *Narrative Discourse: An Essay in Method.* Translated by Jane E. Lewin. Ithaca, NY: Cornell University Press, 1980.

Gilbert, Sandra M., and Susan Gubar. '"Forward into the Past": The Complex Female Affiliation Complex.' In *Historical Studies and Literary Criticism,* edited by Gerome McGann, 240–65. Madison: University of Wisconsin Press, 1985.

– *The Madwoman in the Attic: The Woman Writer and the Nineteenth-Century Literary Imagination.* New Haven: Yale University Press, 1979.

– *No Man's Land: The Place of the Woman Writer in the Twentieth Century.* 3 vols. New Haven: Yale University Press, 1988–94.

Gould, Karen. 'Absence and Meaning in Anne Hébert's *Les fous de Bassan.*' *French Review* 59 (1986): 921–30.

Hébert, Anne. *Aurélien, Clara, Mademoiselle et le Lieutenant anglais.* Paris: Seuil, 1995.

– *L'enfant chargé de songes.* Paris: Seuil, 1992. Translated by Sheila Fischman as *Burden of Dreams* (Concord, ON: Anansi, 1994).

– *Les fous de Bassan.* Paris: Seuil, 1982. Translated by Sheila Fischman as *In the Shadow of the Wind* (Toronto: Stoddart, 1983).

– *Kamouraska.* Paris: Seuil, 1970. Translated by Norman Shapiro as *Kamouraska: A Novel* (New York: Crown, 1973).

– *Le premier jardin.* Paris: Seuil, 1988. Translated by Sheila Fischman as *The First Garden* (Toronto: Anansi, 1990).

– 'Le torrent.' In *Le torrent,* 19–56. Montreal: Hurtubise HMH, 1976 [1950].

Heinich, Nathalie. *L'épreuve de la grandeur: prix littéraires et reconnaissance.* Paris: Découverte, 1999.

Herr, Cheryl. 'Fathers, Daughters, Anxiety, and Fiction.' In *Discontented Discourses: Feminism/Textual Intervention/Psychoanalysis,* edited by Marleen S. Barr and Richard Feldstein, 173–207. Urbana: University of Illinois Press, 1989.

Herrnstein Smith, Barbara. 'Narrative Versions, Narrative Theories.' *Critical Inquiry* 7 (1980): 213–36.

Hestetun, Øyunn. *A Prison-House of Myth? Symptomal Readings in 'Virgin Land,' 'The Madwoman in the Attic,' and 'The Political Unconscious.'* Uppsala, Sweden: Uppsala University, 1993.

Hill, Leslie. *Marguerite Duras: Apocalyptic Desires.* London: Routledge, 1993.

Hutcheon, Linda. 'Metafictional Implications for Novelistic Reference.' In *On Referring in Literature,* edited by Anna Whiteside and Michael Issacharof, 1–13. Bloomington: Indiana University Press, 1987.

Interparliamentary Union. 'Women in National Parliaments: Situation as of November 2005.' 1996–2005. http://www.ipu.org/wmn-e/world.htm.

Irigaray, Luce. 'La "mécanique" des fluides.' In *Ce sexe qui n'en est pas un,* 103–16. Paris: Minuit, 1977. Translated by Catherine Porter with Carolyn Burke as 'The "Mechanics" of Fluids' in *This Sex Which Is Not One,* 23–33 (Ithaca, NY: Cornell University Press, 1985).

Jacobs, Gabriel. 'Spectres of Remorse: Duras's War-Time Autobiography.' *Romance Studies* 30 (1997): 47–57.

Janet, Pierre. *L'automatisme psychologique.* Paris: Société Pierre Janet, 1973 [1889].

– *L'évolution de la mémoire et la notion du temps.* Paris: Cahine, 1928.

– 'Histoire d'une idée fixe.' In vol. 1 of *Névroses et idées fixes.* 2 vols. Paris: Alcan, 1990 [1894].

Jefferson, Ann. *Nathalie Sarraute, Fiction and Theory: Questions of Difference.* Cambridge: Cambridge University Press, 2000.

Johnson, Randal. 'Pierre Bourdieu on Art, Literature and Culture.' Introduction to Pierre Bourdieu, *The Field of Cultural Production: Essays on Art and Literature,* edited by Randal Johnson, 1–28. New York: Columbia University Press, 1995.

Josselin, Jean-François. 'Un gros chagrin.' *Nouvel Observateur* 1418 (9–15 January 1992): 69.

Karnow, Stanley. *Paris in the Fifties.* New York: Random House, 1997.

Kirkey, Sharon. 'Prozac Pushers Target Women – Study.' CanWest News Service, 28 September 2003. http:www.offcmhap.on.ca/addiction/prozac–pushers–target–woen.htm.

Kristeva, Julia. *Desire in Language: A Semiotic Approach to Literature and Art.* Edited by Leon S. Roudiez and translated by Thomas Gora, Alice Jardine, and Leon S. Roudiez. New York: Columbia University Press, 1980.

– *Folle vérité: vérité et vraisemblance du texte psychotique.* Edited by Jean-Michel Ribettes. Paris: Seuil, 1979.

– 'La voie lactée de Jackson Pollack, 1912–1959.' *Art Press* 55 (1982): 6.

– *La révolution du langage poétique.* Paris: Seuil, 1974. Translated by Margaret Waller as *Revolution in Poetic Language* (New York: Columbia University Press, 1984).

Kritzman, Lawrence D. 'Duras' War.' *Esprit Créateur* 33, no. 1 (1993): 63–73.

– 'Ernaux's Testimony of Shame.' *Esprit Créateur* 39, no. 4 (1999): 139–49.

Lacan, Jacques. *Écrits.* Paris: Seuil, 1966.

– *Encore.* Edited by Jacques-Alain Miller. Vol. 20 of *Le séminaire.* Paris: Seuil, 1975.

– 'Le stade du miroir comme formateur de la fonction du Je.' In *Écrits,* 93–100. Paris: Seuil, 1966.

Landes, Joan B. *Women and the Public Sphere in the Age of the French Revolution.* Ithaca, NY: Cornell University Press, 1988.

Lanser, Susan Sniader. *Fictions of Authority: Women Writers and Narrative Voice.* Ithaca, NY: Cornell University Press, 1992.

Langer, Lawrence L. *Holocaust Testimonies: The Ruins of Memory.* New Haven: Yale University Press, 1991.

Laurence, Leslie, and Beth Weinhouse. *Outrageous Practices: The Alarming Truth about How Medicine Mistreats Women.* New York: Fawcett Columbine, 1994.

Lebelley, Frédérique. *Duras ou le poids d'une plume.* Paris: Grasset, 1994.

Lechte, John. *Julia Kristeva.* London: Routledge, 1990.

Lejeune, Philippe. *On Autobiography.* Edited by Paul John Eakin and translated by Katherine Leary. Minneapolis: University of Minnesota Press, 1989.

– *Le pacte autobiographique.* Paris: Seuil, 1975.

Lentricchia, Frank. *After the New Criticism.* London: Athlone, 1980.

– 'Patriarchy against Itself – The Young Manhood of Wallace Stevens.' *Critical Inquiry* 13 (1987): 742–86.

Lévesque, Andrée. *Résistance et transgression: études en histoire des femmes au Québec.* Montreal: Remue-ménage, 1995.

Lionnet, Françoise. *Autobiographical Voices: Race, Gender and Self-Portraiture.* Ithaca, NY: Cornell University Press, 1989.

Mall, Laurence. '"Moins seule et factice": La part autobiographique dans *Une femme* d'Annie Ernaux.' *French Review* 69 (1995): 45–54.

Mallarmé, Stéphane. 'Brise marine.' In *Œuvres complètes*, edited by Henri Mondor and G. Jean-Aubry, 38. Paris: Gallimard, Pléiade, 1945.

Mann, Susan. *The Dream of a Nation: A Social and Intellectual History of Quebec.* Montreal and Kingston: McGill-Queen's University Press, 1982.

Marini, Marcelle. *Territoires du féminin avec Marguerite Duras.* Paris: Minuit, 1977.

Mascolo, Dionys. *Autour d'un effort de mémoire: Sur une lettre de Robert Antelme.* Paris: Nadeau, 1987.

McIlvanney, Siobhán. 'Annie Ernaux: un écrivain dans la tradition du réalisme.' *Revue de l'histoire littéraire française* 2 (1998): 247–66.

Mésavage, Ruth M. 'L'herméneutique de l'écriture: *Les fous de Bassan* d'Anne Hébert.' *Quebec Studies* 5 (1987): 111–24.

Metzl, Jonathan Michel. *Prozac on the Couch: Prescribing Gender in the Era of Wonder Drugs.* Durham, NC: Duke University Press, 2003.

Michaux, Henri. *Plume, précédé de Lointain intérieur.* Paris: Gallimard, 1963.

Miller, Nancy K. '*Madwoman* Revisited.' In *Making Feminist History: The Literary Scholarship of Sandra M. Gilbert and Susan Gubar,* edited by William E. Cain, 87–104. New York: Garland, 1994.

– 'Memory Stains: Annie Ernaux's *Shame.*' *A/b: Auto/Biography Studies* 4 (1999): 38–50.

– *Subject to Change: Reading Feminist Writing.* New York: Columbia University Press, 1988.

Minogue, Valerie. 'Le cheval de Troie: à propos de *Tu ne t'aimes pas.*' *Revue des Sciences Humaines* 217 (1990): 151–61.

– *Nathalie Sarraute and the War of the Words.* Edinburgh: Edinburgh University Press, 1981.

Mitchell, Constantina. 'La symbolique de la surdité dans le *Torrent* d'Anne Hébert.' *Québec Studies* 8 (1989): 65–72.

Modiano, Patrick. *Rue des boutiques obscures*. Paris: Gallimard, 1978.

Moi, Toril. *Sexual/Textual Politics: Feminist Literary Theory.* London: Routledge, 1985.

Moore, Burness E., and Bernard D. Fine, eds. *Psychoanalytic Terms and Concepts.* New Haven: APA and Yale University Press, 1990.

National Institute on Drug Abuse. 'Trends in Prescription Drug Abuse.' http://www.nida.nih.gov/ResearchReports/Prescription/prescription5. html#Gender.

Newman, Beth. *Subjects on Display: Psychoanalysis, Social Expectation, and Victorian Femininity.* Athens: Ohio University Press, 2004.

Observatoire de la parité entre les femmes et les hommes. 'Les modes de scrutin et la parité entre les femmes et les hommes.' http://www.observatoire-parite. gouv.fr/portail/guide.htm.

Oliver, Kelly. 'Introduction: Kristeva's Revolutions.' In *The Portable Kristeva*, edited by Kelly Oliver, xi–xxix. New York: Columbia University Press, 1997.

Pagé, Pierre. *Anne Hébert.* Ottawa: Fides, 1965.

Paterson, Janet M. 'L'envolée de l'écriture: les *Fous de Bassan* d'Anne Hébert.' *Voix et Images* 9 (1984): 143–51.

Pavel, Thomas. *Fictional Worlds.* Cambridge, MA: Harvard University Press, 1986.

Pavese, Cesar. *Bella estate.* Turin: Einaudi, 1958.

Péan, Pierre. *Une jeunesse française: François Mitterrand, 1934–47.* Paris: Fayard, 1994.

Plottel, Jeanine Parisier. 'Memory, Fiction and History.' *Esprit Créateur* 30, no. 1 (1990): 47–55.

Poe, Edgar Allan. 'The Tell-Tale Heart.' In *Collected Works of Edgar Allan Poe*, edited by Thomas Ollive Mabbott, 3:789–99. Cambridge, MA: Harvard University Press, 1978.

Prince, Gerald. *Dictionary of Narratology.* Lincoln: University of Nebraska Press, 1987.

– *Narratology: The Form and Functioning of Narrative.* Berlin: Mouton, 1982.

Proctor, Candice. *Women, Equality, and the French Revolution.* New York: Greenwood Press, 1990.

Proust, Marcel. *À la recherche du temps perdu.* Edited by Pierre Clarac and André Ferré. 3 vols. Paris: Gallimard, Pléiade, 1954. Trans. by Andreas Mayor and Terence Kilmartin as *In Search of Lost Time.* 6 vols. New York: Modern Library, 1993.

Ramsay, Raylene L. *The French New Autobiographies: Sarraute, Duras, and Robbe-Grillet.* Gainesville: University Press of Florida, 1996.

Randall, Marilyn. 'Les énigmes des *Fous de Bassan*: féminisme, narration et clôture.' *Voix et Images* 43 (1989): 66–82.

Rea, Annabelle M. 'The Climate of Viol/Violence and Madness in Anne
Hébert's *Les fous de Bassan*.' *Quebec Studies* 4 (1986): 170–83.

Reid, Gregory. 'Wind in August: *Les fous de Bassan*'s Reply to Faulkner.' *Studies in
Canadian_Literature* 16, no. 2 (1991–2): 112–27.

Reuters Health. 'Anxiety Disorders.' December 2001. http://www.reutershealth.
com/wellconnected/doc28.html.

Ricardou, Jean, and Françoise vos Rossum-Guyon, eds. *Nouveau roman: hier,
aujourd'hui*. Paris: UGE, 1972.

Robbe-Grillet, Alain. *La jalousie*. Paris: Minuit, 1957.

– 'Du réalisme à la réalité.' In *Pour un nouveau roman*, 135–44. Paris: Minuit,
1963.

– *Topologie d'une cité fantôme*. Paris: Minuit, 1976.

Rosenberg, Harold. *The Anxious Object: Art Today and Its Audience*. New York: Collier, 1973.

Rosolato, Guy. 'La voix: entre corps et language.' *Revue française de psychanalyse*
38, no. 1 (1974): 75–94.

Royer, Jean. 'Pour que s'abolisse la barrière entre la littérature et la vie.' *Le
Devoir*, 26 March 1988, D1.

Said, Edward. 'Molestation and Authority in Narrative Fiction.' In *Aspects of Narrative: Selected Papers from the English Institute*, edited by J. Hillis Miller, 47–68.
New York: Columbia University Press, 1971.

Sanders, Carol. 'Stylistic Aspects of Women's Writing: The Case of Annie
Ernaux.' *French Cultural Studies* 4 (1993): 15–29.

Sarraute, Nathalie. 'Ce que je cherche à faire.' In *Nouveau roman: hier,
aujourd'hui*, edited by Jean Ricardou and Françoise vos Rossum-Guyon, 25–58.
Paris: UGE, 1972.

– 'Ce que voient les oiseaux.' In *L'ère du soupçon*, 125–55. Paris: Gallimard, 1956.
Translated by Maria Jolas as "What Birds See," in *Tropisms and The Age of Suspicion*, 121–36 (London: John Calder, 1963).

– 'Conversation et sous-conversation.' In *L'ère du soupçon*, 79–124. Paris: Gallimard, 1956. Translated by Maria Jolas as 'Conversation and Sub-Conversation,' in *Tropisms and the Age of Suspicion*, 97–120 (London: John Calder, 1963).

– 'Dialogue avec Nathalie Sarraute.' Interview by Françoise Dupuy-Sullivan.
Romance Quarterly 37 (1990): 188–92.

– *Enfance*. Paris: Gallimard, Folio, 1983.

– *Entre la vie et la mort*. Paris: Gallimard, Folio, 1968. Translated by Maria Jolas as
Between Life and Death: A Novel (New York: G. Braziller, 1969).

– 'L'ère du soupçon.' In *L'ère du soupçon*, 53–78. Paris: Gallimard, 1956. Translated by Maria Jolas as 'The Age of Suspicion,' in *Tropisms and the Age of Suspicion*, 83–95 (London: John Calder: 1963).

- 'Flaubert le précurseur?' In *Paul Valéry et l'enfant d'éléphant. Flaubert le précurseur*, 61–89. Paris: Gallimard, 1986 [1965].
- *Les fruits d'or.* Paris: Gallimard, Folio, 1963.
- 'Interview: Nathalie Sarraute.' By Pierre Boncenne. *Lire*, June 1983, 92.
- 'La littérature, aujourd'hui – II.' *Tel Quel* 9 (1962): 48–53.
- *Martereau.* Paris: Gallimard, Folio, 1953.
- 'Nathalie Sarraute ne veut rien avoir de commun avec Simone de Beauvoir.' Interview by Thérèse de Saint Phalle. *Le Figaro littéraire*, 5 January 1967, 10.
- 'Nouveau roman et réalité.' *Revue de l'Institut de Sociologie* [Brussels] 2 (1963): 431–41.
- *Œuvres complètes.* Edited by Jean-Yves Tadié. Paris: Gallimard, 1996.
- *Ouvrez.* Paris: Gallimard, Folio, 1997.
- *Le planétarium.* Paris: Gallimard, Folio, 1959.
- *Portrait d'un inconnu.* Paris: Gallimard, Folio, 1948.
- 'Sous-conversation.' In *L'ère du soupçon.* Paris: Gallimard, 1956.
- *Tropismes.* Paris: Denoël, 1939.
- *Tu ne t'aimes pas.* Paris: Gallimard, Folio, 1989.

Sartre, Jean-Paul. *La nausée.* Paris: Gallimard, Folio, 1938.

Schwartz, Paula. 'Redefining Resistance: Women's Activism in Wartime France.' In *Behind the Lines: Gender and the Two World Wars*, edited by Margaret Higonnet, Jane Jenson, Sonya Michel, and Margaret Weitz, 141–53. New Haven: Yale University Press, 1987.

Shakespeare, William. *Macbeth.* New York: Dover, 1993.

Shattuck, Roger. 'The Voice of Nathalie Sarraute.' *French Review* 68 (1995): 955–63.

Sheringham, Michael. 'Changing the Script: Women Writers and the Rise of Autobiography.' In *A History of Women's Writing in France*, edited by Sonya Stephens, 185–203. Cambridge: Cambridge University Press, 2000.

Sherzer, Dina. 'How Discourse Means: A View from Marguerite Duras' *Le vice-consul.*' *Neophilologus* 76 (1992): 370–82.

- *Representation in Contemporary French Fiction.* Lincoln: University of Nebraska Press, 1986.

Silverman, Kaja. *The Acoustic Mirror: The Female Voice in Psychoanalysis and Cinema.* Bloomington: Indiana University Press, 1988.

Slott, Kathryn. 'Submersion and Resurgence of the Female Other in Anne Hébert's *Les fous de Bassan.*' *Quebec Studies* 4 (1986): 158–69.

Suleiman, Susan. 'Nadja, Dora, Lol V. Stein: Women, Madness and Narrative.' In

Discourse in Psychoanalysis and Literature, edited by Shlomith Rimmon-Kenan, 124–51. London: Methuen, 1987.

– *Subversive Intent: Gender, Politics, and the Avant-Garde.* Cambridge, MA: Harvard University Press, 1990.

Têtu de Labsade, Françoise. *Le Québec: un pays, une culture.* 2nd ed. Montreal: Boréal, 2001.

Thomas, Lyn. *Annie Ernaux: An Introduction to the Writer and Her Audience.* Oxford: Berg, 1999.

Tondeur, Claire-Lise. 'Écrire la honte (Annie Ernaux).' In *French Prose in 2000,* edited by Michael Bishop and Christopher Elson, 125–34. Amsterdam: Rodopi, 2002.

The United Kingdom Parliament. 'Statistics of Women in Parliament.' http://www.parliament.uk/commons/lib/research/notes/snsg-01250.pdf.

United States Senate. 'Women in the United States Congress 1917–2005.' http://www.senate.gov/reference/resources/pdf/RL30261.pdf.

Van der Kolk, Bessel A. *Psychological Trauma.* Washington, DC: American Psychiatric Press, 1987.

Van der Kolk, Bessel A., and Onno van der Hart. 'The Intrusive Past: The Flexibility of Memory and the Engraving of Trauma.' In *Trauma: Explorations in Memory,* edited by Cathy Caruth, 158–82. Baltimore, MD: Johns Hopkins University Press, 1995.

Vilain, Philippe. *L'étreinte.* Paris: Gallimard, 1998.

Weedon, Chris. *Feminist Practice and Poststructuralist Theory.* Oxford: Blackwell, 1987.

Willging, Jennifer. 'Annie Ernaux's Shameful Narration.' *French Forum* 26 (2001): 83–103.

– 'Narrative Urge, Narrative Anxiety: Taking Out the Trash in Marguerite Duras's "Madame Dodin."' *French Review* 73 (2000): 699–709.

– 'Partners in Slime: The Liquid and the Viscous in Sartre and Sarraute.' *Romanic Review* 92 (2001): 277–96.

– '"True Down to the Last Detail": Memory and Narrative in Marguerite Duras's "Monsieur X."' *Twentieth Century Literature* 46 (2000): 369–86.

Winston, Jane Bradley. *Postcolonial Duras: Cultural Memory in Postwar France.* New York: Palgrave, 2001.

Wolman, Benjamin B., ed. *Encyclopedia of Psychiatry, Psychology and Psychoanalysis.* New York: Aesculapius, 1996.

Index